DEMOSTHENES: Six Private Speeches

D1316596

AMERICAN PHILOLOGICAL ASSOCIATION

TEXTBOOK SERIES

NUMBER 1
DEMOSTHENES:
SIX PRIVATE SPEECHES
Introduction and Commentary
by Lionel Pearson

DEMOSTHENES
Six Private Speeches

INTRODUCTION AND COMMENTARY BY
LIONEL PEARSON

FOREWORD BY
HELEN F. NORTH

Scholars Press
Atlanta, Georgia

INTERNATIONAL STANDARD BOOK NUMBER: 0–8061–0974–2

LIBRARY OF CONGRESS CATALOG CARD NUMBER: 72–160502

Copyright © 1972 by The American Philological Association
Reprinted, 1987

FOREWORD

ANCIENT CRITICS agreed that Demosthenes (384–322 B.C.) was the greatest of the Attic orators, and modern readers have rarely dissented from this view. But such judgments are usually based on the public orations—especially the *Philippics*, the *Olynthiacs*, and *On the False Embassy*—all delivered between 351–340 B.C., and all concerned with the great political crisis that confronted Athens at that time, the threat that Philip of Macedon would make himself master of the Greek city-states and wipe out for ever the liberties that had been preserved by the "men of Marathon" and the victors at Salamis and Plataea in the Persian Wars of the early fifth century. Demosthenes aroused the Athenians to their desperate peril and inspired the Greek resistance that was ultimately crushed at Chaeronea in 338 B.C.

The subsequent domination of Athens by Philip and then by his son and successor Alexander did not prevent Demosthenes from continuing to play a leading part in Athenian politics, or from speaking with incomparable eloquence on issues connected with public life. His most famous oration, *On the Crown*, delivered in 330 B.C., reviewed and justified his policies as leader of the anti-Macedonian party in the years before Chaeronea. It was this speech above all, together with the famous *Third*

Philippic, that won Demosthenes his reputation as the master of the grand style and the model for the supreme oratorical quality that the Greeks called *deinotes*, awe-inspiring forcefulness—an excellence sought by all who aimed at eloquence in the Greek and Roman schools.

By comparison with the intense scrutiny to which the public orations have been subjected, Demosthenes' private speeches, composed earlier in his career and concerned with civil litigation, have been, if not precisely ignored, at least neglected, save by historians of Athenian life in the fourth century, who have found in them a treasury of information about domestic relations, commercial trans-actions, legal and political institutions, economic and social life. Yet they deserve to be more widely read, not only because of the light they cast on Demosthenes' early career in the courts and his growing mastery of the art of rhetoric, but because of their intrinsic interest—their stylistic grace and subtle argumentation, their feeling of life and immediacy, above all the vivid glimpses they afford of the legal tangles involving ordinary Athenian citizens. It has been said that what Aristophanes is to the private life of the Athenians half a century earlier, the same for his own times is Demosthenes.

An edition of the best of these speeches, with an up-to-date commentary in English, has long been desired, to replace Sandys and Paley's *Select Private Orations*, first published in the Victorian era (only recently reprinted). Professor Pearson has filled the gap admirably with the present volume, which, in addition to providing essential (but not excessive) help with difficulties of grammar and syntax, offers an illuminating commentary on the legal complexities, the domestic and social conventions, and the rhetorical techniques that are most in need of elucidation.

His close knowledge of the historical background, especially the peculiarities of the Athenian courts, makes him an invaluable guide through the litigation that called forth the earliest efforts of the orator who was to become the last great champion of Greek freedom.

HELEN F. NORTH
Swarthmore College

Note to Revised Edition

In preparing this revised edition, we have striven to correct errors in the original and to bring the bibliography up to date, adding some titles published since 1972 and substituting recent works in English for the older French and German standard texts on Athenian law and legal procedure.

John Ramsey   Lionel Pearson

CONTENTS

DEMOSTHENES: Six Private Speeches

INTRODUCTION

THE SPEECHES which Demosthenes composed and delivered in the lawsuit against his guardians, soon after he reached the age of eighteen, in 364/3 B.C., are of special interest because his skill and success in this first adventure in the courts must have influenced his choice of a career.   It was his own legal troubles which showed him where his tastes and talents lay.   He became a professional speechwriter; but since litigants in Athens normally spoke for themselves, even though their speeches were written for them by professional speechwriters, he had no further opportunity of trying out his talents as a speaker, unless he actually delivered the speech *For Phormio* (36), as some people are tempted to believe, which was spoken by "a friend," after the inarticulate Phormio had stumbled through a brief formal statement.   It was not until nearly ten years later that he ventured to make his first speech in the Assembly, if Oration 14 is in fact his first speech. Plutarch's account is that his first attempt in the Assembly was a dismal failure and that he had to follow a strict discipline of training (speaking with pebbles in his mouth and so on) before he mastered the art of addressing large audiences.

Whatever the truth of this may be, it was during the decade 349–339 that he reached the height of his powers

3

and reputation as a political speaker, urging continued resistance to the aggressive Philip of Macedon. He entered the courts again in 343 to prosecute Aeschines for misconduct as a member of the embassy to Philip; but this prosecution failed to achieve his object, and it was not until 330 that he obtained his revenge, when Aeschines took the initiative as prosecutor and the speech *On the Crown*, which Demosthenes delivered in reply, won him a decisive victory. The speech *Against Meidias*, which later critics regarded as one of his finest speeches, belongs to an earlier date, but it appears never to have been actually delivered. His personal quarrel with Meidias goes back to the time of his lawsuit against his guardians and came to a climax in 348. In that year he was choregus at the Greater Dionysia and responsible for the expense of providing and training a tragic chorus for the festival. Meidias is supposed to have assaulted him publicly in the theatre, when he was acting in his official capacity, and Demosthenes went through the elaborate process of indicting him for this gross offence against the dignity of the festival; but eventually he seems to have agreed to accept his offer to settle the case out of court.

The charges against Meidias and Aeschines are what we should call criminal charges—γραφαί as they were called in Athens. If such prosecutions had been successful, the defendant could have been sentenced to a severe fine or even to banishment; and the charges were intended to ruin the defendant's public career, since Aeschines and Meidias were both politicians. The case against the guardians, on the other hand, is a civil case, a δίκη, in which the plaintiff seeks restitution or damages. Aphobus is not charged with embezzling public funds, but with the dishonest or incompetent management of a trust fund.

The issues involved are personal not political, and Demosthenes will declare himself content if he can recover the money which he says is due to him.

The distinction between δίκαι and γραφαί is not quite the same as between civil and criminal actions, since the state did not undertake responsibility for prosecution even when very serious offences were thought to have been committed; it was always a private individual who took the risk and sought the credit. It is therefore more correct to speak of private and public cases, and the speeches which Demosthenes wrote for private cases are commonly known as his Private Orations. It was with such cases that speechwriters were mainly concerned, writing speeches for individuals with little or no experience of the courts or of public speaking; the men who undertook prosecution in public cases were more likely to be politicians, with enough experience and enough confidence in their oratorical powers to prepare their own speeches.

The biographical tradition about Demosthenes, as we find it in Plutarch's life or in the *Lives of the Ten Orators* wrongly attributed to him, tells us hardly anything that we can trust about the orator's youthful troubles that we cannot learn from these speeches. Plutarch writes:

"He was seven years old when his father died, leaving him well provided for; the value of the estate amounted altogether to nearly fifteen talents. But he was badly served by his guardians, who misappropriated money and managed the estate badly; they even refused to pay his teachers' fees. This seems to be the reason why he missed receiving the education that was usual and appropriate to a freeborn boy; because of his physical weakness and

softness his mother did not let him exert himself stren-
uously and his *paidagogoi* did not force him to; he was in
fact feeble and sickly from infancy."

When we read in Demosthenes' speech *On the Crown*
about the undignified and "ungentlemanly" way in
which Aeschines was supposed to have spent his boyhood
—wiping down the tables in his father's school and
assisting his mother in religious services not supposed to
be quite respectable—we wonder how much of this is
totally false; and we may well wonder how much truth
there is in this story that Demosthenes lacked a regular
education. But it will not surprise us to read about an
incident in his boyhood which was supposed to have fired
him with the ambition to be an orator; he contrives to be
present when the politician Callistratus defends himself
in an important trial, and the experience is supposed to
have settled his choice of a career. This is the kind of
romantic detail that we are under no obligation to
believe; it is not quite so easy to dismiss the story that he
received instruction from Isaeus, the speechwriter who
specialized in cases concerning inheritance. There is a
passage in one of the speeches in this case (30.37) that
appears to have been borrowed directly from Isaeus, and
the story might simply be an inference from the passage,
as the biographies of literary men in antiquity are often
based on arbitrary interpretations of passages in their
works; early biographers of Demosthenes may be no
different in this respect from biographers of Horace and
Virgil.

Plutarch takes it for granted that the guardians were
severely at fault, and certainly Demosthenes was successful
in his case against them—successful in the courts, at

least, though that was only the beginning of the battle; actual recovery of the money was not so easy. Any attempt to reconstruct exactly what the guardians did, what happened to the various properties, and how much Demosthenes might reasonably expect to receive when he came of age—any such attempt is very precarious, since we know very little of what the defendants had to say for themselves; we shall notice details in which Demosthenes is surely not telling the precise truth and appears to be claiming more than he should, and we shall do well to maintain a healthy and judicial scepticism about a good many things that he says; but this should not lead us to conclude that he had a poor case in law. Even under the best conducted legal systems a scrupulously accurate and modest statement of one's grievances is not always the best way to obtain reasonable restitution; and no one would pretend that forensic oratory in Athens erred on the side of understatement. Rather than attempt to play judge and jury, with no more knowledge of the facts than plaintiff or defendant wishes us to have, readers of Demosthenes will find it more profitable to admire his skill in presenting a case that, at first sight, may look incontrovertible; part of the skill in presenting such a case is not to avoid difficulties and awkward details, but to present them in such a way that the jury will not think them important. And sometimes a false or inexact statement may force one's adversary to deal with topics that he would prefer to have left alone.

Modern critics of the Athenian legal system always point out how uncertain the result of a case must be when the jury was left to decide matters of law as well as matters of fact, without the legal instruction that an experienced presiding judge can provide. One side may ask the jury

7

to give its verdict "in accordance with what the law demands," the other may ask for "what is only fair and reasonable"; and a skilful orator may easily persuade a jury of men without legal training that the second alternative is the right verdict. It is with such considerations in mind that one should learn to appreciate the skill and ingenuity of the Attic orators.

Most persons contemplating legal action first attempted to obtain a settlement out of court. One way was to persuade the other party to let the case be submitted to an arbitrator, whose decision both parties could agree to accept; his verdict was then legally binding, and the case could not be submitted to a court. Alternatively there were official arbitrators (διαιτηταί), men of over sixty who were apparently obliged to perform the service for a nominal fee, and we hear constantly in the orators of the procedure before one of these men. If his decision was not acceptable to both parties, then he would refer the case to the courts, all the documents which had been submitted to him being sealed up in a special container (ἐχῖνος), so that they would be ready for production at the trial. This was the normal prelude to a trial in court, where private disputes were concerned. Only questions involving very small sums (under ten drachmae) could be settled by local courts (the δικασταὶ κατὰ δήμους, as they were called); all other disputes which were not settled privately or by official arbitration had to be submitted to the Heliastic courts in Athens.

Application for trail by jury was made through one of the nine archons—the six thesmothetai and the archon eponymos, basileus, and polemarch. Different branches of the law were the special concern of different members of the board; for example, the archon eponymos

8

was responsible for matters concerning orphans and the polemarch for matters concerning non-citizens.

The Athenian system of jury courts had been established in the fifth century, and the courts were kept particularly busy when members of the Athenian confederacy were bound to come to Athens if they became involved in litigation of any importance at all. We have to be careful not to take too literally the scenes of Athenian life which are presented to us in the comedies of Aristophanes; but we cannot forget that the *Wasps*, which is a satire on the judicial system, shows great crowds of men struggling to find a place on the day's quota of jurymen and taking an enormous malicious pleasure in their work. Various modifications were introduced over the years, but the system was essentially the same in the time of Demosthenes as in the Periclean age. Pay for jury duty was introduced by Pericles and reinstated in the fourth century, after the oligarchic revolutions of 411 and 403 had abolished payment for all civic duties. But it was not a princely wage; three obols (half a drachma) was hardly enough to provide food for a single man. It does not of course follow that only unemployed idlers volunteered for the duty, and there is no real evidence (apart from Aristophanes) that it was ever keenly sought after. But large numbers of men were required and there is never any suggestion that it was difficult to recruit them. We are told that 6000 men were supposed to be available on any day when the courts were in session; and since the normal number for a jury in private cases (δίκαι) was 201, in public cases (γραφαί) 501, and in specially important cases 1001, the total does not seem excessive.

There are references in the literature of the fifth and fourth centuries to various places where the courts sat, and in the fourth century, as we might have expected, it appears that trials were held in buildings in the Agora. Excavations in the Agora have uncovered a building complex which is very reasonably identified as "the law courts" (δικαστήρια), and further evidence may be forthcoming in the course of time. Various objects used in the "machinery" of the law courts have also been found in the Agora; for example, part of an allotment machine (κληρωτήριον) which was used to decide which jurymen would be employed on any particular day, a water clock (κλεψύδρα) which timed the speeches of plaintiff and defendant, and jurors' voting ballots and tickets, marked with letters to show the number of the court room to which they were assigned. For illustrations see *Excavations of the Athenian Agora*, Picture Book No. 4, "The Athenian citizen" (Princeton, 1960).

By the use of large numbers on juries and making sure that no one could know in advance who would be sitting in any given trial, it was possible to avoid the danger of bribery or intimidation; charges of interfering with juries are never made seriously by the orators, in great contrast to what we find in Cicero's time in Rome, when the integrity of the courts had been seriously undermined. On the other hand Cicero's speeches make it clear that, though Roman juries may have been easily corrupted, their level of education and intelligence was expected to be quite high. Roman juries were chosen from a particular class, which was supposed (rightly or wrongly) to be financially responsible. In Athens the orators had no such guarantee that the jurors would have any considerable understanding of business or the law, though it is always taken for granted that they are familiar with and interested in contemporary politics. It was of course in keeping with Athenian democratic tradition to insist that there must be no ruling class, chosen on the basis of wealth or social standing, just as it was considered right to have large juries, to avoid any suggestion that power was being given to oligarchic committees.

It was also part of Athenian democratic theory that no special intelligence or training was required to understand and interpret the law. Thucydides (3.37) represents Cleon as insisting that men of average, or less than average, intelligence will respect it more and uphold it more faithfully than clever men; and this attitude cannot have been unusual, since speakers are always ready to complain that their adversary is an ingenious practitioner, with experience of litigation, who will try to deceive the jury into giving a verdict which is not in accordance with law. Though Demosthenes may magnify the powers of the courts when he chooses, and tell them that they can "pass any sentence they like" (24.151), he is always quick to remind them that they have sworn to uphold the laws and not to pass judgment contrary to the law. The courts are constantly upheld as defenders of the law, not only because they are expected to enforce it against persons guilty of crimes and defend the innocent against the dishonest, but because they are also interpreters of the law at all levels, of constitutional law as well as all other branches of it. Politicians could be prosecuted on the charges of introducing illegal (i.e. unconstitutional) legislation, under a γραφὴ παρανόμων, and the charge was sufficiently serious to drive a man into exile if it could be proved against him. It may seem shocking to us that large untrained juries should be given the power to decide issues which we consider fit only for learned professional jurists. But it would be just as undemocratic, in Athenian theory, to make a special group of citizens responsible for such decisions as to substitute privileged officials for juries of ordinary men.

These are considerations which must constantly be borne in mind as we read the work of the Attic orators. It is easy to criticize speeches by saying that they violate the Anglo-American traditions of the bar and to point out passages at which, in our courts, opposing counsel would certainly raise an objection and which a judge might order to be stricken from the record, after a stern rebuke to the speaker. The speeches of Demosthenes and his contemporaries are not intended for our courts, but for the Athenian courts of the fourth century, and they must be judged and appreciated with regard for the audience that the speaker expected to face. When we disapprove of the method or tone of the argument, it is the judicial system of Athens with which we should find fault, not the orator.

The weakness of the Athenian courts, from the modern or the Roman point of view, is that a litigant could not be sure whether they would enforce the law or be so strongly affected by an appeal to their emotions as to give a verdict that seemed to them "right and fair," but was not in accordance with the law. The orators take full advantage of this weakness, and the well-known contest of the Just Argument and the Unjust Argument, in Aristophanes' *Clouds*, reminds us that it may often have seemed easier to obtain a favourable verdict by inviting the jury to disregard the law and be guided solely by considerations of equity.

The *Clouds* shows little respect for the art of rhetoric, just as the law courts are satirized unmercifully in the *Wasps*; Plato's more direct attack on it is another indication that it was regarded with hostility and suspicion in some quarters. The litigants for whom Demosthenes writes speeches often present themselves as simple people, who are afraid that their more experienced and cunning opponents will deceive the jury with clever speeches; there was always the possibility that the jury might be prejudiced against someone who appeared to have reached a professional standard of oratory. The "simple" speaker, delivering a speech prepared for him by an accomplished artist, has to avoid giving the impression of conscious artistry. What a man with a good case had most to fear was not so much that his opponent would mislead the jury with plausible sophistic argument, as that he would misrepresent the law by references to parallels and precedents which were not strictly applicable, or attempt to divert them from the legal issue by emotional appeals and ingenious misrepresentations of his own and his opponent's character.

In any trial the chances of a favourable verdict are good if "the facts" can be presented to the jury in such a way that no lengthy argument is needed to show which side is in the right. We cannot tell to what extent a speaker has twisted or distorted detail in order to achieve this end, since we cannot question the witnesses or even read their written depositions; and when one speaker complains of the lies that the opposing speaker has told or will tell, we cannot know how far we should believe him. The art of an orator in these private disputes consists to a great extent in lucid narrative, presented in such a way as to show his client in a favourable light and blacken the character of his opponent unmercifully. This was a lesson that Demosthenes had already learnt when he entered on the case against Aphobus. This need not mean that he simply "tells the truth," though he may be claiming to be doing just this. He may be telling less than the truth, or he may not know the whole truth. The second alternative, indeed, is more likely. Modern scholars have striven to discover what the whole truth is, but with no more evidence than Demosthenes allows them to have before them, they face a very difficult, if not an impossible, task and their conclusions cannot really be trusted. The discussion of Schwahn and his critics (see Bibliographical Note) is most interesting, but there are numerous points that must remain uncertain.

The "facts" as Demosthenes presents them in *Against Aphobus* are simple. His father left an estate in trust for him, to be administered by trustees until he came of age, which was worth about 14 talents; when he came of age ten years later, all that the trustees handed over to him was little more than a talent. The estate included two small businesses, which had brought in a steady income in the past, and Demosthenes is not going to offer any reasons why they should cease to be successful—a cutlery business, making swords or knives, and a furniture business, making beds or couches. These businesses have been made to "disappear" by the trustees; we might suppose that sheer misfortune or inefficient management was the cause, but Demosthenes takes for granted that the trustees have been grossly dishonest and tricked him out of his due inheritance.

The story as he tells it is easy to follow, and no purpose would be served by giving a summary here. His statement of what the trustees ought to have done is also easy to understand, though his reasoning is not always as accurate as it might be. Details are better left for the commentary, as they occur in the text. All that remains to be done in this introduction is to discuss the rhetorical arrangement of the speeches and explain a few technical points of Athenian business (including the currency) and procedure.

If Demosthenes had received lessons from Isaeus or some other experienced practitioner in the courts, we must ask what form this is likely to have taken. Handbooks of rhetoric existed in Aristotle's time, and he speaks of them with scant respect. His own *Rhetoric* is a book of enormous interest, but it was not yet written, and since (as he makes clear) it is written quite differently from current handbooks and concerned with different topics, we must look elsewhere for information about what rhetoricians actually taught. By combining the detail that we find in the only extant handbook from the fourth century—the *Rhetorica ad Alexandrum* by a contemporary of Aristotle and mistakenly attributed to him in late antiquity—and what can be read in Latin in the *De Inventione* of Cicero and the *Rhetorica ad Herennium*, which are adaptations of Greek handbooks, we can reasonably conclude that pupils were taught to make their speeches conform to certain rules of composition.

In an introductory section (προοίμιον) a speaker tries to acquire the good will of his hearers, and the recognized methods of establishing oneself in the jury's favour are well illustrated in surviving speeches. If possible the speaker stresses his inexperience in litigation, his unworldly, generous, and patriotic character in contrast with that of his opponent, his need of a sympathetic hearing though he may not express himself very well, his unlucky situation which is due to no fault of his own. This introduction is generally quite brief, and leads into a narrative (διήγησις), more or less detailed according to the circumstances. Then, after giving his version of "the facts of the case," the speaker will set to work explaining why his version

must be accepted as true or at least considered more
likely to be true than any alternative account that his
adversary may produce. This is his "argument" (πίστις).
Sometimes he may have to argue that his interpretation
of the observable or admitted actions is the true interpretation; for example, that when A struck B he did so
with deliberate intent to cause bodily harm, after careful
planning, while the other side may plead that he struck
him accidentally or in an excusable outburst of rage or
believing him to be someone else, and that the injury to
B should be considered an accident. Proofs or arguments
(πίστεις), as Aristotle reminds us, are either ἄτεχνοι or
ἔντεχνοι, two very difficult adjectives to translate,
because they do not mean "non-technical" and "technical." A proof is ἄτεχνος if it is not the product of the
speaker's τέχνη, his skill or ingenuity, but a "fact"
attested to by witnesses or a document of some kind; it is
ἔντεχνος if it is the product of his own ingenuity, a piece
of deductive reasoning or a comparison. Then, after
presenting the arguments on his side, he will want to meet
those presented by his adversary.

Often a Greek orator, after telling his story and presenting his evidence, may think it necessary to show that
his version is more likely to have happened than what his
adversary says, using the argument from probability (τὸ
εἰκός). Thus after presenting witnesses to his absence
from Athens at the time when a theft was committed, he
will show that he was not the kind of person to have done
such a thing or that it would not have been to his advantage or that, being an intelligent wealthy man, he
would not have risked detection for such a small advantage.
Then after refuting his adversary's arguments, he may
finish with some emotional appeals—for example, hint at

the consequences to law and order if such a treacherous criminal is allowed to go free, or call attention to the terrible disaster it will mean to himself and his family if he does not obtain a favourable verdict. Alternatively, he may ridicule his opponent for indulging in such a melodramatic display, or be content with a recapitulation or summary of his case.

If all speeches by Greek orators followed this pattern, they would not hold our attention for long. In the speeches of Demosthenes the structure and composition is often much less regular. The narrative is often combined with argument, so that formal analysis is neither necessary nor satisfactory. And he shows special skill in his economical handling of detail, sometimes postponing a telling point until a later stage of the speech, a technical device on which Quintilian still prides himself four centuries later (4.283). One thing that makes the private speeches of Demosthenes attractive is that the formal composition is never so obvious as to seem artificial or forced; even in his earliest speeches he has already learnt this lesson.

We are given just enough detail about business and finance in the speeches against Aphobus to make us wish for more. The question arises whether Demosthenes could have told us more. Was he in fact unable to understand what had happened to his inheritance, was his command of detail as limited as it appears to be? It is possible that his guardians had covered their tracks carefully and blocked his investigation, and it is also possible that he had not yet become familiar with the devices used by businessmen, especially dishonest businessmen. But there is also the possibility that he carefully tells the story in the simplest possible terms, so that the jury cannot fail to follow him; and that he leaves it to his opponent to baffle and irritate the jury by more abstruse and detailed argument. From the story as he tells it a plain man will be disposed to conclude that the guardians must be dishonest; there is always the chance that their efforts to prove the contrary will be unintelligible.

Demosthenes' father, also called Demosthenes, is represented as a careful man, and since no apology or explanation of his arrangements is offered, we may presume that they are not unusual. The two businesses or workshops that he owns—"factory" is really too elaborate a term to describe them—are valued purely in terms of the workers (who, as slaves, are capital assets) and material in stock; nothing is said of tools or premises. Any attempt to offer valuations in modern currency or to establish any comparison between the drachma and the dollar or the pound is largely worthless, since our knowledge of the cost of living in Athens is very sketchy indeed. A drachma, certainly, was what an Athenian sailor on some occasions received as his daily wage, so that a crew of 200 would receive 6000 drachmas, i.e. one talent, in a month of thirty days.

A talent is a measure of weight, which in Athens was reckoned at about 57 pounds avoirdupois, and the cash value of a talent which will be found in old grammars (£50 or $200) is based on the price of silver about 1900; it is absurdly misleading when it reduces the drachma, a daily wage, to the value of a few cents. It is more useful to remember that a talent was suitable dowry for a woman of fairly wealthy parents or that half a talent was a reasonable price for a house. Sums less than a talent are sometimes reckoned in drachmas, sometimes in minas; a mina (μνᾶ) was 100 drachmas, 60 to the talent. As a measure of weight, therefore, about a pound.

18

The workshop which manufactured swords or knives, consisting of thirty workers, a capital value estimated at about 100 minas, is said to have brought in an annual net income of 30 minas, and Demosthenes claims that he should receive the annual income that ought to have been earned over ten years, plus interest at 12%—the standard rate. This may seem an excessive claim, based on a simple man's conception of business, since nothing is said of the various expenses which would cut into this so-called "net income." For one thing the slaves would grow old and have to be replaced. It does not follow that Demosthenes is unaware of such considerations, but his opponent will have to take time to explain them; and since every speaker's time was limited, measured by the water clock (see note on 27.12), it was often good tactics to set such tasks for one's opponent that would force him to "waste time" and use up part of his allotted time which he would prefer to employ differently. Indeed Demosthenes sometimes complains that an opponent is treating him in this way.

Efforts have been made to work out in more accurate and realistic detail the financial basis and prospects of the cutlery business and the furniture workshop, but since we are given only a limited amount of information, any attempts at more detailed reconstruction are bound to be largely conjectural. For further discussion see the works of Schwahn, Oertel, and Finley listed in the Bibliographical Note.

In addition to the income from the workshops there were sums of money invested in loans and deposited in banks. The intention of the elder Demosthenes was that the guardians should take care of his son's upbringing and education out of the income, which would be more than enough for the purpose, and if they did not mismanage things, should be able to present him with a substantial nest-egg when he came of age. His widow and little daughter were also provided for, in a manner which seems to have been quite orthodox. Aphobus was to marry the widow, and a dowry was set aside for her; this does not mean that he and she were obliged to marry against their will, but if he did not marry her, he was charged with the responsibility of finding a husband for her, which with a substantial dowry provided was not an unreasonable task for a trustee. Likewise a husband was to be found for the little girl, when she grew up, and a dowry set aside for her. As we shall see, the guardians are accused of taking the cash but making no more effort to provide for the widow and daughter than they did for the son.

There is no need to take up space with further analysis or description, because the speeches are written in such a way as to be intelligible to a jury with no previous knowledge of the case. Points of Attic law that are raised in particular passages are better discussed in the commentary as the need arises, but a few remarks on the orator's skill in composing his speeches may be worthwhile. Like any competent writer, Demosthenes knows how to be economical in presenting the relevant facts; he does not confuse the minds of the jury by offering irrelevant detail, though we may regret that he omits much that we should like to know. He never makes a situation appear more complicated than is necessary to make his point clear. The aim of a forensic speaker is not necessarily to reveal all the facts, but only such facts as will prove his case, show his adversary's guilt or his own innocence while appearing to conceal nothing of importance. Demosthenes tells us very little of the private lives of Aphobus and his fellow trustees. If details of their occupations or their public careers might suggest to the jury some special need for money or special opportunities of acquiring and disposing of property without attracting notice, we might well have expected to be told about them. His object after all is to present the story in such a way that there appears to be no explanation of his own misfortune except gross dishonesty on their part.

This is why he combines narrative with commentary, frequently interposing remarks on their character—their meanness, cruelty, heartlessness, lack of all scruples. If the story does not of itself prove them guilty of such baseness, the presumption of baseness may make the story more credible. For the purposes of obtaining a verdict it will be just as useful to convince the jury that the defendants are criminally guilty because of their character, as to make them conclude that they are base characters because of their criminal actions. It certainly will not be enough to satisfy jurors that the narrative of events is true; they must also be satisfied that the responsibility for his misfortune rests on the defendants and that their failure to prevent it is both legally and morally reprehensible. When there is no learned judge to explain the law to the jury, pleaders will inevitably exploit the tendency of a jury to jump to conclusions. Aristotle recognizes that weakness in the Athenian judicial system and gives it as his opinion, in the opening paragraphs of the *Rhetoric*, that it is not proper for the litigating parties to tell the jury what is right and what is wrong. We may well agree with what he says; but we must admit that the Attic orators who understood this weakness have produced more interesting speeches than might have resulted in more strictly controlled courts.

The preceding remarks have been mainly concerned with the two speeches *Against Aphobus*, in which Demosthenes begins his lawsuit against his guardians. He obtained judgment against Aphobus, and in the two speeches *Against Onetor* we see some of the difficulties he encountered in trying to collect the sum that was awarded to him. In all these speeches he is presenting his own case, when he is still a very young man. *For Phormio*, which follows in this collection, was written more than twelve years later for an ex-slave, a banker's trusted assistant, whom the banker in his will appointed as one of the trustees of his estate and as guardian of his younger son, and who became involved in a bitter controversy with the elder son. The speech *Against Zenothemis*, of which only the first part survives, is even later in date and was delivered by a relative of Demosthenes. It reveals a remarkable story of an attempt to defraud him of his investment in a shipload of grain. More detailed introduction to these speeches will be found in the commentary.

BIBLIOGRAPHICAL NOTE

The Greek text in this edition is based to a large extent on that of W. Rennie, Demosthenes, II ii, Oxford Classical Texts (Oxford, 1921). The more recent edition of Louis Gernet, Démosthène, *Plaidoyers Civils*, i–ii (Collection Budé, Paris, 1954–1957), differs only occasionally in its text readings, but its admirable French translation, brief explanatory notes, and introductions to each speech make it an indispensable guide for every student of Demosthenes.

In addition to the English translation by A. T. Murray in the Loeb Classical Library mention should be made of the older translation by C. R. Kennedy, in Bohn's Classical Library (London, 1882). In addition to an accurate translation, made with due regard to points of law (Kennedy was a London barrister), the volume contains good essays on Athenian law and legal practice.

The edition of *Select Private Orations of Demosthenes*, by J. E. Sandys and F. A. Paley, 2 volumes (3rd edition, Cambridge, 1896, reprinted, New York, 1979), includes the speech *For Phormio*, and is still very valuable. It includes a bibliography which is a useful guide to earlier work. There is a Dutch edition of the speech *Against Zenothemis* by A. C. Cosman, *Demosthenes' Rede tegen Zenothemis, met Inleiding en Commentaar* (Leiden, 1939). *Selected Private Speeches* of Demosthenes by Carey and Reed (Cambridge, 1985) and *Three Private Speeches* by Doherty (Oxford, 1927, now o.p.) contain none of the speeches in the present collection.

23

Among works concerned with Demosthenes' political career and his speeches, with Greek Oratory in general and Athenian law and legal procedure, the following should be mentioned:

Friedrich Blass, *Die attische Beredsamkeit,* 3 volumes (Leipzig, 1893, reprinted, Hildesheim, 1962), vol. III i, Demosthenes.

A. W. Pickard-Cambridge, *Demosthenes and the Last Days of Greek Freedom* (London and New York, 1914, reprinted, New York, 1978).

W. Jaeger, *Demosthenes, the Origin and Growth of his Policy* (Sather Classical Lectures, Berkeley, 1938, reprinted, New York, 1963).

Paul Cloché, *Démosthènes et la fin de la démocratie athénienne* (Paris, 1937).

Lionel Pearson, *The Art of Demosthenes* (Meisenheim, 1976, reprinted, Chico, California, 1981).

Lionel Pearson, "Demosthenes," in *Ancient Writers: Greece and Rome,* edited by T. J. Luce (New York, 1983) pp. 417–433.

George Kennedy, *The Art of Persuasion in Greece* (Princeton, 1963).

J. H. Lipsius, *Das attische Recht und Rechtsverfahren,* 3 volumes (Leipzig, 1905–1915).

R. J. Bonner and Gertrude Smith, *The Administration of Justice from Homer to Aristotle,* 2 volumes (Chicago, 1930–1938).

A. R. W. Harrison, *The Law of Athens,* 2 volumes (Oxford, 1968–71).

Douglas M. MacDowell, *The Law in Classical Athens* (London and Ithaca, 1978).

A. H. M. Jones, *Athenian Democracy* (Oxford, 1960).

W. K. Lacey, *The Family in Classical Greece* (London, 1968).

G. M. Calhoun, *The Business Life of Ancient Athens* (Chicago, 1926).

R. J. Bonner, *Lawyers and Litigants in Ancient Athens* (Chicago, 1927).

T. R. Glover, *From Pericles to Philip* (London, 1917), Chap. X, "The House of Pasion."

American School of Classical Studies in Athens, *Excavations of the Athenian Agora*, Picture Book No. 4, "The Athenian Citizen" (Princeton, 1960).

More complete bibliographical information will be found in Gernet's edition and in the survey by D. F. Jackson and G. O. Rowe covering the years 1915 to 1965, *Lustrum* 14 (1969) 5–109. The following short list of special studies may also be useful:

H. J. Wolff, *Die attische Paragraphe* (Weimar, 1966).

W. Schwahn, *Demosthenes gegen Aphobos, Ein Beitrag zur Geschichte der griechischen Wirtschaft* (Leipzig-Berlin, 1929).

M. I. Finley, *Studies in Land and Credit in Ancient Athens* (New Brunswick, N.J., 1952).

J. Korver, "Demosthenes gegen Aphobos," *Mnemosyne* 10 (1941–2), 8–22.

F. Oertel, "Zur Frage der attischen Grossindustrie," *Rheinisches Museum* 79 (1930), 230–252.

G. M. Calhoun, "Risk in sea loans in ancient Athens," *Journal of economic and business history* 2 (1929–30), 561–584.

L. Gernet, "Sur les actions commerciales en droit athénien," *Revue des études grecques* 51 (1938), 1–44.

AGAINST APHOBUS I (XXVII)

The outline or *hypothesis*, which precedes each speech in the text, was written in late antiquity. These *hypotheses* very rarely contain any information beyond what is in the speech itself, and the student is not recommended to study them as introductions; they are often difficult to understand, until the vocabulary and the arguments of the speech have become familiar, but may be useful at a later stage as a means of recalling detail. No commentary on them will be given; they are self-explanatory to anyone who is familiar with the speech.

References to speeches of Demosthenes will be by number—this is Oration 27.

XXVII

ΚΑΤ' ΑΦΟΒΟΥ ΕΠΙΤΡΟΠΗΣ Α

Δημοσθένης ὁ Παιανιεύς, Δημοσθένους τοῦ ῥήτορος πατήρ,
τελευτῶν ἐπὶ δύο παισί, τῷ τε Δημοσθένει καὶ θυγατρί, ἐπιτρόπους καθίστησι καὶ τῶν παίδων καὶ τῶν χρημάτων τρεῖς, δύο
μὲν συγγενεῖς, Ἄφοβόν τε καὶ Δημοφῶντα, ἕνα δὲ φίλον ἐκ 5
παίδων, Θηριππίδην. καὶ Θηριππίδῃ μὲν δίδωσιν ἑβδομήκοντα
καρποῦσθαι μνᾶς, ἄχρις ἂν Δημοσθένης εἰς ἄνδρας ἐγγραφῇ·
Δημοφῶντι δ' ἐγγυᾷ τὴν θυγατέρα, προστάξας αὐτὸν προῖκα δύο
τάλαντα λαβεῖν· Ἄφόβῳ δὲ τὴν ἑαυτοῦ μὲν γυναῖκα, τῶν δὲ
παίδων μητέρα, Κλεοβούλην τὴν Γύλωνος, ἀξιοῖ γήμασθαι μνᾶς 10
ἐπιδοὺς ὀγδοήκοντα, καὶ χρῆσθαι κελεύει τῇ τ' οἰκίᾳ καὶ τοῖς ἐν
αὐτῇ σκεύεσι μέχρι τῆς Δημοσθένους εἰς ἄνδρας ἐγγραφῆς.
2 οὗτοι τὰ μὲν δοθέντα χρήματα αὐτοῖς εὐθὺς λαμβάνουσι, γαμεῖ δ'
οὔτ' Ἄφοβος τὴν γυναῖκα τοῦ τελευτήσαντος οὔτε Δημοφῶν τὴν
θυγατέρα. διαχειρίσαντες δὲ τὴν οὐσίαν τεττάρων καὶ δέκα 15
ταλάντων, ὡς ὁ ῥήτωρ ἐπιδείκνυσιν, ὀφείλοντες τριάκοντα τάλαντ'
ἐκτῖσαι ἐπικαρπίας καὶ ἀποδοῦναι, μικρὰ παντελῶς παρέδωκαν εἰς
ἄνδρας ἐγγραφέντι τῷ Δημοσθένει. διὸ πρὸς τὸν Ἄφοβον
εἰσελήλυθεν ἐπιτροπῆς δέκα ταλάντων τὴν δίκην λαχών, ἐπειδὴ
τρίτος ὢν ἐπίτροπος τὸ τρίτον ὀφείλει τῶν χρημάτων· ἃ καὶ 20
συντίθησιν ὁ ῥήτωρ ἔκ τε τῶν ἀρχαίων καὶ τῆς ἐπικαρπίας.
3 Κατ' Ἀφόβου Β. Πρός τινας ἀντιρρήσεις εἰσαγομένας ὑπὸ
τοῦ Ἀφόβου οὗτος ὁ λόγος ἐπηγώνισται, ἔχει δὲ καὶ τῶν
προειρημένων ἐπανάμνησιν.

Εἰ μὲν ἐβούλετ' Ἄφοβος, ὦ ἄνδρες δικασταί, τὰ δίκαια   1
ποιεῖν ἢ περὶ ὧν διεφερόμεθα τοῖς οἰκείοις ἐπιτρέπειν,
οὐδὲν ἂν ἔδει δικῶν οὐδὲ πραγμάτων· ἀπέχρη γὰρ ἂν τοῖς
ὑπ' ἐκείνων γνωσθεῖσιν ἐμμένειν, ὥστε μηδεμίαν ἡμῖν εἶναι
5 πρὸς τοῦτον διαφοράν. ἐπειδὴ δ' οὗτος τοὺς μὲν σαφῶς
εἰδότας τὰ ἡμέτερ' ἔφυγε μηδὲν διαγνῶναι περὶ αὐτῶν, εἰς
δ' ὑμᾶς τοὺς οὐδὲν τῶν ἡμετέρων ἀκριβῶς ἐπισταμένους
ἐλήλυθεν, ἀνάγκη ἐστὶν ἐν ὑμῖν παρ' αὐτοῦ πειρᾶσθαι τῶν
δικαίων τυγχάνειν. οἶδα μὲν οὖν, ὦ ἄνδρες δικασταί, ὅτι   2
10 πρὸς ἄνδρας καὶ λέγειν ἱκανοὺς καὶ παρασκευάσασθαι δυνα-
μένους χαλεπόν ἐστιν εἰς ἀγῶνα καθίστασθαι περὶ τῶν
ὄντων ἁπάντων, ἄπειρον ὄντα παντάπασι πραγμάτων διὰ
τὴν ἡλικίαν· ὅμως δέ, καίπερ πολὺ τούτων καταδεέστερος
ὤν, πολλὰς ἐλπίδας ἔχω καὶ παρ' ὑμῖν τεύξεσθαι τῶν δι-
15 καίων καὶ μέχρι γε τοῦ τὰ γεγενημένα διεξελθεῖν καὶ αὐτὸς
ἀρκούντως ἐρεῖν, ὥσθ' ὑμᾶς μήτ' ἀπολειφθῆναι τῶν πραγμάτων μηδὲ καθ' ἓν μήτ' ἀγνοῆσαι περὶ ὧν δεήσει τὴν
ψῆφον ἐνεγκεῖν. δέομαι δ' ὑμῶν, ὦ ἄνδρες δικασταί, μετ'   3
εὐνοίας τέ μου ἀκοῦσαι, κἂν ἠδικῆσθαι δοκῶ, βοηθῆσαί μοι
20 τὰ δίκαια. ποιήσομαι δ' ὡς ἂν δύνωμαι διὰ βραχυτάτων
τοὺς λόγους. ὅθεν οὖν ῥᾷστα μαθήσεσθε περὶ αὐτῶν, ἐντεῦθεν ὑμᾶς καὶ ἐγὼ πρῶτον πειράσομαι διδάσκειν.

Δημοσθένης γὰρ οὑμὸς πατήρ, ὦ ἄνδρες δικασταί, κατέ-   4
λιπεν οὐσίαν μὲν σχεδὸν τεττάρων καὶ δέκα ταλάντων, ἐμὲ
25 δ' ἕπτ' ἐτῶν ὄντα καὶ τὴν ἀδελφὴν πέντε, ἔτι δὲ τὴν ἡμετέ-
ραν μητέρα πεντήκοντα μνᾶς εἰς τὸν οἶκον εἰσενηνεγμένην.
βουλευσάμενος δὲ περὶ ἡμῶν, ὅτ' ἔμελλε τελευτᾶν, ἅπαντα
ταῦτ' ἐνεχείρισεν Ἀφόβῳ τε τουτῳὶ καὶ Δημοφῶντι τῷ
Δήμωνος υἱεῖ, τούτοιν μὲν ἀδελφιδοῖν ὄντοιν, τῷ μὲν ἐξ ἀδελ-
30 φοῦ, τῷ δ' ἐξ ἀδελφῆς γεγονότοιν, ἔτι δὲ Θηριππίδῃ τῷ
Παιανιεῖ, γένει μὲν οὐδὲν προσήκοντι, φίλῳ δ' ἐκ παιδὸς
ὑπάρχοντι. κἀκείνῳ μὲν ἔδωκεν ἐκ τῶν ἐμῶν ἑβδομήκοντα   5
μνᾶς καρπώσασθαι τοσοῦτον χρόνον, ἕως ἐγὼ ἀνὴρ εἶναι

δοκιμασθείην, ὅπως μὴ δι' ἐπιθυμίαν χρημάτων χεῖρόν τι
τῶν ἐμῶν διοικήσειεν· Δημοφῶντι δὲ τὴν ἐμὴν ἀδελφὴν
καὶ δύο τάλαντ' εὐθὺς ἔδωκεν ἔχειν, αὐτῷ δὲ τούτῳ τὴν
μητέρα τὴν ἐμὴν καὶ προῖκ' ὀγδοήκοντα μνᾶς, καὶ τὴν οἰκίαν
⟨οἰκεῖν⟩ καὶ σκεύεσι χρῆσθαι τοῖς ἐμοῖς, ἡγούμενος, καὶ τού- 5
τους ἔτ' οἰκειοτέρους εἴ μοι ποιήσειεν, οὐκ ἂν χεῖρόν μ' ἐπι-
6 τροπευθῆναι ταύτης τῆς οἰκειότητος προσγενομένης. λαβόντες
δ' οὗτοι ταῦτα πρῶτον σφίσιν αὐτοῖς ἐκ τῶν χρημάτων, καὶ
τὴν ἄλλην οὐσίαν ἅπασαν διαχειρίσαντες, καὶ δέκ' ἔτη ἡμᾶς
ἐπιτροπεύσαντες, τὰ μὲν ἄλλα πάντ' ἀπεστερήκασιν, τὴν 10
οἰκίαν δὲ καὶ ἀνδράποδα τέτταρα καὶ δέκα καὶ ἀργυρίου μνᾶς
τριάκοντα, μάλιστα σύμπαντα ταῦτ' εἰς ἑβδομήκοντα μνᾶς
7 παραδεδώκασι. καὶ τὸ μὲν κεφάλαιον τῶν ἀδικημάτων, ὡς
ἂν συντομώτατ' εἴποι τις, τοῦτ' ἔστιν, ὦ ἄνδρες δικασταί·
τὸ δὲ πλῆθος τῆς οὐσίας ὅτι τοῦτ' ἦν τὸ καταλειφθέν, μέ- 15
γιστοι μὲν αὐτοὶ μάρτυρές μοι γεγόνασιν· εἰς γὰρ τὴν συμμορίαν ὑπὲρ ἐμοῦ συνετάξαντο κατὰ τὰς πέντε καὶ εἴκοσι
μνᾶς πεντακοσίας δραχμὰς εἰσφέρειν, ὅσονπερ Τιμόθεος ὁ
Κόνωνος καὶ οἱ τὰ μέγιστα κεκτημένοι τιμήματ' εἰσέφερον·
δεῖ δὲ καὶ καθ' ἕκαστον ὑμᾶς ἀκοῦσαι τά τ' ἐνεργὰ αὐτῶν 20
καὶ ὅσ' ἦν ἀργὰ καὶ ὅσου ἦν ἄξι' ἕκαστα. ταῦτα γὰρ μα-
θόντες ἀκριβῶς εἴσεσθε, ὅτι τῶν πώποτ' ἐπιτροπευσάντων
οὐδένες ἀναιδέστερον οὐδὲ περιφανέστερον ἢ οὗτοι τὰ ἡμέ-
8 τερα διηρπάκασιν. πρῶτον μὲν οὖν ὡς συνετιμήσανθ' ὑπὲρ
ἐμοῦ ταύτην τὴν εἰσφορὰν εἰς τὴν συμμορίαν, παρέξομαι 25
τούτων μάρτυρας, ἔπειθ' ὅτι οὐ πένητα κατέλιπέν μ' ὁ πατὴρ
οὐδ' ἑβδομήκοντα μνῶν οὐσίαν κεκτημένον, ἀλλὰ τοσαύτην
ὅσην οὐδ' αὐτοὶ οὗτοι ἀποκρύψασθαι διὰ τὸ μέγεθος πρὸς
τὴν πόλιν ἐδυνήθησαν. καί μοι ἀναγίγνωσκε λαβὼν ταύτην
τὴν μαρτυρίαν. 30

MΑΡΤΥΡΙΑ.

9   Δῆλον μὲν τοίνυν καὶ ἐκ τούτων ἐστὶν τὸ πλῆθος τῆς

οὐσίας. πεντεκαίδεκα ταλάντων γὰρ τρία τάλαντα τίμημα·
ταύτην ἠξίουν εἰσφέρειν τὴν εἰσφοράν. ἔτι δ' ἀκριβέστερον
εἴσεσθε τὴν οὐσίαν αὐτὴν ἀκούσαντες· ὁ γὰρ πατήρ, ὦ ἄνδρες δικασταί, κατέλιπεν δύ' ἐργαστήρια, τέχνης οὐ μικρᾶς
5 ἑκάτερον, μαχαιροποιοὺς μὲν τριάκοντα, καὶ δύ' ἢ τρεῖς ἀνὰ
πέντε μνᾶς καὶ ἕξ, τοὺς δ' οὐκ ἐλάττονος ἢ τριῶν μνῶν
ἀξίους, ἀφ' ὧν τριάκοντα μνᾶς ἀτελεῖς ἐλάμβανεν τοῦ
ἐνιαυτοῦ τὴν πρόσοδον, κλινοποιοὺς δ' εἴκοσι τὸν ἀριθμόν,
τετταράκοντα μνῶν ὑποκειμένους, οἳ δώδεκα μνᾶς ἀτελεῖς
10 αὐτῷ προσέφερον, ἀργυρίου δ' εἰς τάλαντον ἐπὶ δραχμῇ
δεδανεισμένου, οὗ τόκος ἐγίγνετο τοῦ ἐνιαυτοῦ ἑκάστου πλεῖν
ἢ ἑπτὰ μναῖ. καὶ ταῦτα μὲν ἐνεργὰ κατέλιπεν, ὡς καὶ 10
αὐτοὶ οὗτοι ὁμολογήσουσιν· ὧν γίγνεται τοῦ μὲν ἀρχαίου
κεφάλαιον τέτταρα τάλαντα καὶ πεντακισχίλιαι, τὸ δ' ἔργον
15 αὐτῶν πεντήκοντα μναῖ τοῦ ἐνιαυτοῦ ἑκάστου. χωρὶς δὲ
τούτων ἐλέφαντα μὲν καὶ σίδηρον, ὃν κατηργάζοντο, καὶ
ξύλα κλίνει' εἰς ὀγδοήκοντα μνᾶς ἄξια, κηκῖδα δὲ καὶ χαλ-
κὸν ἑβδομήκοντα μνῶν ἐωνημένα, ἔτι δ' οἰκίαν τρισχιλίων,
ἔπιπλα δὲ καὶ ἐκπώματα καὶ χρυσία καὶ ἱμάτια, τὸν κόσμον
20 τῆς μητρός, ἄξια σύμπαντα ταῦτ' εἰς μυρίας δραχμάς, ἀργυρίου δ' ἔνδον ὀγδοήκοντα μνᾶς. καὶ ταῦτα μὲν οἴκοι 11
κατέλιπεν πάντα, ναυτικὰ δ' ἑβδομήκοντα μνᾶς, ἔκδοσιν
παρὰ Ξούθῳ, τετρακοσίας δὲ καὶ δισχιλίας ἐπὶ τῇ τραπέζῃ
τῇ Πασίωνος, ἑξακοσίας δ' ἐπὶ τῇ Πυλάδου, παρὰ Δημο-
25 μέλει δὲ τῷ Δήμωνος υἱεῖ χιλίας καὶ ἑξακοσίας, κατὰ διακοσίας δὲ καὶ τριακοσίας ὁμοῦ τι τάλαντον διακεχρημένον.
καὶ τούτων αὖ τῶν χρημάτων τὸ κεφάλαιον πλέον ἢ ὀκτὼ
τάλαντα καὶ πεντήκοντα μναῖ γίγνονται. συμπάντων δ' εἰς
τέτταρα καὶ δέκα τάλανθ' εὑρήσετε σκοποῦντες.
30 Καὶ τὸ μὲν πλῆθος τῆς οὐσίας τοῦτ' ἦν τὸ καταλειφθέν, 12
ὦ ἄνδρες δικασταί. ὅσα δ' αὐτῆς διακέκλεπται καὶ ὅσ' ἰδίᾳ
ἕκαστος εἴληφεν καὶ ὁπόσα κοινῇ πάντες ἀποστεροῦσιν, οὐκ
ἐνδέχεται πρὸς ταὐτὸ ὕδωρ εἰπεῖν, ἀλλ' ἀνάγκη χωρὶς ἕκα-

στον διελεῖν ἐστίν. ἃ μὲν οὖν Δημοφῶν ἢ Θηριππίδης
ἔχουσι τῶν ἐμῶν, τότ᾽ ἐξαρκέσει περὶ αὐτῶν εἰπεῖν, ὅταν
κατ᾽ αὐτῶν τὰς γραφὰς ἀπενέγκωμεν· ἃ δὲ τοῦτον ἔχοντ᾽
ἐξελέγχουσιν ἐκεῖνοι καὶ ἐγὼ οἶδ᾽ αὐτὸν εἰληφότα, περὶ τούτων ἤδη ποιήσομαι τοὺς λόγους πρὸς ὑμᾶς. πρῶτον μὲν 5
οὖν ὡς ἔχει τὴν προῖκα, τὰς ὀγδοήκοντα μνᾶς, τοῦθ᾽ ὑμῖν
ἐπιδείξω, μετὰ δὲ ταῦτα καὶ περὶ τῶν ἄλλων, ὡς ἂν δύνωμαι διὰ βραχυτάτων.

13 Οὗτος γὰρ εὐθὺς μετὰ τὸν τοῦ πατρὸς θάνατον ᾤκει τὴν
οἰκίαν εἰσελθὼν κατὰ τὴν ἐκείνου διαθήκην, καὶ λαμβάνει 10
τά τε χρυσία τῆς μητρὸς καὶ τὰ ἐκπώματα τὰ καταλειφθέντα.
καὶ ταῦτα μὲν ὡς εἰς πεντήκοντα μνᾶς εἶχεν, ἔτι δὲ τῶν
ἀνδραπόδων τῶν πιπρασκομένων παρά τε Θηριππίδου καὶ
Δημοφῶντος τὰς τιμὰς ἐλάμβανεν, ἕως ἀνεπληρώσατο τὴν
14 προῖκα, τὰς ὀγδοήκοντα μνᾶς. καὶ ἐπειδὴ εἶχεν, ἐκπλεῖν 15
μέλλων εἰς Κέρκυραν τριήραρχος, ἀπέγραψε ταῦτα πρὸς
Θηριππίδην ἔχονθ᾽ ἑαυτὸν καὶ ὡμολόγει κεκομίσθαι τὴν
προῖκα. καὶ πρῶτον μὲν τούτων Δημοφῶν καὶ Θηριππίδης,
οἱ τούτου συνεπίτροποι, μάρτυρές εἰσιν· ἔτι δὲ καὶ ὡς αὐτὸς
ὡμολόγει ταῦτ᾽ ἔχειν, Δημοχάρης θ᾽ ὁ Λευκονοεύς, ὁ τὴν 20
τηθίδα τὴν ἐμὴν ἔχων, καὶ ἄλλοι πολλοὶ μάρτυρες γεγόνασιν.
15 οὐ γὰρ διδόντος τούτου σῖτον τῇ μητρί, τὴν προῖκ᾽ ἔχοντος,
οὐδὲ τὸν οἶκον μισθοῦν ἐθέλοντος, ἀλλὰ μετὰ τῶν ἄλλων
ἐπιτρόπων διαχειρίζειν ἀξιοῦντος, ἐποιήσατο λόγους περὶ
τούτων ὁ Δημοχάρης. οὗτος δ᾽ ἀκούσας οὔτ᾽ ἠμφεσβήτησεν 25
μὴ ἔχειν οὔτε χαλεπῶς ἤνεγκεν ὡς οὐκ εἰληφώς, ἀλλ᾽ ὡμολόγει καὶ ἔτι μικρὸν ἔφη πρὸς τὴν ἐμὴν μητέρα περὶ χρυσι-
δίων ἀντιλέγεσθαι· τοῦτ᾽ οὖν διευκρινησάμενος, καὶ περὶ
τῆς τροφῆς καὶ περὶ τῶν ἄλλων ποιήσειν οὕτως ὥστ᾽ ἔχειν
16 μοι πάντα καλῶς. καίτοι εἰ φανήσεται πρός τε τὸν Δημο- 30
χάρη ταῦθ᾽ ὡμολογηκὼς καὶ πρὸς τοὺς ἄλλους οἳ παρῆσαν,
παρά τε τοῦ Δημοφῶντος καὶ τοῦ Θηριππίδου τῶν ἀνδραπόδων εἰς τὴν προῖκα τὰς τιμὰς εἰληφώς, αὐτός θ᾽ ἑαυτὸν

ἔχειν τὴν προῖκ' ἀπογράψας πρὸς τοὺς συνεπιτρόπους, οἰκῶν
τε τὴν οἰκίαν ἐπειδὴ τάχιστ' ἐτελεύτησεν ὁ πατήρ, πῶς οὐκ
ἐκ πάντων ὁμολογουμένου τοῦ πράγματος εὑρεθήσεται φανερῶς τὴν προῖκα, τὰς ὀγδοήκοντα μνᾶς, κεκομισμένος, καὶ
5 λίαν ἀναιδῶς μὴ λαβεῖν ἐξαρνούμενος; ἀλλὰ μὴν ὡς ἀληθῆ 17
λέγω, λαβὲ τὰς μαρτυρίας καὶ ἀνάγνωθι.

MΑΡΤΥΡΙΑΙ.

Τὴν μὲν τοίνυν προῖκα τοῦτον τὸν τρόπον ἔχει λαβών.
μὴ γήμαντος δ' αὐτοῦ τὴν μητέρα τὴν ἐμήν, ὁ μὲν νόμος
10 κελεύει τὴν προῖκ' ὀφείλειν ἐπ' ἐννέ' ὀβολοῖς, ἐγὼ δ' ἐπὶ
δραχμῇ μόνον τίθημι. γίγνεται δ', ἐάν τις συντιθῇ τό τ'
ἀρχαῖον καὶ τὸ ἔργον τῶν δέκ' ἐτῶν, μάλιστα τρία τάλαντα.
καὶ ταῦτα μὲν οὕτως ὑμῖν ἐπιδείκνυμι λαβόντα καὶ ἔχειν 18
ὁμολογήσαντα μαρτύρων ἐναντίον τοσούτων· ἄλλας τοίνυν
15 ἔχει τριάκοντα μνᾶς, τοῦ ἐργαστηρίου λαβὼν τὴν πρόσοδον,
καὶ ἀναισχυντότατ' ἀνθρώπων ἀποστερεῖν ἐπικεχείρηκεν.
ἐμοὶ δ' ὁ πατὴρ κατέλιπεν τριάκοντα μνᾶς ἀπ' αὐτῶν τὴν
πρόσοδον· ἀποδομένων δὲ τούτων τὰ ἡμίσεα τῶν ἀνδραπόδων, πεντεκαίδεκά μοι μνᾶς γίγνεσθαι κατὰ λόγον προσῆκε.
20 Θηριππίδης μὲν οὖν ἔπτ' ἔτη τῶν ἀνδραπόδων ἐπιμεληθεὶς 19
ἕνδεκα μνᾶς τοῦ ἐνιαυτοῦ ἀπέφηνε, τέτταρσι μναῖς καθ'
ἕκαστον ἐνιαυτὸν ἔλαττον ἢ ὅσον προσῆκε λογιζόμενος.
οὗτος δὲ δύ' ἔτη τὰ πρῶτ' ἐπιμεληθεὶς οὐδ' ὁτιοῦν ἀποδείκνυσιν, ἀλλ' ἐνίοτε μέν φησιν ἀργῆσαι τὸ ἐργαστήριον,
25 ἐνίοτε δ' ὡς αὐτὸς μὲν οὐκ ἐπεμελήθη τούτων, ὁ δ' ἐπίτροπος Μιλύας, ὁ ἀπελεύθερος ὁ ἡμέτερος, διῴκησεν αὐτά, καὶ
παρ' ἐκείνου μοι προσήκει λόγον λαβεῖν. ἂν οὖν καὶ νῦν
εἴπῃ τινὰ τούτων τῶν λόγων, ῥᾳδίως ἐξελεγχθήσεται ψευδό-
μενος. ἂν μὲν οὖν ἀργὸν φῇ γενέσθαι, λόγον αὐτὸς ἀπε- 20
30 νήνοχεν ἀναλωμάτων οὐκ εἰς σιτία τοῖς ἀνθρώποις, ἀλλ' εἰς
ἔργα, τὸν εἰς τὴν τέχνην ἐλέφαντα καὶ μαχαιρῶν λαβὰς καὶ
ἄλλας ἐπισκευάς, ὡς ἐργαζομένων τῶν δημιουργῶν. ἔτι δὲ

Θηριππίδῃ τριῶν ἀνδραπόδων, ἃ ἦν αὐτῷ ἐν τῷ ἐμῷ ἐργα-
στηρίῳ, μισθὸν ἀποδεδωκέναι λογίζεται. καίτοι μὴ γενομένης ἐργασίας οὔτ' ἐκείνῳ λαβεῖν μισθὸν οὔτ' ἐμοὶ τὰ
21 ἀναλώματα ταῦτα λογισθῆναι προσῆκεν. εἰ δ' αὖ γενέσθαι
μὲν φήσει, τῶν δ' ἔργων ἀπρασίαν εἶναι, δεῖ δήπου τά γ' 5
ἔργ' αὐτὸν ἀποδεδωκότα μοι φαίνεσθαι, καὶ ὧν ἐναντίον
ἀπέδωκε παρασχέσθαι μάρτυρας. εἰ δὲ μηδὲν τούτων
πεποίηκεν, πῶς οὐκ ἔχει τὴν πρόσοδον δυοῖν ἐτοῖν τὴν ἐκ
τοῦ ἐργαστηρίου, τὰς τριάκοντα μνᾶς, φανερῶς οὕτως τῶν
22 ἔργων γεγενημένων; εἰ δ' αὖ τούτων μὲν μηδὲν ἐρεῖ, Μι- 10
λύαν δ' αὐτὰ φήσει πάντα διῳκηκέναι, πῶς χρὴ πιστεύειν,
ὅταν φῇ τὰ μὲν ἀναλώματ' αὐτὸς ἀνηλωκέναι, πλέον ἢ
πεντακοσίας δραχμάς, λῆμμα δ' εἴ τι γέγονεν, ἐκεῖνον ἔχειν;
ἐμοὶ μὲν γὰρ δοκεῖ τοὐναντίον ἂν γενέσθαι τούτων, εἰ καὶ
Μιλύας αὐτῶν ἐπεμελεῖτο, τὰ μὲν ἀναλώματ' ἐκεῖνος ἀνα- 15
λῶσαι, τὰ δὲ λήμμαθ' οὗτος λαβεῖν, εἴ τι δεῖ τεκμαίρεσθαι
πρὸς τὸν ἄλλον αὐτοῦ τρόπον καὶ τὴν ἀναίδειαν. λάβ' οὖν
τὰς μαρτυρίας ταύτας, καὶ ἀνάγνωθ' αὐτοῖς.

MΑΡΤΥΡΙΑΙ.

23   Ταύτας τοίνυν ἔχει τριάκοντα μνᾶς ἀπὸ τοῦ ἐργαστηρίου, 20
καὶ τὸ ἔργον αὐτῶν ὀκτὼ ἐτῶν· ὃ ἂν ἐπὶ δραχμῇ τις τιθῇ
μόνον, ἄλλας τριάκοντα μνᾶς εὑρήσει. καὶ ταῦτα μὲν ἰδίᾳ
μόνος εἴληφεν· ἃ συντεθέντα πρὸς τὴν προῖκα μάλιστα τέτταρα τάλαντα γίγνεται σὺν τοῖς ἀρχαίοις. ἃ δὲ μετὰ τῶν
ἄλλων ἐπιτρόπων κοινῇ διήρπακεν, καὶ ὅσ' ἔνια μηδὲ καταλει- 25
φθῆναι παντάπασιν ἠμφεσβήτηκεν, ταῦθ' ὑμῖν ἤδη ἐπιδείξω
24 καθ' ἕκαστον. πρῶτον μὲν οὖν περὶ τῶν κλινοποιῶν, οὓς
κατέλιπεν μὲν ὁ πατήρ, ἀφανίζουσι δ' οὗτοι, τετταράκοντα
μὲν μνῶν ὑποκειμένους, εἴκοσι δ' ὄντας τὸν ἀριθμόν, ἐπιδείξω ὑμῖν ὡς λίαν ἀναιδῶς καὶ φανερῶς μ' ἀποστεροῦσι. 30
τούτους γὰρ καταλειφθῆναι μὲν οἴκοι παρ' ἡμῖν πάντες ὁμολογοῦσιν, καὶ τὰς δώδεκα μνᾶς ἑκάστου τοῦ ἐνιαυτοῦ τῷ πατρὶ

34

γίγνεσθαί φασιν· αὐτοὶ δὲ λῆμμα μὲν παρ' αὐτῶν ἐν
δέκ' ἔτεσιν οὐδὲν ἐμοὶ γεγενημένον ἀποφαίνουσιν ἀλλ' οὐδὲ
μικρόν, ἀναλώματος δὲ κεφάλαιον εἰς αὐτοὺς οὗτος ὀλίγου
δεῖν λογίζεται χιλίας· εἰς τοῦτ' ἀναιδείας ἐλήλυθεν. αὐτοὺς 25
5 δὲ τοὺς ἀνθρώπους, εἰς οὓς ταῦτ' ἀνηλωκέναι φησίν, οὐδα-
μοῦ μοι παραδεδώκασιν, ἀλλὰ πάντων κενότατον λόγον
λέγουσιν, ὡς ὁ ὑποθεὶς τῷ πατρὶ τἀνδράποδα πονηρότατος
ἀνθρώπων ἐστὶν καὶ ἐράνους τε λέλοιπε πλείστους καὶ
ὑπέρχρεως γέγονε, καὶ τούτων οὐκ ὀλίγους κεκλήκασι κατ'
10 ἐκείνου μάρτυρας. τὰ δ' ἀνδράποδ' ὅστις ἐστὶν ὁ λαβών,
ἢ πῶς ἐκ τῆς οἰκίας ἐξῆλθεν, ἢ τίς ἀφείλετο, ἢ πρὸς τίνα
δίκην ἥττηνται περὶ αὐτῶν, οὐκ ἔχουσιν εἰπεῖν. καίτοι εἴ 26
τι ἔλεγον ὑγιές, οὐκ ἂν κατὰ τῆς ἐκείνου πονηρίας παρεί-
χοντο μάρτυρας, ἧς οὐδέν μοι προσήκει φροντίζειν, ἀλλὰ
15 τούτων ἂν ἀντελαμβάνοντο καὶ τοὺς λαβόντας ἀπεδείκνυσαν
καὶ οὐδὲν ἂν αὐτῶν παρέλειπον. νῦν δ' ὠμότατ' ἀνθρώπων,
ὁμολογοῦντες καταλειφθῆναι καὶ λαβόντες ὡς αὐτοὺς καὶ
καρπωσάμενοι δέκ' ἔτη τοὺς ἀνθρώπους, ἄρδην ὅλον τὸ
ἐργαστήριον ἀφανίζουσι. καὶ ταῦθ' ὡς ἀληθῆ λέγω, λαβέ
20 μοι τὰς μαρτυρίας καὶ ἀναγίγνωσκε.

ΜΑΡΤΥΡΙΑΙ.

Ὅτι τοίνυν οὐκ ἄπορος ἦν ὁ Μοιριάδης, οὐδ' ἦν τῷ 27
πατρὶ τοῦτο τὸ συμβόλαιον εἰς τἀνδράποδ' ἠλιθίως συμ-
βεβλημένον, μεγίστῳ τεκμηρίῳ γνώσεσθε· λαβὼν γὰρ ὡς
25 ἑαυτὸν Ἄφοβος τοῦτο τὸ ἐργαστήριον, ὡς αὐτοὶ τῶν μαρτύρων ἠκούσατε, καὶ δέον αὐτόν, εἰ καί τις ἄλλος ἐβούλετ'
εἰς ταῦτα συμβαλεῖν, τοῦτον διακωλύειν ἐπίτροπόν γ' ὄντα,
αὐτὸς ἐπὶ τούτοις τοῖς ἀνδραπόδοις τῷ Μοιριάδῃ πεντακοσίας δραχμὰς ἐδάνεισεν, ἃς ὀρθῶς καὶ δικαίως παρ' ἐκείνου
30 κεκομίσθαι ὡμολόγηκεν. καίτοι πῶς οὐ δεινόν, εἰ ἡμῖν 28
μὲν πρὸς τῷ λήμμ' ἀπ' αὐτῶν μηδὲν γεγονέναι καὶ αὐτὰ τὰ
ὑποτεθέντ' ἀπόλωλεν, οἳ πρότερον συνεβάλομεν, τῷ δ' εἰς

τὰ ἡμέτερα δανείσαντι καὶ τοσούτῳ χρόνῳ πράξαντι καὶ οἱ
τόκοι καὶ τἀρχαῖ᾿ ἐκ τῶν ἡμετέρων ἀποδέδοται καὶ οὐδεμί᾿
ἀπορία γέγονεν; ἀλλὰ μὴν ὡς ἀληθῆ λέγω, λαβὲ τὴν
μαρτυρίαν καὶ ἀνάγνωθι.

MΑΡΤΥΡΙΑ.   5

29   Σκέψασθε τοίνυν ὅσον ἀργύριον οὗτοι παρὰ τοὺς κλινοποιοὺς κλέπτουσι, τετταράκοντα μὲν μνᾶς αὐτὸ τὸ ἀρχαῖον,
δέκα δ᾿ ἐτῶν τὸ ἔργον αὐτῶν δύο τάλαντα· δώδεκα γὰρ
μνᾶς ἑκάστου τοῦ ἐνιαυτοῦ τὴν πρόσοδον αὐτῶν ἐλάμβανον.
ἆρα μικρόν τι καὶ ἐξ ἀφανοῦς ποθεν καὶ παραλογίσασθαι   10
ῥᾴδιον, ἀλλ᾿ οὐ φανερῶς οὑτωσὶ μικροῦ δεῖν τρία τάλαντα
ταῦτ᾿ ἀνηρπάκασιν; ὧν κοινῇ διαπεφορημένων τὸ τρίτον
δήπου μέρος παρὰ τούτου μοι προσήκει κεκομίσθαι.

30   Καὶ μήν, ὦ ἄνδρες δικασταί, καὶ τὰ περὶ τοῦ ἐλέφαντος
καὶ σιδήρου τοῦ καταλειφθέντος παραπλήσιά πως τούτοις   15
πεποιήκασιν· οὐδὲ γὰρ ταῦτ᾿ ἀποφαίνουσιν. καίτοι κεκτημένον μὲν τοσούτους κλινοποιούς, κεκτημένον δὲ μαχαιροποιοὺς οὐχ οἷόν τε μὴ οὐχὶ καὶ σίδηρον καὶ ἐλέφαντα
καταλιπεῖν, ἀλλ᾿ ἀνάγκη ταῦτά γ᾿ ὑπάρχειν· τί γὰρ ἂν
31 ἠργάζοντο τούτων μὴ ὑπαρξάντων; τὸν τοίνυν πλέον ἢ   20
πεντήκοντ᾿ ἀνδράποδα κεκτημένον καὶ δυοῖν τέχναιν ἐπιμε-
λούμενον, ὧν θάτερον ἐργαστήριον εἰς τὰς κλίνας ῥᾳδίως
δύο μνᾶς τοῦ μηνὸς ἀνήλισκεν ἐλέφαντος, τὸ δὲ μαχαιρο-
ποιεῖον οὐκ ἔλαττον ἢ τοσοῦτον ἕτερον σὺν σιδήρῳ, τοῦτον
οὔ φασιν καταλιπεῖν οὐδὲν τούτων· εἰς τοῦτ᾿ ἀναιδείας   25
32 ἐληλύθασιν. ὅτι μὲν οὖν οὐ πιστὰ λέγουσιν, καὶ ἐκ τούτων
αὐτῶν ῥᾴδιόν ἐστι μαθεῖν· ὅτι δ᾿ ἐκεῖνος κατέλιπε τοσοῦτον
τὸ πλῆθος ὥστε μὴ μόνον ἱκανὸν εἶναι κατεργάζεσθαι τοῖς
ἑαυτοῦ δημιουργοῖς, ἀλλὰ καὶ τῷ βουλομένῳ πρὸς ὠνεῖσθαι
τῶν ἄλλων, ἐκεῖθεν φανερόν, ὅτι αὐτός τ᾿ ἐπώλει ζῶν καὶ   30
Δημοφῶν καὶ οὗτος τοῦ πατρὸς ἤδη τετελευτηκότος ἐκ τῆς
33 οἰκίας τῆς ἐμῆς ἀπεδίδοντο τοῖς βουλομένοις. καίτοι πόσον

τινὰ χρὴ τὸν καταλειφθέντα νομίζειν εἶναι, ὅταν φαίνηται
τηλικούτοις τ' ἐργαστηρίοις ἐξαρκῶν καὶ χωρὶς ὑπὸ τῶν
ἐπιτρόπων πιπρασκόμενος; ἆρ' ὀλίγον, ἀλλ' οὐ πολλῷ
πλείω τῶν ἐγκεκλημένων; λαβὲ τοίνυν τὰς μαρτυρίας ταυ-
5 τασὶ καὶ ἀνάγνωθ' αὐτοῖς.

MΑΡΤΥΡΙΑΙ.

Τούτου τοίνυν τοῦ ἐλέφαντός ἐστι πλέον ἢ τάλαντον, ὃν
οὔτ' αὐτὸν οὔτε τὸ ἔργον μοι ἀποφαίνουσιν, ἀλλὰ καὶ τοῦτον
ἄρδην ἀφανίζουσιν ὅλον.

10 Ἔτι τοίνυν, ὦ ἄνδρες δικασταί, παρὰ τὸν λόγον ὃν ἀπο- 34
φέρουσιν, ἐξ ὧν αὐτοὶ λαβεῖν ὁμολογοῦσιν, ἐπιδείξω ὑμῖν
τρεῖς μὲν ὄντας αὐτοὺς πλέον ἢ ὀκτὼ τάλαντ' ἐκ τῶν ἐμῶν
ἔχοντας, ἰδίᾳ δ' ἐκ τούτων Ἄφοβον τρία τάλαντα καὶ
χιλίας εἰληφότα, τά τ' ἀνηλωμένα χωρὶς τούτων πλείω
15 τιθεὶς καὶ ὅσ' ἐκ τούτων ἀπέδοσαν ἀφαιρῶν, ἵν' εἰδῆθ' ὅτι
οὐ μικρᾶς ἀναιδείας τὰ ἐγχειρήματ' αὐτῶν ἐστιν. λαβεῖν 35
γὰρ ἐκ τῶν ἐμῶν ὁμολογοῦσιν οὗτος μὲν ὀκτὼ καὶ ἑκατὸν
μνᾶς, χωρὶς ὧν ἔχοντ' αὐτὸν ἐγὼ ἐπιδείξω νῦν, Θηριππίδης
δὲ δύο τάλαντα, Δημοφῶν δ' ἑπτὰ καὶ ὀγδοήκοντα μνᾶς.
20 τοῦτο δ' ἐστὶ πέντε τάλαντα καὶ πεντεκαίδεκα μναῖ. τούτου
τοίνυν ὃ μὲν οὐχ ἄθρουν ἐλήφθη, σχεδόν εἰσιν ἑβδομήκοντα
μναῖ καὶ ἑπτά, ἡ πρόσοδος ἡ ἀπὸ τῶν ἀνδραπόδων, ὃ δ'
εὐθὺς ἔλαβον οὗτοι, μικροῦ δέοντα τέτταρα τάλαντα· οἷς
τὸ ἔργον ἂν προσθῆτ' ἐπὶ δραχμῇ μόνον τῶν δέκ' ἐτῶν,
25 ὀκτὼ τάλανθ' εὑρήσετε σὺν τοῖς ἀρχαίοις καὶ χιλίας γιγνομένας. τὴν μὲν τοίνυν τροφὴν ἀπὸ τῶν ἑβδομήκοντα μνῶν 36
καὶ ἑπτὰ λογιστέον τῶν ἀπὸ τοῦ ἐργαστηρίου γενομένων.
Θηριππίδης γὰρ ἑπτὰ μνᾶς ἐδίδου καθ' ἕκαστον τὸν ἐνιαυτὸν
εἰς ταῦτα, καὶ ἡμεῖς τοῦτο λαβεῖν ὁμολογοῦμεν. ὥσθ'
30 ἑβδομήκοντα μνῶν ἐν τοῖς δέκ' ἔτεσιν τροφὴν τούτων ἡμῖν
ἀνηλωκότων, τὸ περιὸν τὰς ἑπτακοσίας προστίθημ' αὐτοῖς,
καὶ τούτων πλείω εἰμὶ τεθηκώς. ὃ δ' ἐμοὶ δοκιμασθέντι

37

παρέδοσαν καὶ ὅσον εἰς τὴν πόλιν εἰσενηνόχασιν, τοῦτ' ἀπὸ
τῶν ὀκτὼ ταλάντων καὶ τοῦ προσόντος ἀφαιρετέον ἐστίν.
37 ἀπέδοσαν μὲν τοίνυν οὗτος καὶ Θηριππίδης μίαν καὶ τριάκοντα μνᾶς, εἰσφορὰς δ' εἰσενηνοχέναι λογίζονται δυοῖν δεού-
σας εἴκοσι μνᾶς. ἐγὼ δ' ὑπερβαλὼν τοῦτο ποιήσω τριάκοντα 5
μνᾶς, ἵνα πρὸς ταῦτα μηδ' ἀντειπεῖν ἔχωσιν. οὐκοῦν ἂν
ἀφέλητε τὸ τάλαντον ἀπὸ τῶν ὀκτὼ ταλάντων, ἑπτὰ τὰ
λειπόμεν' ἐστί, καὶ ταῦτα, ἐξ ὧν αὐτοὶ λαβεῖν ὁμολογοῦσι,
τούτους ἔχειν ἐστὶν ἀναγκαῖον. τοῦτο τοίνυν, εἰ καὶ τἄλλα
πάντ' ἀποστεροῦσιν ἀρνούμενοι μὴ ἔχειν, ἀποδοῦναι προσῆ- 10
38 κεν, ὁμολογοῦντάς γε λαβεῖν ταῦτ' ἐκ τῶν ἐμῶν. νῦν
δὲ τί ποιοῦσιν; ἔργον μὲν οὐδὲν ἀποφαίνουσι τοῖς χρήμασιν, αὐτὰ δὲ τὰ ἀρχαῖα πάντ' ἀνηλωκέναι φασὶ σὺν ταῖς
ἑπτὰ καὶ ἑβδομήκοντα μναῖς· Δημοφῶν δὲ καὶ πρὸς ὀφεί-
λοντας ἡμᾶς ἐνέγραψε. ταῦτ' οὐ μεγάλη καὶ περιφανὴς 15
ἀναισχυντία; ταῦτ' οὐχ ὑπερβολὴ δεινῆς αἰσχροκερδίας;
τί οὖν ποτ' ἐστὶ τὸ δεινόν, εἰ μὴ ταῦτα δόξει τηλικαύτας
39 ὑπερβολὰς ἔχοντα; οὗτος τοίνυν τὸ καθ' αὑτὸν ὀκτὼ καὶ
ἑκατὸν μνᾶς λαβεῖν ὁμολογῶν, ἔχει καὶ αὐτὰς καὶ τὸ ἔργον
δέκ' ἐτῶν, μάλιστα τρία τάλαντα καὶ χιλίας. καὶ ταῦθ' 20
ὡς ἀληθῆ λέγω, καὶ ἐν τοῖς λόγοις τῆς ἐπιτροπῆς τὸ λῆμμ'
ἕκαστος τοῦθ' ὁμολογῶν λαβεῖν ἅπαν ἀνηλωκέναι λογίζεται,
λαβὲ τὰς μαρτυρίας καὶ ἀνάγνωθι.

MAPTYPIAI.

40 Νομίζω τοίνυν, ὦ ἄνδρες δικασταί, περὶ τούτων ἱκανῶς 25
μὲν ὑμᾶς μεμαθηκέναι, καὶ ὅσα κλέπτουσιν καὶ κακουργοῦσιν
ἕκαστος αὐτῶν· ἔτι δ' ἀκριβέστερον ἔγνωτ' ἄν, εἴ μοι τὰς
διαθήκας, ἃς ὁ πατὴρ κατέλιπεν, οὗτοι ἀποδοῦναι ἠθέλησαν.
ἐν γὰρ ἐκείναις ἐγέγραπτο, ὥς φησιν ἡ μήτηρ, ἃ κατέλιπεν
ὁ πατὴρ πάντα, καὶ ἐξ ὧν ἔδει τούτους λαβεῖν τὰ δοθέντα, 30
41 καὶ τὸν οἶκον ὅπως μισθώσουσι. νῦν δ' ἀπαιτοῦντος ἐμοῦ
καταλειφθῆναι μὲν ὁμολογοῦσιν, αὐτὰς δ' οὐκ ἀποφαίνουσι.

ταῦτα δὲ ποιοῦσι τό τε πλῆθος οὐ βουλόμενοι καταφανὲς
ποιῆσαι τῆς οὐσίας τὸ καταλειφθέν, ὃ διηρπάκασιν οὗτοι,
τάς τε δωρεὰς ἵνα μὴ δοκῶσιν ἔχειν, ὥσπερ οὐκ ἐξ αὐτοῦ
τοῦ πράγματος ἐξελεγχθησόμενοι ῥᾳδίως. λαβὲ δ' αὐτοῖς
5 τὰς μαρτυρίας ὧν ἐναντίον ἀπεκρίναντο, καὶ ἀνάγνωθι.

ΜΑΡΤΥΡΙΑΙ.

Οὗτος διαθήκην μὲν γενέσθαι φησίν, καὶ τὰ δύο τάλαντα 42
Δημοφῶντι καὶ τὰς ὀγδοήκοντα μνᾶς τούτῳ δοθῆναι μαρτυ-
ρεῖ· τὰς δ' ἑβδομήκοντα μνᾶς, ἃς Θηριππίδης ἔλαβεν, οὐ
10 προσγραφῆναί φησιν, οὐδὲ τὸ πλῆθος τῆς οὐσίας τὸ καταλειφθέν, οὐδὲ τὸν οἶκον ὅπως μισθώσουσιν· οὐ γὰρ αὐτῷ
συμφέρει προσομολογῆσαι ταῦτα. λαβὲ δὴ τὴν τούτου
ἀπόκρισιν.

ΜΑΡΤΥΡΙΑ.

15 Οὗτος αὖ τὴν μὲν διαθήκην γενέσθαι φησίν, καὶ τὸ 43
ἀργύριον ἐκ τοῦ χαλκοῦ καὶ τῆς κηκῖδος ἀποδοθῆναι τῷ
Θηριππίδῃ, ὃ ἐκεῖνος οὔ φησιν, καὶ τὰ δύο τάλαντα τῷ
Δημοφῶντι· περὶ δὲ τῶν αὐτῷ δοθέντων γραφῆναι μέν
φησιν, οὐχ ὁμολογῆσαι δ' αὐτός, ἵνα μὴ δοκῇ λαβεῖν. τὸ
20 δὲ πλῆθος τῆς οὐσίας οὐδ' οὗτος ἀποφαίνει καθόλου, οὐδὲ
τὸ μισθοῦν τὸν οἶκον· οὐδὲ γὰρ οὐδὲ τούτῳ συμφέρει προσομολογῆσαι ταῦτα. δῆλον τοίνυν ἐστὶν οὐδὲν ἧττον τὸ 44
πλῆθος τῶν καταλειφθέντων, καίπερ ἀφανιζόντων τούτων
τὴν οὐσίαν ἐκ τῶν διαθηκῶν, ἐξ ὧν τοσαῦτα χρήματ' ἀλλή-
25 λοις φασὶ δοθῆναι. ὅστις γὰρ ἐκ τεττάρων ταλάντων καὶ
τρισχιλίων τοῖς μὲν τρία τάλαντα καὶ δισχιλίας προῖκα
δέδωκεν, τῷ δ' ἑβδομήκοντα μνᾶς καρποῦσθαι, φανερὸν
δήπου πᾶσιν ὅτι οὐκ ἀπὸ μικρᾶς οὐσίας, ἀλλὰ πλέον ἢ
διπλασίας ἧς ἐμοὶ κατέλειπεν ταῦτ' ἀφεῖλεν. οὐ γὰρ δήπου 45
30 τὸν μὲν υἱὸν ἐμὲ πένητ' ἐβούλετο καταλιπεῖν, τούτους δὲ
πλουσίους ὄντας ἔτι πλουσιωτέρους ποιῆσαι ἐπεθύμησεν,

39

ἀλλ' ἔνεκα τοῦ πλήθους τῶν ἐμοὶ καταλειπομένων Θηριππίδῃ
τε τοσοῦτον ἀργύριον καὶ Δημοφῶντι τὰ δύο τάλαντα, οὔπω
μέλλοντι τῇ ἀδελφῇ τῇ ἐμῇ συνοικήσειν, καρποῦσθαι ἔδωκεν,
ἵνα δυοῖν θάτερον διαπράξαιτο, ἢ διὰ τὰ διδόμενα βελτίους
αὐτοὺς εἶναι τὰ περὶ τὴν ἐπιτροπὴν προτρέψειεν, ἢ εἰ κακοὶ 5
γίγνοιντο, μηδεμιᾶς συγγνώμης παρ' ὑμῶν τυγχάνοιεν, εἰ
46 τοσούτων ἀξιωθέντες τοιαῦτ' εἰς ἡμᾶς ἐξαμαρτάνοιεν. οὗτος
τοίνυν καὶ αὐτὸς πρὸς τῇ προικὶ καὶ θεραπαίνας λαβὼν καὶ
τὴν οἰκίαν οἰκῶν, ἐπειδὴ δεῖ λόγον αὐτὸν δοῦναι τούτων, τὰ
ἑαυτοῦ πράττειν φησίν· καὶ εἰς τοσοῦτον αἰσχροκερδίας 10
ἦλθεν, ὥστε καὶ τοὺς διδασκάλους τοὺς μισθοὺς ἀπεστέρηκεν
καὶ τῶν εἰσφορῶν ἔστιν ἃς οὐ κατέθηκεν, ἐμοὶ δὲ λογίζεται.
λαβὲ δὴ καὶ ταύτας αὐτοῖς τὰς μαρτυρίας καὶ ἀνάγνωθι.

MΑΡΤΥΡΙΑΙ.

47 Πῶς οὖν ἄν τις σαφέστερον ἐπιδείξειεν πάντα διηρπακότα 15
καὶ μηδὲ τῶν μικρῶν ἀπεσχημένον, ἢ τοῦτον τὸν τρόπον
ἐπιδεικνὺς μετὰ τοσούτων μαρτύρων καὶ τεκμηρίων; τὴν
μὲν προῖκα λαβεῖν ὁμολογήσαντα καὶ ἔχειν αὐτὸν πρὸς τοὺς
ἐπιτρόπους ἀπογράψαντα, τὸ δ' ἐργαστήριον κεκαρπωμένον
48 αὐτὸν καὶ τὴν πρόσοδον οὐκ ἀποφαίνοντα, τῶν δ' ἄλλων τὰ 20
μὲν πεπρακότα καὶ τὰς τιμὰς οὐκ ἀποδεδωκότα, τὰ δ' ὡς
ἑαυτὸν λαβόντα καὶ ταῦτ' ἠφανικότα, ἔτι δὲ παρὰ τὸν λόγον
ὃν αὐτὸς ἀπέδωκε τοσαῦτα κλέπτοντα, πρὸς δὲ τούτοις τὴν
διαθήκην ἠφανικότα, τὰ ἀνδράποδα πεπρακότα, τἄλλ' οὕτω
πάντα διῳκηκότα, ὡς οὐδ' ἂν οἱ ἔχθιστοι διοικήσειαν; ἐγὼ 25
μὲν οὐκ οἶδ' ὅπως ἄν τις σαφέστερον ἐπιδείξειεν.

49 Ἐτόλμα τοίνυν πρὸς τῷ διαιτητῇ λέγειν, ὡς ἀπὸ τῶν
χρημάτων χρέα τε πάμπολλ' ἐκτέτεικεν ὑπὲρ ἐμοῦ Δημοφῶντι καὶ Θηριππίδῃ τοῖς συνεπιτρόποις, καὶ ὡς πολλὰ τῶν
ἐμῶν λάβοιεν, οὐδέτερ' ἔχων ἐπιδεικνύαι τούτων. οὔτε 30
γὰρ ὡς ὀφείλοντά με κατέλιπεν ὁ πατὴρ ἐν τοῖς γράμμασιν
ἀπέφηνεν, οὐδ' οἷς ἀποδεδωκέναι ταῦτ' ἔφη παρέσχηται μάρ-

τυρας, οὔτ' αὖ τὸν ἀριθμὸν τῶν χρημάτων εἰς τοὺς συνεπιτρόπους ἐπανέφερεν ὅσον αὐτὸς φαίνεται λαβών, ἀλλὰ
πολλοῖς ἐλάττω χρήμασιν. ἐρωτηθεὶς δ' ὑπὸ τοῦ διαιτητοῦ 50
ταῦτά τε καθ' ἕκαστον, καὶ τὴν οὐσίαν τὴν αὐτοῦ πότερον
5 ἐκ τῶν ἐπικαρπιῶν ἢ τἀρχαῖ' ἀναλίσκων διῴκηκεν, καὶ
πότερον ἐπιτροπευθεὶς ἀπεδέξατ' ἂν τοῦτον τὸν λόγον παρὰ
τῶν ἐπιτρόπων ἢ τἀρχαῖ' ἂν ἀπολαβεῖν ἠξίου σὺν τοῖς
ἔργοις τοῖς γεγενημένοις, πρὸς μὲν ταῦτ' ἀπεκρίνατ' οὐδέν,
προὐκαλεῖτο δ' ἐθέλειν ἐπιδεῖξαί μοι τὴν οὐσίαν δέκα ταλάν-
10 των οὖσαν· εἰ δέ τι ἐλλείποι, αὐτὸς ἔφη προσθήσειν. κε- 51
λεύοντος δ' ἐμοῦ πρὸς τὸν διαιτητὴν ἐπιδεικνύναι ταῦτ' οὐκ
ἐπέδειξεν, οὐδ' ὡς οἱ συνεπίτροποι παρέδοσαν (οὐ γὰρ ἂν
αὐτοῦ κατεδιῄτησεν), μαρτυρίαν δ' ἐνεβάλετο τοιαύτην, περὶ
ἧς πειράσεταί τι λέγειν. ἂν μὲν οὖν καὶ νῦν ἔχειν με φῇ,
15 τίνος παραδόντος ἐρωτᾶτ' αὐτόν, καὶ καθ' ἕκαστον παρασχέσθαι μάρτυρας ἀξιοῦτε. ἐὰν δ' εἶναί μοι φῇ τοῦτον τὸν 52
τρόπον, λογιζόμενος τὰ παρ' ἑκατέρῳ τῶν ἐπιτρόπων, διπλασίοις ἐλάττω φανήσεται λέγων, ἔχοντα δ' οὐδὲν μᾶλλον
ἀποφαίνων. ἐγὼ γὰρ ὥσπερ καὶ τοῦτον τοσαῦτ' ἔχοντ'
20 ἐξήλεγξα, οὕτως κἀκείνων ἑκάτερον οὐκ ἐλάττω τούτων
ἔχοντ' ἐπιδείξω. ὥστ' οὐ τοῦτ' αὐτῷ λεκτέον, ἀλλ' ὡς ἢ
αὐτὸς ἢ οἱ συνεπίτροποι παρέδοσαν. εἰ δὲ μὴ τοῦτ' ἐπι-
δείξει, πῶς χρὴ ταύτῃ τῇ προκλήσει προσέχειν ὑμᾶς τὸν
νοῦν; οὐδὲν γὰρ μᾶλλον ἔχοντά μ' ἐπιδείκνυσι.

25 Πολλὰ τοίνυν ἀπορηθεὶς πρὸς τῷ διαιτητῇ περὶ πάντων 53
τούτων, καὶ καθ' ἕκαστον ἐξελεγχόμενος ὥσπερ νυνὶ παρ'
ὑμῖν, ἐτόλμησε ψεύσασθαι πάντων δεινότατον, ὡς τέτταρά
μοι τάλανθ' ὁ πατὴρ κατέλιπε κατορωρυγμένα καὶ τούτων
κυρίαν τὴν μητέρ' ἐποίησεν. ταῦτα δ' εἶπεν, ἵν' εἰ μὲν καὶ
30 νῦν προσδοκήσαιμ' αὐτὸν ἐρεῖν, ἀπολογούμενος περὶ αὐτῶν
διατρίβοιμι, δέον ἕτερά μ' αὐτοῦ κατηγορεῖν πρὸς ὑμᾶς· εἰ
δ' ὡς οὐ ῥηθησομένων παραλίποιμι, νῦν αὐτὸς εἴποι, ἵνα
δοκῶν εἶναι πλούσιος ἧττον ὑφ' ὑμῶν ἐλεοίμην. καὶ μαρ- 54

41

τυρίαν μὲν οὐδεμίαν ἐνεβάλετο τούτων ὁ ταῦτ' εἰπεῖν ἀξιώσας,
ψιλῷ δὲ λόγῳ χρησάμενος ὡς πιστευθησόμενος δι' ἐκείνων.
καὶ ὅταν μὲν ἔρηταί τις αὐτόν, εἰς τί τῶν ἐμῶν τοσαῦτα
χρήματ' ἀνήλωκεν, χρέα φησὶν ὑπὲρ ἐμοῦ ἐκτετεικέναι καὶ
πένητ' ἐνταυθοῖ ζητεῖ ποιεῖν· ὅταν δὲ βούληται, πλούσιον 5
ὡς ἔοικεν, εἴπερ γε καὶ τοσοῦτον ἐκεῖνος ἀργύριον οἴκοι κατέλιπεν. ὡς δ' οὐκ ἀληθῆ λέγειν οἷόν τ' αὐτόν, ἀλλ' ἀδύνατόν
55 τι γενέσθαι τούτων, ἐκ πολλῶν ῥᾴδιον μαθεῖν. εἰ μὲν γὰρ
ὁ πατὴρ ἠπίστει τούτοις, δῆλον ὅτι οὔτ' ἂν τἄλλ' ἐπέτρεπεν
οὔτ' ἂν ταῦθ' οὕτω καταλείπων αὐτοῖς ἔφραζε· μανία γὰρ 10
δεινὴ τὰ κεκρυμμέν' εἰπεῖν, μηδὲ τῶν φανερῶν μέλλοντ' ἐπιτρόπους καταστήσειν. εἰ δ' ἐπίστευεν, οὐκ ἂν δήπου τὰ μὲν
πλεῖστ' αὐτοῖς τῶν χρημάτων ἐνεχείρισεν, τῶν δ' οὐκ ἂν
κυρίους ἐποίησεν. οὐδ' ἂν τῇ μὲν μητρί μου ταῦτα φυλάτ-
τειν ἔδωκεν, αὐτὴν δ' ἐκείνην ἑνὶ τῶν ἐπιτρόπων τούτῳ 15
γυναῖκ' ἔδωκεν· οὐ γὰρ ἔχει λόγον, σῴζειν μὲν τὰ χρήματα
διὰ τῆς ἐμῆς μητρὸς ζητεῖν, ἕνα δὲ τῶν ἀπιστουμένων καὶ
56 αὐτῆς καὶ τῶν χρημάτων κύριον ποιεῖν. ἔτι δέ, τούτων εἴ τι
ἦν ἀληθές, οἴεσθ' οὐκ ἂν αὐτὴν λαβεῖν δοθεῖσαν ὑπὸ τοῦ
πατρός; ὃς τὴν μὲν προῖκ' αὐτῆς ἤδη, τὰς ὀγδοήκοντα μνᾶς, 20
ἔχων ὡς συνοικήσων αὐτῇ, τὴν Φιλωνίδου τοῦ Μελιτέως
θυγατέρ' ἔγημεν· τεττάρων δὲ ταλάντων ἔνδον ὄντων, καὶ
ταῦτ' ἐκείνης ἐχούσης, ὡς οὗτός φησιν, οὐκ ἂν ἡγεῖσθ' αὐτὸν
κἂν ἐπιδραμεῖν, ὥστε γενέσθαι μετ' ἐκείνης αὐτῶν κύριον;
57 ἢ τὴν μὲν φανερὰν οὐσίαν, ἣν καὶ ὑμῶν οἱ πολλοὶ συνῄδεσαν 25
ὅτι κατελείφθη, μετὰ τῶν συνεπιτρόπων οὕτως αἰσχρῶς
διήρπασεν, ὧν δ' οὐκ ἐμέλλεθ' ὑμεῖς ἔσεσθαι μάρτυρες,
ἀπέσχετ' ἂν ἐξὸν αὐτῷ λαβεῖν; καὶ τίς ἂν πιστεύσειεν; οὐκ
ἔστιν ταῦτ', ὦ ἄνδρες δικασταί, οὐκ ἔστιν, ἀλλὰ τὰ μὲν
χρήματα, ὅσα κατέλιπεν ὁ πατήρ, πάντα τούτοις παρέδωκεν, 30
οὗτος δ', ἵν' ἧττον ἐλεηθῶ παρ' ὑμῖν, τούτοις τοῖς λόγοις
χρήσεται.
58 Πολλὰ μὲν οὖν ἔγωγ' ἔχω καὶ ἄλλα τούτου κατηγορεῖν·

ἐν δὲ περὶ πάντων κεφάλαιον εἰπών, πάσας αὐτοῦ διαλύσω
τὰς ἀπολογίας. τούτῳ γὰρ ἐξῆν μηδὲν ἔχειν τούτων τῶν
πραγμάτων, μισθώσαντι τὸν οἶκον κατὰ τουτουσὶ τοὺς νόμους.
λαβὲ τοὺς νόμους καὶ ἀνάγνωθι.

5   ΝΟΜΟΙ.

Κατὰ τούτους τοὺς νόμους Ἀντιδώρῳ μὲν ἐκ τριῶν ταλάντων καὶ τρισχιλίων ἐν ἓξ ἔτεσιν ἓξ τάλαντα καὶ πλέον
ἐκ τοῦ μισθωθῆναι παρεδόθη, καὶ ταῦθ' ὑμῶν τινες εἶδον·
Θεογένης γὰρ ὁ Προβαλίσιος, ὁ μισθωσάμενος αὐτοῦ τὸν
10 οἶκον, ἐν τῇ ἀγορᾷ ταῦτα τὰ χρήματ' ἐξηρίθμησεν. ἐμοὶ δ' 59
ἐκ τεττάρων καὶ δέκα ταλάντων ἐν δέκ' ἔτεσιν πρὸς τὸν
χρόνον τε καὶ τὴν ἐκείνου μίσθωσιν πλέον ἢ τριπλάσια κατὰ
τὸ εἰκὸς προσῆκον γενέσθαι, τοῦτο διὰ τί οὐκ ἐποίησεν, ἐρωτᾶτ' αὐτόν. εἰ μὲν γάρ φησι βέλτιον εἶναι μὴ μισθωθῆναι
15 τὸν οἶκον, δειξάτω μὴ διπλάσια μηδὲ τριπλάσιά μοι γεγενημένα, ἀλλ' αὐτὰ τὰ ἀρχαῖ' ἐμοὶ πάντ' ἀποδεδομένα. εἰ δ'
ἐκ τεττάρων καὶ δέκα ταλάντων ἐμοὶ μὲν μηδ' ἑβδομήκοντα
μνᾶς παραδεδώκασιν, ὁ δὲ καὶ πρὸς ὀφείλοντά μ' αὐτῷ ἀπέγραψεν, πῶς ἀποδέξασθαί τι προσήκει τούτων λεγόντων;
20 οὐδαμῶς δήπουθεν.

Τοσαύτης τοίνυν οὐσίας μοι καταλειφθείσης ὅσην ἐξ 60
ἀρχῆς ἠκούσατε, καὶ τοῦ τρίτου μέρους πρόσοδον αὐτῆς
φερούσης πεντήκοντα μνᾶς, ἐξὸν τούτοις τοῖς ἀπληστοτάτοις
χρημάτων, καὶ εἰ μὴ μισθοῦν τὸν οἶκον ἐβούλοντο, ἀπὸ μὲν
25 τούτων τῶν προσιόντων, ἐῶντας ὥσπερ εἶχεν κατὰ χώραν,
ἡμᾶς τε τρέφειν καὶ τὰ πρὸς τὴν πόλιν διοικεῖν, καὶ ὅσ' ἐξ
αὐτῶν περιεγίγνετο, ταῦτα προσπεριποιεῖν, τὴν δ' ἄλλην 61
οὐσίαν ἐνεργὸν ποιήσασιν, οὖσαν ταύτης διπλασίαν, αὐτοῖς
τε, εἰ χρημάτων ἐπεθύμουν, μέτρι' ἐξ αὐτῶν λαβεῖν, ἐμοί τε
30 σὺν τοῖς ἀρχαίοις τὸν οἶκον ἐκ τῶν προσόδων μείζω ποιῆσαι,
τούτων μὲν οὐδὲν ἐποίησαν, ἀποδόμενοι δ' ἀλλήλοις τὰ
πλείστου ἄξια τῶν ἀνδραπόδων, τὰ δὲ παντάπασιν ἀφανί-

43

σαντες, ἐμοῦ μὲν ἀνεῖλον καὶ τὴν ὑπάρχουσαν πρόσοδον,
σφίσι δ᾽ αὐτοῖς οὐ μικρὰν ἐκ τῶν ἐμῶν κατεσκευάσαντο.

62 λαβόντες δὲ καὶ τἄλλ᾽ αἰσχρῶς οὑτωσὶ πάντα, πλέον ἢ τὰ
ἡμίσεα τῶν χρημάτων μηδὲ καταλειφθῆναι κοινῇ πάντες
ἀμφισβητοῦσιν, ὡς πεντεταλάντου δὲ μόνον τῆς οὐσίας οὔ- 5
σης ἐκ τοσαύτης τοὺς λόγους ἀπενηνόχασιν, οὐ πρόσοδον
μὲν ἐξ αὐτῶν οὐκ ἀποφαίνοντες, τὰ δὲ κεφάλαια φανερὰ
ἀποδεικνύντες, ἀλλ᾽ αὐτὰ τὰ ἀρχαῖ᾽ οὕτως ἀναιδῶς ἀνηλῶ-
σθαι φάσκοντες. καὶ οὐδ᾽ αἰσχύνονται ταῦτα τολμῶντες.

63 καίτοι τί ποτ᾽ ἂν ἔπαθον ὑπ᾽ αὐτῶν, εἰ πλείω χρόνον ἐπε- 10
τροπεύθην; οὐκ ἂν ἔχοιεν εἰπεῖν. ὅπου γὰρ δέκ᾽ ἐτῶν
διαγενομένων παρὰ μὲν τῶν οὕτω μικρὰ κεκόμισμαι, τῷ δὲ
καὶ πρὸς ὀφείλων ἐγγέγραμμαι, πῶς οὐκ ἄξιον διαγανακτεῖν;
δῆλον δὲ παντάπασιν· εἰ κατελείφθην μὲν ἐνιαύσιος, ἓξ ἔτη
δὲ πρὸς ἐπετροπεύθην ὑπ᾽ αὐτῶν, οὐδ᾽ ἂν τὰ μικρὰ ταῦτα 15
παρ᾽ αὐτῶν ἀπέλαβον. εἰ γὰρ ἐκεῖν᾽ ἀνήλωται ὀρθῶς, οὐδὲν
ἂν τῶν νῦν παραδοθέντων ἐξήρκεσεν εἰς ἕκτον ἔτος, ἀλλ᾽ ἢ
παρ᾽ αὐτῶν ἄν μ᾽ ἔτρεφον ἢ τῷ λιμῷ περιεῖδον ἀπολόμενον.

64 καίτοι πῶς οὐ δεινόν, εἰ ἕτεροι μὲν οἶκοι ταλαντιαῖοι καὶ
διτάλαντοι καταλειφθέντες ἐκ τοῦ μισθωθῆναι διπλάσιοι καὶ 20
τριπλάσιοι γεγόνασιν, ὥστ᾽ ἀξιοῦσθαι λητουργεῖν, ὁ δ᾽ ἐμὸς
τριηραρχεῖν εἰθισμένος καὶ μεγάλας εἰσφορὰς εἰσφέρειν μηδὲ
μικρὰς δυνήσεται διὰ τὰς τούτων ἀναισχυντίας; τίνας δ᾽
οὗτοι λελοίπασιν ὑπερβολὰς εἰπεῖν; οἳ καὶ τὴν διαθήκην
ἠφανίκασιν ὡς λήσοντες, καὶ τὰς μὲν σφετέρας αὐτῶν οὐσίας 25
ἐκ τῶν ἐπικαρπιῶν διῳκήκασι καὶ τἀρχαῖα τῶν ὑπαρχόντων
ἐκ τῶν ἐμῶν πολλῷ μείζω πεποιήκασι, τῆς δ᾽ ἐμῆς οὐσίας,
ὥσπερ τὰ μέγισθ᾽ ὑφ᾽ ἡμῶν ἀδικηθέντες, ὅλον τὸ κεφάλαιον

65 ἀνῃρήκασι; καὶ ὑμεῖς μὲν οὐδὲ τῶν εἰς ὑμᾶς ἁμαρτανόντων
ὅταν τινὸς καταψηφίσησθε, οὐ πάντα τὰ ὄντ᾽ ἀφείλεσθε, 30
ἀλλ᾽ ἢ γυναῖκας ἢ παιδί᾽ αὐτῶν ἐλεήσαντες μέρος τι κἀκεί-
νοις ὑπελίπετε· οὗτοι δὲ τοσοῦτον διαφέρουσιν ὑμῶν, ὥστε
καὶ δωρεὰς παρ᾽ ἡμῶν προσλαβόντες ἵνα δικαίως ἐπιτροπεύ-

σωσι, τοιαῦτ' εἰς ἡμᾶς ὑβρίκασι. καὶ οὐδ' ᾐσχύνθησαν, εἰ
μὴ ἠλέησαν, τὴν ἐμὴν ἀδελφήν, εἰ δυοῖν ταλάντοιν ὑπὸ τοῦ
πατρὸς ἀξιωθεῖσα, μηδενὸς τεύξεται τῶν προσηκόντων, ἀλλ'
ὥσπερ ἔχθιστοί τινες, ἀλλ' οὐ φίλοι καὶ συγγενεῖς κατα-
5 λειφθέντες οὐδὲν τῆς οἰκειότητος ἐφρόντισαν. ἀλλ' ἐγὼ μὲν 66
ὁ πάντων ταλαιπωρότατος πρὸς ἀμφότερ' ἀπορῶ, ταύτην θ'
ὅπως ἐκδῶ καὶ τἄλλ' ὁπόθεν διοικῶ. προσεπίκειται δ' ἡ
πόλις ἀξιοῦσ' εἰσφέρειν, δικαίως· οὐσίαν γὰρ ἱκανὴν πρὸς
ταῦτα κατέλιπέν μοι ὁ πατήρ. τὰ δὲ χρήματα τὰ κατα-
10 λειφθένθ' οὗτοι πάντ' εἰλήφασιν. καὶ νῦν κομίσασθαι τἀ- 67
μαυτοῦ ζητῶν εἰς κίνδυνον καθέστηκα τὸν μέγιστον. ἂν γὰρ
ἀποφύγῃ μ' οὗτος, ὃ μὴ γένοιτο, τὴν ἐπωβελίαν ὀφλήσω
μνᾶς ἑκατόν. καὶ τούτῳ μέν, ἐὰν καταψηφίσησθε, τιμητόν,
κοὐκ ἐκ τῶν ἑαυτοῦ χρημάτων, ἀλλ' ἐκ τῶν ἐμῶν ποιήσεται
15 τὴν ἔκτεισιν· ἐμοὶ δ' ἀτίμητον τοῦτ' ἔστιν, ὥστ' οὐ μόνον
ἔσομαι τῶν πατρῴων ἀπεστερημένος, ἀλλὰ καὶ πρὸς ἠτιμωμένος, ἂν μὴ νῦν ἡμᾶς ὑμεῖς ἐλεήσητε. δέομαι οὖν ὑμῶν, 68
ὦ ἄνδρες δικασταί, καί ἱκετεύω καὶ ἀντιβολῶ, μνησθέντας
καὶ τῶν νόμων καὶ τῶν ὅρκων οὓς ὀμόσαντες δικάζετε, βοη-
20 θῆσαι ἡμῖν τὰ δίκαια, καὶ μὴ περὶ πλείονος τὰς τούτου
δεήσεις ἢ τὰς ἡμετέρας ποιήσασθαι. δίκαιοι δ' ἔστ' ἐλεεῖν
οὐ τοὺς ἀδίκους τῶν ἀνθρώπων, ἀλλὰ τοὺς παραλόγως δυσ-
τυχοῦντας, οὐδὲ τοὺς ὠμῶς οὕτως τἀλλότρι' ἀποστεροῦντας,
ἀλλ' ἡμᾶς τοὺς πολὺν χρόνον ὧν ὁ πατὴρ ἡμῖν κατέλιπεν
25 στερομένους καὶ πρὸς ὑπὸ τούτων ὑβριζομένους καὶ νῦν περὶ
ἀτιμίας κινδυνεύοντας. μέγα δ' ἂν οἶμαι στενάξαι τὸν πατέρ' 69
ἡμῶν, εἰ αἴσθοιτο τῶν προικῶν καὶ τῶν δωρεῶν ὧν αὐτὸς
τούτοις ἔδωκεν, ὑπὲρ τούτων τῆς ἐπωβελίας τὸν αὐτοῦ υἱὸν
ἐμὲ κινδυνεύοντα, καὶ ἄλλους μέν τινας ἤδη τῶν πολιτῶν
30 οὐ μόνον συγγενῶν, ἀλλὰ καὶ φίλων ἀνδρῶν ἀπορούντων
θυγατέρας παρὰ σφῶν αὐτῶν ἐκδόντας, Ἄφοβον δὲ μηδ' ἣν
ἔλαβεν προῖκ' ἐθέλοντ' ἀποδοῦναι, καὶ ταῦτ' ἔτει δεκάτῳ.

XXVIII

KAT' ΑΦΟΒΟΥ Β

Πολλὰ καὶ μεγάλ' ἐψευσμένου πρὸς ὑμᾶς Ἀφόβου, τοῦτ' αὐτὸν ἐλέγξαι πειράσομαι πρῶτον, ἐφ' ᾧ μάλιστ' ἠγανάκτησα τῶν ῥηθέντων. εἶπεν γὰρ ὡς ὁ πάππος ὤφειλε τῷ δημοσίῳ, καὶ διὰ ταῦθ' ὁ πατὴρ οὐκ ἐβούλετο μισθωθῆναι τὸν οἶκον,
5 ἵνα μὴ κινδυνεύσῃ. καὶ τὴν μὲν πρόφασιν ποιεῖται ταύτην, ὡς δ' ὀφείλων ἐτελεύτησεν ἐκεῖνος, οὐδεμίαν παρέσχετο μαρτυρίαν· ἀλλ' ὡς μὲν ὤφλεν, ἐνεβάλετο τηρήσας τὴν τελευταίαν ἡμέραν, ταύτην δ' εἰς τὸν ὕστερον λόγον ὑπελίπετο, ὡς διαβαλεῖν τὸ πρᾶγμ' ἐξ αὐτῆς δυνησόμενος. ἐὰν οὖν 2
10 ἀναγνῷ, προσέχετ' αὐτῇ τὸν νοῦν· εὑρήσετε γὰρ οὐχ ὡς ὀφείλει μεμαρτυρημένην, ἀλλ' ὡς ὤφλεν. τοῦτ' οὖν ἐλέγξαι πειράσομαι πρῶτον, ἐφ' ᾧ φρονεῖ μάλιστα· ὃ καὶ ἡμεῖς ἀμφισβητοῦμεν. εἰ μὲν οὖν τότ' ἐξεγένετο καὶ μὴ τῷ χρόνῳ τοῦτ' ἐνηδρεύθημεν, παρεσχόμεθ' ἂν μάρτυρας ὡς ἐξετείσθη
15 τὰ χρήματα καὶ πάντ' αὐτῷ διελέλυτο τὰ πρὸς τὴν πόλιν· νῦν δὲ τεκμηρίοις μεγάλοις ἐπιδείξομεν ὡς οὔτ' ὤφειλεν οὔτ' ἦν κίνδυνος οὐδεὶς ἡμῖν φανερὰ κεκτημένοις τὰ ὄντα. πρῶ- 3 τον μὲν γὰρ Δημοχάρης, ἔχων ἀδελφὴν τῆς ἐμῆς μητρός, θυγατέρα δὲ Γύλωνος, οὐκ ἀποκέκρυπται τὴν οὐσίαν, ἀλλὰ
20 χορηγεῖ καὶ τριηραρχεῖ καὶ τὰς ἄλλας λῃτουργίας λῃτουργεῖ καὶ οὐδὲν τῶν τοιούτων δέδοικεν. ἔπειτ' αὐτὸς ὁ πατὴρ τήν τ' ἄλλην οὐσίαν καὶ τέτταρα τάλαντα καὶ τρισχιλίας φανε- ρὰς ἐποίησεν, ἃς οὗτοι γραφῆναί τ' ἐν ταῖς διαθήκαις καὶ λαβεῖν σφᾶς αὐτοὺς κατ' ἀλλήλων καταμαρτυροῦσιν. ἔτι δὲ 4
25 καὶ αὐτὸς Ἄφοβος μετὰ τῶν συνεπιτρόπων τῇ πόλει τὸ πλῆθος τῶν καταλειφθέντων χρημάτων ἐμφανὲς ἐποίησεν, ἡγεμόνα με τῆς συμμορίας καταστήσας οὐκ ἐπὶ μικροῖς τιμή- μασιν, ἀλλ' ἐπὶ τηλικούτοις ὥστε κατὰ τὰς πέντε καὶ εἴκοσι μνᾶς πεντακοσίας εἰσφέρειν. καίτοι εἴ τι τούτων ἦν ἀληθές,
30 οὐδὲν ἂν αὐτῶν ἐποίησεν, ἀλλὰ πάντ' ἂν ηὐλαβήθη. νῦν δὲ καὶ Δημοχάρης καὶ ὁ πατὴρ καὶ αὐτοὶ οὗτοι φαίνονται φανερὰ ποιοῦντες, καὶ οὐδένα τοιοῦτον κίνδυνον δεδιότες.

Πάντων δ' ἀτοπώτατόν ἐστιν, λέγοντας ὡς ὁ πατὴρ οὐκ 5

εἴα μισθοῦν τὸν οἶκον, τὴν μὲν διαθήκην μηδαμοῦ ταύτην
ἀποφαίνειν, ἐξ ἧς ἦν εἰδέναι τἀκριβές, τηλικαύτην δ' ἀνε-
λόντας μαρτυρίαν οὕτως οἴεσθαι δεῖν εἰκῇ πιστεύεσθαι παρ'
ὑμῖν. ἀλλ' ἐχρῆν, ἐπειδὴ τάχιστ' ἐτελεύτησεν ὁ πατήρ,
εἰσκαλέσαντας μάρτυρας πολλοὺς παρασημήνασθαι κελεῦσαι 5
τὰς διαθήκας, ἵν' εἴ τι ἐγίγνετ' ἀμφισβητήσιμον, ἦν εἰς τὰ
γράμματα ταῦτ' ἐπανελθεῖν καὶ τὴν ἀλήθειαν πάντων εὑρεῖν.
6 νῦν δ' ἕτερα μὲν παρασημήνασθαι ἠξίωσαν, ἐν οἷς πολλὰ
τῶν καταλειπομένων οὐκ ἐγέγραπτο, ὑπομνήματα δ' ἦν·
αὐτὴν δὲ τὴν διαθήκην, δι' ἧς τούτων ὧν ἐσημήναντο γραμ- 10
μάτων καὶ τῶν ἄλλων ἁπάντων χρημάτων ἐγίγνοντο κύριοι,
καὶ τοῦ μὴ μισθοῦν τὸν οἶκον τῆς αἰτίας ἀπελέλυντο, ταύτην δ' οὐκ ἐσημήναντο, οὐδ' αὐτὴν ἀπέδοσαν. ἄξιόν γε
πιστεύειν αὐτοῖς ὅ τι ἂν περὶ τούτων λέγωσιν.
7 Ἀλλ' ἐγὼ οὐκ οἶδ' ὅ τι τοῦτ' ἔστιν. οὐκ εἴα μισθοῦν 15
τὸν οἶκον οὐδ' ἐμφανῆ τὰ χρήματα ποιεῖν ὁ πατήρ. πότερον
ἐμοί; ἢ τῇ πόλει; φαίνεσθε γὰρ τοὐναντίον ἐκείνῃ μὲν
φανερὰ ποιήσαντες, ἐμοὶ δὲ παντάπασιν ἀφανῆ πεποιηκότες,
καὶ οὐδὲ ταῦτ' ἀποφαίνοντες ἐξ ὧν τιμησάμενοι τὰς εἰσφορὰς εἰσεφέρετε. δείξατε γὰρ ταύτην τὴν οὐσίαν, τίς ἦν 20
8 καὶ ποῦ παρέδοτέ μοι καὶ τίνος ἐναντίον. τὰ μὲν γὰρ δύο
τάλαντα καὶ τὰς ὀγδοήκοντα μνᾶς ἀπὸ τῶν τεττάρων ταλάντων καὶ τρισχιλίων ἐλάβετε, ὥστ' οὐδὲ ταύτας ὑπὲρ ἐμοῦ
εἰς τὸ δημόσιον ἐτιμήσασθε· ὑμέτεραι γὰρ ἦσαν ἐν ἐκείνοις
τοῖς χρόνοις. ἀλλὰ μὴν ἔκ γε τῆς οἰκίας καὶ τῶν τεττάρων 25
καὶ δέκ' ἀνδραπόδων καὶ τῶν τριάκοντα μνῶν, ἅ μοι παρε-
δώκατε, τὴν εἰσφορὰν οὐχ οἷόν τε γενέσθαι τοσαύτην ὅσην
9 ὑμεῖς συνετάξασθε πρὸς τὴν συμμορίαν. ἀλλ' ἀνάγκη
μεγάλη τὰ καταλειφθέντα, πολλῷ πλείον' ὄντα τούτων,
πάνθ' ὑμᾶς ἔχειν ἐστίν, ἃ φανερῶς ὅτι διηρπάκατ' ἐξε- 30
λεγχόμενοι τοιαῦτα πλάττεσθαι τολμᾶτε. καὶ τοτὲ μὲν εἰς
ἀλλήλους ἀναφέρετε, πάλιν δ' εἰληφέναι κατ' ἀλλήλων
μαρτυρεῖτε. φάσκοντες δ' οὐ πολλὰ λαβεῖν μεγάλων

ἀναλωμάτων λόγους ἀπενηνόχατε. πάντες δὲ κοινῇ μ' 10
ἐπιτροπεύσαντες ἰδίᾳ μετὰ ταῦθ' ἕκαστος μηχανᾶσθε. καὶ
τὴν μὲν διαθήκην ἠφανίκατε, ἐξ ἧς ἦν εἰδέναι περὶ πάντων
τὴν ἀλήθειαν, φαίνεσθε δ' οὐδέποτε ταὐτὰ περὶ ἀλλήλων
5 λέγοντες.

Λαβὲ δὴ τὰς μαρτυρίας καὶ ἀνάγνωθ' αὐτοῖς πάσας
ἐφεξῆς, ἵνα μνησθέντες καὶ τῶν μεμαρτυρημένων καὶ τῶν
εἰρημένων ἀκριβέστερον διαγιγνώσκωσι περὶ αὐτῶν.

ΜΑΡΤΥΡΙΑΙ.

10 Ταῦθ' οὗτοι πρὸς πεντεκαιδεκαταλάντους οἴκους συνετι- 11
μήσανθ' ὑπὲρ ἐμοῦ· μνῶν δ' οὐδ' ἑβδομήκοντ' ἀξίαν μοι
παραδεδώκασι τὴν οὐσίαν τρεῖς ὄντες. λέγε τὰς ἐφεξῆς.

ΜΑΡΤΥΡΙΑΙ.

Ταύτην τὴν προῖκα οἵ τ' ἐπίτροποι καταμαρτυροῦσιν
15 αὐτὸν λαβεῖν, ἄλλοι τε πρὸς οὓς ἔχειν ὡμολόγησεν. ταύτην
οὔτ' αὐτὴν οὔτε τὸν σῖτον ἀποδέδωκεν. λαβὲ τὰς ἄλλας
καὶ ἀναγίγνωσκε.

ΜΑΡΤΥΡΙΑΙ.

Δύ' ἔτη τὸ ἐργαστήριον διοικήσας Θηριππίδη μὲν ἀπο- 12
20 δέδωκε τὴν μίσθωσιν· ἐμοὶ δέ, δυοῖν ἐτοῖν λαβών τὴν
πρόσοδον, τριάκοντα μνᾶς, οὔτ' αὐτὰς οὔτε τὸ ἔργον ἀποδέδωκεν. λάβ' ἑτέραν καὶ ἀνάγνωθι.

ΜΑΡΤΥΡΙΑ.

Ταῦτα τἀνδράποδ' ὡς αὐτὸν λαβὼν οὗτος, καὶ τἄλλα τὰ
25 μετὰ τούτων ὑποτεθένθ' ἡμῖν, ἀνάλωμα μὲν εἰς αὐτὰ τοσοῦτο
λελόγισται, λῆμμα δ' ἀπ' αὐτῶν οὐδ' ὁτιοῦν, καὶ αὐτοὺς δὲ
τοὺς ἀνθρώπους ἠφάνικεν, οἳ δώδεκα μνᾶς ἀτελεῖς ἑκάστου
τοῦ ἐνιαυτοῦ προσέφερον. λέγ' ἑτέραν.

ΜΑΡΤΥΡΙΑ.

13 Τοῦτον τὸν ἐλέφαντα καὶ τὸν σίδηρον πεπρακὼς οὐδὲ καταλειφθῆναί φησιν, ἀλλὰ καὶ τούτων τὴν τιμὴν ἀποστερεῖ με, μάλιστα τάλαντον. λέγε ταυτασί.

ΜΑΡΤΥΡΙΑΙ.

Ταῦθ' οὗτος τρία τάλαντα καὶ χιλίας ἔχει χωρὶς τῶν ἄλλων. τοῦ μὲν οὖν ἀρχαίου πέντε τάλανθ' ἃ εἴληφεν· σὺν δὲ τοῖς ἔργοις, ἂν ἐπὶ δραχμῇ τις τιθῇ μόνον, πλέον ἢ δέκα τάλαντ' ἔχει. λέγε τὰς ἐφεξῆς.

ΜΑΡΤΥΡΙΑΙ.

14 Ταῦθ' οὗτοι γραφῆναι μὲν ἐν ταῖς διαθήκαις καὶ λαβεῖν σφᾶς αὐτοὺς κατ' ἀλλήλων μαρτυροῦσιν. οὗτος δὲ καὶ μεταπεμφθῆναι φάσκων ὑπὸ τοῦ πατρός, καὶ ἐλθὼν εἰς τὴν οἰκίαν, εἰσελθεῖν μὲν οὔ φησιν ὡς τὸν μεταπεμψάμενον, οὐδ' ὁμολογῆσαι περὶ τούτων οὐδέν, Δημοφῶντος δ' ἀκοῦσαι γραμματεῖον ἀναγιγνώσκοντος καὶ Θηριππίδου λέγοντος ὡς ἐκεῖνος ταῦτα διέθετο, καὶ προεισεληλυθὼς καὶ ἅπαντα διωμολογημένος πρὸς τὸν πατέρα, ὅσαπερ ἐκεῖνος γράψας

15 κατέλιπεν. ὁ γὰρ πατήρ, ὦ ἄνδρες δικασταί, ὡς ᾔσθετο τὴν νόσον οὐκ ἀποφευξόμενος, συγκαλέσας τούτους τρεῖς ὄντας, καὶ συμπαρακαθισάμενος Δήμωνα τὸν ἀδελφόν, τὰ σώμαθ' ἡμῶν εἰς τὰς χεῖρας ἐνέθηκεν παρακαταθήκην ἐπονομάζων, τὴν μὲν ἀδελφὴν Δημοφῶντι καὶ δύο τάλαντα προῖκα διδοὺς εὐθύς, καὶ γυναῖκ' αὐτῷ ταύτην ἐγγυῶν, ἐμὲ δὲ πᾶσιν κοινῇ μετὰ τῶν χρημάτων παρακατατιθέμενος, καὶ ἐπισκήπτων μισθῶσαί τε τὸν οἶκον καὶ συνδιασῶσαί μοι

16 τὴν οὐσίαν, διδοὺς ἅμα τε Θηριππίδῃ τὰς ἑβδομήκοντα μνᾶς, καὶ τούτῳ τήν τ' ἐμὴν μητέρ' ἐγγυῶν ἐπὶ ταῖς ὀγδοήκοντα μναῖς, κἄμ' εἰς τὰ τούτου γόνατα τιθείς· ὧν οὗτος ὁ πάντων ἀνθρώπων ἀνοσιώτατος οὐδένα λόγον ἐποιήσατο, κύριος τῶν ἐμῶν γενόμενος ἐπὶ τούτοις, ἀλλὰ τὰ χρήματά με πάντ'

52

ἀπεστερηκὼς μετὰ τῶν συνεπιτρόπων, ἐλεεῖσθαι νῦν ὑφ'
ὑμῶν ἀξιώσει, μνῶν οὐδ' ἑβδομήκοντ' ἄξια τρίτος αὐτὸς
ἀποδεδωκώς, εἶτα καὶ τούτοις αὐτοῖς πάλιν ἐπιβεβουλευκώς.
ὡς γὰρ τὰς δίκας ταύτας ἔμελλον εἰσιέναι κατ' αὐτῶν, 17
5 ἀντίδοσιν ἐπ' ἐμὲ παρεσκεύασαν, ἵν' εἰ μὲν ἀντιδοίην, μὴ
ἐξείη μοι πρὸς αὐτοὺς ἀντιδικεῖν, ὡς καὶ τῶν δικῶν τούτων
τοῦ ἀντιδόντος γιγνομένων, εἰ δὲ μηδὲν τούτων ποιοίην, ἵν'
ἐκ βραχείας οὐσίας λητουργῶν παντάπασιν ἀναιρεθείην.
καὶ τοῦτ' αὐτοῖς ὑπηρέτησε Θρασύλοχος ὁ Ἀναγυράσιος·
10 ᾧ τούτων οὐδὲν ἐνθυμηθεὶς ἀντέδωκα μέν, ἀπέκλεισα δ' ὡς
διαδικασίας τευξόμενος· οὐ τυχὼν δὲ ταύτης, τῶν χρόνων
ὑπογύων ὄντων, ἵνα μὴ στερηθῶ τῶν δικῶν, ἀπέτεισα τὴν
λητουργίαν ὑποθεὶς τὴν οἰκίαν καὶ τἀμαυτοῦ πάντα, βουλόμενος εἰς ὑμᾶς εἰσελθεῖν τὰς πρὸς τουτουσὶ δίκας.
15 Ἆρ' οὐ μεγάλα μὲν ἐξ ἀρχῆς ἠδίκημαι, μεγάλα δ', ὅτι 18
δίκην ζητῶ λαβεῖν, νῦν ὑπ' αὐτῶν βλάπτομαι; τίς δ' οὐκ
ἂν ὑμῶν τούτῳ μὲν φθονήσειε δικαίως, ἡμᾶς δ' ἐλεήσειεν,
ὁρῶν τῷ μὲν πρὸς τῇ οὐσίᾳ τῇ παραδοθείσῃ πλεῖν ἢ δέκα
ταλάντων τὴν ἐμὴν τοσαύτην οὖσαν προσγεγενημένην, ἡμᾶς
20 δὲ μὴ μόνον τῶν πατρῴων διημαρτηκότας, ἀλλὰ καὶ τῶν
νῦν παραδοθέντων διὰ τὴν τούτων πονηρίαν ἀπεστερημένους;
ποῖ δ' ἂν τραποίμεθα, εἴ τι ἄλλο ψηφίσαισθ' ὑμεῖς περὶ
αὐτῶν; εἰς τὰ ὑποκείμενα τοῖς δανείσασιν; ἀλλὰ τῶν ὑποθεμένων ἐστίν. ἀλλ' εἰς τὰ περιόντ' αὐτῶν; ἀλλὰ τούτου
25 γίγνεται, τὴν ἐπωβελίαν ἐὰν ὄφλωμεν. μηδαμῶς, ὦ 19
ἄνδρες δικασταί, γένησθ' ἡμῖν τοσούτων αἴτιοι κακῶν· μηδὲ
τὴν μητέρα κἀμὲ καὶ τὴν ἀδελφὴν ἀνάξια παθόντας περιίδητε, οὓς ὁ πατὴρ οὐκ ἐπὶ ταύταις ταῖς ἐλπίσιν κατέλιπεν,
ἀλλὰ τὴν μὲν ὡς Δημοφῶντι συνοικήσουσαν ἐπὶ δυοῖν
30 ταλάντοιν προικί, τὴν δ' ἐπ' ὀγδοήκοντα μναῖς τούτῳ τῷ
σχετλιωτάτῳ πάντων ἀνθρώπων, ἐμὲ δ' ὑμῖν διάδοχον ἀνθ'
αὑτοῦ τῶν λητουργιῶν ἐσόμενον. βοηθήσατ' οὖν ἡμῖν, 20
βοηθήσατε, καὶ τοῦ δικαίου καὶ ὑμῶν αὐτῶν ἕνεκα καὶ ἡμῶν

καὶ τοῦ πατρὸς τοῦ τετελευτηκότος. σώσατε, ἐλεήσατε,
ἐπειδή μ' οὗτοι συγγενεῖς ὄντες οὐκ ἠλέησαν. εἰς ὑμᾶς
καταπεφεύγαμεν. ἱκετεύω, ἀντιβολῶ πρὸς παίδων, πρὸς
γυναικῶν, πρὸς τῶν ὄντων ἀγαθῶν ὑμῖν. οὕτως ὄναισθε
τούτων, μὴ περιίδητέ με, μηδὲ ποιήσητε τὴν μητέρα καὶ τῶν 5
ἐπιλοίπων ἐλπίδων εἰς τὸν βίον στερηθεῖσαν ἀνάξιον αὑτῆς
21 τι παθεῖν· ἢ νῦν μὲν οἴεται τυχόντα με τῶν δικαίων παρ'
ὑμῖν ὑποδέξεσθαι καὶ τὴν ἀδελφὴν ἐκδώσειν· εἰ δ' ὑμεῖς
ἄλλο τι γνώσεσθε, ὃ μὴ γένοιτο, τίν' οἴεσθ' αὐτὴν ψυχὴν
ἕξειν, ὅταν ἐμὲ μὲν ἴδῃ μὴ μόνον τῶν πατρῴων ἀπεστερη- 10
μένον, ἀλλὰ καὶ πρὸς ἠτιμωμένον, περὶ δὲ τῆς ἀδελφῆς μηδ'
ἐλπίδ' ἔχουσαν ὡς τεύξεταί τινος τῶν προσηκόντων διὰ τὴν
22 ἐσομένην ἀπορίαν; οὐκ ἄξιος, ὦ ἄνδρες δικασταί, οὔτ' ἐγὼ
δίκης ἐν ὑμῖν μὴ τυχεῖν, οὔθ' οὗτος τοσαῦτα χρήματ' ἀδίκως
κατασχεῖν. ἐμοῦ μὲν γὰρ εἰ καὶ μήπω πεῖραν εἰλήφατε, 15
ποῖός τις ἂν εἰς ὑμᾶς εἴην, ἐλπίζειν προσήκει μὴ χείρω τοῦ
πατρὸς ἔσεσθαι. τούτου δὲ πεῖραν ἔχετε, καὶ σαφῶς ἴσθ'
ὅτι πολλὴν οὐσίαν παραλαβὼν οὐ μόνον οὐδὲν πεφιλοτίμη-
ται πρὸς ὑμᾶς, ἀλλὰ καὶ τἀλλότρι' ἀποστερῶν ἀποδέδεικται.
23 ταῦτ' οὖν σκοποῦντες καὶ τἆλλα μνησθέντες, ᾗ δίκαιόν ἐστι, 20
ταύτῃ ψηφίσασθε. πίστεις δ' ἔχεθ' ἱκανὰς ἐκ μαρτύρων,
ἐκ τεκμηρίων, ἐκ τῶν εἰκότων, ἐξ ὧν οὗτοι λαβεῖν ὁμολογοῦντες ἀθρόα τἀμά, ταῦτ' ἀνηλωκέναι φασὶν οὐκ ἀνηλω-
24 κότες, ἀλλ' αὐτοὶ πάντ' ἔχοντες. ὧν ἐνθυμουμένους χρὴ
ποιήσασθαί τιν' ἡμῶν πρόνοιαν, εἰδότας ὅτι ἐγὼ μὲν τἀμαυ- 25
τοῦ δι' ὑμῶν κομισάμενος εἰκότως λῃτουργεῖν ἐθελήσω,
χάριτας ὀφείλων ὅτι μοι δικαίως ἀπέδοτε τὴν οὐσίαν, οὗτος
δ', ἐὰν αὐτὸν ποιήσητε τῶν ἐμῶν κύριον, οὐδὲν ποιήσει
τοιοῦτον. μὴ γὰρ οἴεσθ' αὐτόν, ὑπὲρ ὧν ἤρνηται μὴ λαβεῖν,
ὑπὲρ τούτων ὑμῖν λῃτουργεῖν ἐθελήσειν, ἀλλ' ἀποκρύψεσθαι 30
μᾶλλον, ἵνα δικαίως ἀποπεφευγέναι δοκῇ.

XXX

ΠΡΟΣ ΟΝΗΤΟΡΑ ΕΞΟΥΛΗΣ Α

Ἄφοβος, μέλλοντος αὐτῷ Δημοσθένους τὰς τῆς ἐπιτροπῆς δίκας λαγχάνειν, ἔγημεν Ὀνήτορος ἀδελφὴν ἐκδοθεῖσαν αὐτῷ παρὰ Τιμοκράτους τοῦ προτέρου ἀνδρός, ἐπειδὴ ἐκεῖνος ἐπίκληρον λαμβάνειν ἔμελλε. μετὰ δὲ ταῦτ' Ὀνήτωρ, ἤδη φεύγοντος 5 Ἀφόβου τὴν τῆς ἐπιτροπῆς δίκην, ὡς ὁ ῥήτωρ ἀποδείκνυσι, πλασάμενος ἀπόλειψιν τὴν ἀδελφὴν παρ' ἑαυτὸν ἀπήγαγεν. ἐπεὶ δ' Ἄφοβος ἑάλω, ἐπὶ τὴν οὐσίαν αὐτοῦ τὸν ῥήτορ' ἀφικνούμενον καὶ εἰς τὰ χωρί' εἰσιόντ' ἐξήλασεν Ὀνήτωρ, φάσκων τῆς 2 ἀδελφῆς εἶναι τὰ χωρία, εἰς τὴν προῖκ' ἀποτιμηθέντα. διόπερ 10 ἐξούλης αὐτῷ δικάζεται ὁ Δημοσθένης, ὡς ἐκ τῶν Ἀφόβου πρότερον, νῦν δ' ἑαυτῷ γεγενημένων ἐξεληλαμένος, φάσκων οὐκ εἰληφέναι τὴν προῖκ' Ἄφοβον, ἀλλὰ τὴν γυναῖκα μόνον· τὴν γὰρ προῖκα μὴ βουληθῆναι Ὀνήτορα δοῦναι, διότι κινδυνεύοντα τὸν Ἄφοβον ἑώρα καὶ τὴν οὐσίαν αὐτοῦ. νῦν οὖν, φησί, πλαστὴ 15 μὲν ἡ ἀπόλειψις, ὑπὲρ δ' ὧν οὐκ εἴληφεν Ἄφοβος, τὸ χωρίον ἀποτετίμηται ἐπ' ἀποστερήσει τῶν ἐμῶν. τὸ δὲ τῆς ἐξούλης ὄνομα Ἀττικόν· ἐξίλλειν γὰρ ἔλεγον τὸ ἐξωθεῖν καὶ ἐκβάλλειν βίᾳ.

Περὶ πολλοῦ ποιούμενος, ὦ ἄνδρες δικασταί, μήτε πρὸς
Ἄφοβόν μοι συμβῆναι τὴν γενομένην διαφορὰν μήτε τὴν
νῦν οὖσαν πρὸς Ὀνήτορα τουτονί, κηδεστὴν ὄντ' αὐτοῦ,
πολλὰ καὶ δίκαια προκαλεσάμενος ἀμφοτέρους, οὐδενὸς ἐδυ-
5 νήθην τυχεῖν τῶν μετρίων, ἀλλ' ηὕρηκα πολὺ τοῦτον ἐκείνου
δυσκολώτερον καὶ μᾶλλον ἄξιον ὄντα δοῦναι δίκην. τὸν μὲν 2
γὰρ οἰόμενος δεῖν ἐν τοῖς φίλοις διαδικάσασθαι τὰ πρὸς ἐμὲ
καὶ μὴ λαβεῖν ὑμῶν πεῖραν οὐχ οἷός τ' ἐγενόμην πεῖσαι·
τοῦτον δ' αὐτὸν αὐτῷ κελεύων γενέσθαι δικαστήν, ἵνα μὴ
10 παρ' ὑμῖν κινδυνεύσῃ, τοσοῦτον κατεφρονήθην, ὥστ' οὐχὶ
μόνον λόγου τυχεῖν οὐκ ἠξιώθην, ἀλλὰ καὶ ἐκ τῆς γῆς, ἣν
Ἄφοβος ἐκέκτηθ' ὅτ' ὠφλίσκανέ μοι τὴν δίκην, ὑβριστικῶς
ὑπ' αὐτοῦ πάνυ ἐξεβλήθην. ἐπειδὴ οὖν συναποστερεῖ τέ με 3
τῶν ὄντων τῷ ἑαυτοῦ κηδεστῇ, πιστεύων τ' εἰς ὑμᾶς εἰσελή-
15 λυθεν ταῖς αὐτοῦ παρασκευαῖς, ὑπόλοιπόν ἐστιν ἐν ὑμῖν
πειρᾶσθαι παρ' αὐτοῦ τῶν δικαίων τυγχάνειν. οἶδα μὲν οὖν,
ὦ ἄνδρες δικασταί, ὅτι μοι πρὸς παρασκευὰς λόγων καὶ
μάρτυρας οὐ τἀληθῆ μαρτυρήσοντας ὁ ἀγών ἐστιν· ὅμως
μέντοι τοσοῦτον οἶμαι διοίσειν τῷ δικαιότερα τούτου λέγειν,
20 ὥστ' εἰ καί τις ὑμῶν πρότερον τοῦτον ἡγεῖτ' εἶναι μὴ πονηρόν, 4
ἔκ γε τῶν πρὸς ἐμὲ πεπραγμένων γνώσεσθαι, ὅτι καὶ τὸν
ἄλλον χρόνον ἐλάνθανεν αὐτὸν κάκιστος ὢν καὶ ἀδικώτατος
ἁπάντων. ἀποδείξω γὰρ αὐτὸν οὐ μόνον τὴν προῖκ' οὐ δεδω-
κότα, ἧς φησι νῦν ἀποτετιμῆσθαι τὸ χωρίον, ἀλλὰ καὶ ἐξ
25 ἀρχῆς τοῖς ἐμοῖς ἐπιβουλεύσαντα, καὶ πρὸς τούτοις τὴν μὲν
γυναῖκ' οὐκ ἀπολελοιπυῖαν, ὑπὲρ ἧς ἐξήγαγέ μ' ἐκ ταύτης
τῆς γῆς, προϊστάμενον δ' ἐπ' ἀποστερήσει τῶν ἐμῶν Ἀφόβου 5
καὶ τούτους ὑπομένοντα τοὺς ἀγῶνας, οὕτω μεγάλοις τεκμηρίοις καὶ φανεροῖς ἐλέγχοις ὥσθ' ὑμᾶς ἅπαντας εἴσεσθαι
30 σαφῶς ὅτι δικαίως καὶ προσηκόντως οὗτος φεύγει ταύτην
ὑπ' ἐμοῦ τὴν δίκην. ὅθεν δὲ ῥᾷστα μαθήσεσθε περὶ αὐτῶν,
ἐντεῦθεν ὑμᾶς καὶ ἐγὼ πρῶτον πειράσομαι διδάσκειν.

Ἐγὼ γάρ, ὦ ἄνδρες δικασταί, πολλούς τ' ἄλλους Ἀθη- 6

57

ναίων καὶ τοῦτον οὐκ ἐλάνθανον κακῶς ἐπιτροπευόμενος,
ἀλλ' ἦν καταφανὴς εὐθὺς ἀδικούμενος· τοσαῦται πραγματεῖαι
καὶ λόγοι καὶ παρὰ τῷ ἄρχοντι καὶ παρὰ τοῖς ἄλλοις ἐγί-
γνονθ' ὑπὲρ τῶν ἐμῶν. τό τε γὰρ πλῆθος τῶν καταλειφθέντων ἦν φανερόν, ὅτι τ' ἀμίσθωτον τὸν οἶκον ἐποίουν 5
οἱ διαχειρίζοντες, ἵν' αὐτοὶ τὰ χρήματα καρποῖντο, οὐκ ἄδη-
λον ἦν. ὥστ' ἐκ τῶν γιγνομένων οὐκ ἔσθ' ὅστις οὐχ ἡγεῖτο
τῶν εἰδότων δίκην με λήψεσθαι παρ' αὐτῶν, ἐπειδὴ τάχιστ'
7 ἀνὴρ εἶναι δοκιμασθείην. ἐν οἷς καὶ Τιμοκράτης καὶ Ὀνήτωρ
ταύτην ἔχοντες διετέλεσαν τὴν διάνοιαν. τεκμήριον δὲ 10
πάντων μέγιστον· οὗτος γὰρ ἐβουλήθη μὲν Ἀφόβῳ δοῦναι
τὴν ἀδελφήν, ὁρῶν τῆς θ' αὑτοῦ πατρῴας οὐσίας καὶ τῆς
ἐμῆς οὐκ ὀλίγης αὐτὸν κύριον γεγενημένον, προέσθαι δὲ τὴν
προῖκ' οὐκ ἐπίστευσεν, ὥσπερ εἰ τὰ τῶν ἐπιτροπευόντων
χρήματ' ἀποτίμημα τοῖς ἐπιτροπευομένοις καθεστάναι νομί- 15
ζων. ἀλλὰ τὴν μὲν ἀδελφὴν ἔδωκεν, τὴν δὲ προῖκ' αὐτῷ
Τιμοκράτης ἐπὶ πέντ' ὀβολοῖς ὀφειλήσειν ὡμολόγησεν, ᾧ
8 πρότερον ἡ γυνὴ συνοικοῦσ' ἐτύγχανεν. ὀφλόντος δέ μοι
τὴν δίκην Ἀφόβου τῆς ἐπιτροπῆς καὶ οὐδὲν δίκαιον ποιεῖν
ἐθέλοντος, διαλύειν μὲν ἡμᾶς Ὀνήτωρ οὐδ' ἐπεχείρησεν, οὐκ 20
ἀποδεδωκὼς δὲ τὴν προῖκα, ἀλλ' αὐτὸς κύριος ὤν, ὡς ἀπο-
λελοιπυίας τῆς ἀδελφῆς καὶ δοὺς κομίσασθαι δ' οὐ δυνάμενος,
ἀποτιμήσασθαι φάσκων τὴν γῆν ἐξάγειν μ' ἐξ αὐτῆς ἐτόλ-
μησεν· τοσοῦτον καὶ ἐμοῦ καὶ ὑμῶν καὶ τῶν κειμένων νόμων
9 κατεφρόνησεν. καὶ τὰ μὲν γενόμενα, καὶ δι' ἃ φεύγει τὴν 25
δίκην καὶ περὶ ὧν οἴσετε τὴν ψῆφον, ταῦτ' ἐστίν, ὦ ἄνδρες
δικασταί· παρέξομαι δὲ μάρτυρας πρῶτον μὲν αὐτὸν Τιμοκράτην, ὡς ὡμολόγησεν ὀφειλήσειν τὴν προῖκα καὶ τὸν τόκον
ἀπεδίδου τῆς προικὸς Ἀφόβῳ κατὰ τὰς ὁμολογίας, ἔπειθ'
ὡς αὐτὸς Ἄφοβος ὡμολόγει κομίζεσθαι τὸν τόκον παρὰ 30
Τιμοκράτους. καί μοι λαβὲ τὰς μαρτυρίας.

MAPTYPIAI.

10 Ἐξ ἀρχῆς μὲν τοίνυν ὁμολογεῖται μὴ δοθῆναι τὴν προῖκα

μηδὲ γενέσθαι κύριον αὐτῆς Ἄφοβον. δῆλον δὲ καὶ ἐκ τῶν
εἰκότων ὅτι τούτων ἕνεχ' ὧν εἴρηκα ὀφείλειν εἴλοντο μᾶλλον
ἢ καταμεῖξαι τὴν προῖκ' εἰς τὴν οὐσίαν τὴν Ἀφόβου τὴν
οὕτω κινδυνευθήσεσθαι μέλλουσαν. οὔτε γὰρ δι' ἀπορίαν
5 οἷόν τ' εἰπεῖν ὡς οὐκ εὐθὺς ἀπέδοσαν (Τιμοκράτει τε γάρ
ἐστιν οὐσία πλέον ἢ δέκα ταλάντων, Ὀνήτορί τε πλέον ἢ
τριάκοντα, ὥστ' οὐκ ἂν διὰ τοῦτό γ' εἶεν οὐκ εὐθὺς δεδωκότες),
οὔτε κτήματα μὲν ἦν αὐτοῖς, ἀργύριον δ' οὐκ ἔτυχεν παρόν, 11
ἡ γυνὴ δ' ἐχήρευεν, διὸ πρᾶξαι ταῦτ' ἠπείχθησαν οὐχ ἅμα
10 τὴν προῖκα διδόντες· ἀργύριόν τε γὰρ οὗτοι δανείζουσιν
ἄλλοις οὐκ ὀλίγον, συνοικοῦσάν τε ταύτην, ἀλλ' οὐ χηρεύου-
σαν παρὰ Τιμοκράτους ἐξέδοσαν, ὥστ' οὐδ' ἂν ταύτην τὴν
σκῆψιν εἰκότως αὐτῶν τις ἀποδέξαιτο. καὶ μὲν δή, ὦ ἄνδρες 12
δικασταί, κἀκεῖν' ἂν πάντες ὁμολογήσαιτε, ὅτι τοιοῦτον
15 πρᾶγμα συναλλάττων ὁστισοῦν ἔλοιτ' ἂν ἑτέρῳ μᾶλλον ὀφείλειν ἢ κηδεστῇ τὴν προῖκα μὴ ἀποδοῦναι. μὴ διαλυσάμενος
μὲν γὰρ γίγνεται χρήστης ἄδηλος εἴτ' ἀποδώσει δικαίως εἴτε
μή, μετὰ δὲ τῆς γυναικὸς τἀκείνης ἀποδοὺς οἰκεῖος καὶ κη-
δεστής· ἐν οὐδεμιᾷ γάρ ἐστιν ὑποψίᾳ τὰ δίκαια πάντα 13
20 ποιήσας. ὥσθ' οὕτως τοῦ πράγματος ἔχοντος, καὶ τούτων
οὐδὲ καθ' ἓν ὧν εἶπον ὀφείλειν ἀναγκασθέντων, οὐδὲ βουληθέντων ἄν, οὐκ ἔστ' εἰπεῖν ἄλλην πρόφασιν δι' ἣν οὐκ
ἀπέδοσαν, ἀλλ' ἀνάγκη ταύτην εἶναι τὴν αἰτίαν, δι' ἣν δοῦναι
τὴν προῖκ' οὐκ ἐπίστευσαν.

25 Ἐγὼ τοίνυν ὁμολογουμένως οὕτω ταῦτ' ἐξελέγχων, ὡς 14
οὐδ' ὕστερον ἀπέδοσαν, οἶμαι ῥᾳδίως ἐπιδείξειν ἐξ αὐτῶν τῶν
πεπραγμένων, ὥσθ' ὑμῖν γενέσθαι φανερόν, ὅτι κἂν εἰ μὴ
ἐπὶ τούτοις, ἀλλ' ἐπὶ τῷ διὰ ταχέων ἀποδοῦναι τἀργύριον
εἶχον, οὐκ ἄν ποτ' ἀπέδοσαν οὐδ' ἂν προεῖντο· τοιαύτας
30 ἀνάγκας εἶχεν αὐτοῖς τὸ πρᾶγμα. δύο μὲν γάρ ἐστιν ἔτη 15
τὰ μεταξὺ τοῦ συνοικίσαί τε τὴν γυναῖκα καὶ φῆσαι τούτους
πεποιῆσθαι τὴν ἀπόλειψιν· ἐγήματο μὲν γὰρ ἐπὶ Πολυζήλου
ἄρχοντος σκιροφοριῶνος μηνός, ἡ δ' ἀπόλειψις ἐγράφη ποσι-
δεῶνος μηνὸς ἐπὶ Τιμοκράτους· ἐγὼ δ' εὐθέως μετὰ τοὺς

γάμους δοκιμασθεὶς ἐνεκάλουν καὶ λόγον ἀπῄτουν, καὶ πάντων
ἀποστερούμενος τὰς δίκας ἐλάγχανον ἐπὶ τοῦ αὐτοῦ ἄρχοντος.
16 ὁ δὴ χρόνος οὗτος ὀφειλῆσαι μὲν ἐνδέχεται κατὰ τὰς ὁμολογίας, ἀποδοῦναι δ' οὐκ ἔχει πίστιν. ὃς γὰρ διὰ ταῦτ' ἐξ
ἀρχῆς ὀφείλειν εἵλετο καὶ τόκον φέρειν, ἵνα μὴ κινδυνεύοι 5
ἡ προὶξ μετὰ τῆς ἄλλης οὐσίας, πῶς οὗτος ἂν ἀπέδωκεν ἤδη
τὴν δίκην φεύγοντος; ὃς εἰ καὶ τότ' ἐπίστευσεν, τηνικαῦτ'
ἂν ἀπολαβεῖν ἐζήτησεν. οὐκ ἔνεστι δήπουθεν, ὦ ἄνδρες
17 δικασταί. ἀλλὰ μὴν ὡς ἐγήματο μὲν ἡ γυνὴ καθ' ὃν ἐγὼ
λέγω χρόνον, ἀντίδικοι δ' ἡμεῖς ἤδη πρὸς ἀλλήλους ἐν τῷ 10
μεταξὺ χρόνῳ κατέστημεν, ὕστερον δ' ἢ ἐγὼ τὴν δίκην
ἔλαχον τὴν ἀπόλειψιν οὗτοι πρὸς τὸν ἄρχοντ' ἀπεγράψαντο,
λαβέ μοι καθ' ἕκαστον ταύτας τὰς μαρτυρίας.

MΑΡΤΥΡΙΑ.

Μετὰ τοίνυν τοῦτον τὸν ἄρχοντα Κηφισόδωρος, Χίων. 15
ἐπὶ τούτων ἐνεκάλουν δοκιμασθείς, ἔλαχον δὲ τὴν δίκην ἐπὶ
Τιμοκράτους. λαβὲ ταύτην τὴν μαρτυρίαν.

MΑΡΤΥΡΙΑ.

18 Ἀνάγνωθι δὲ καὶ ταύτην τὴν μαρτυρίαν.

MΑΡΤΥΡΙΑ.   20

Δῆλον μὲν τοίνυν καὶ ἐκ τῶν μεμαρτυρημένων, ὅτι τὴν
προῖκ' οὐ δόντες, ἀλλ' ἐπὶ τῷ διασῴζειν Ἀφόβῳ τὴν οὐσίαν
ταῦτα τολμῶσι πράττειν. οἳ γὰρ ἐν τοσούτῳ χρόνῳ καὶ
ὀφειλῆσαι καὶ ἀποδοῦναι καὶ τὴν γυναῖκ' ἀπολιπεῖν καὶ οὐ
κομίσασθαι καὶ τὸ χωρίον ἀποτιμήσασθαί φασιν, πῶς οὐ 25
φανερὸν ὅτι προστάντες τοῦ πράγματος τὰ γνωσθένθ' ὑφ'
19 ὑμῶν ἀποστερῆσαί με ζητοῦσιν; ὡς δὲ καὶ ἐξ ὧν αὐτὸς
οὗτος καὶ Τιμοκράτης καὶ Ἄφοβος ἀπεκρίναντο, οὐχ οἷόν τ'
ἀποδεδόσθαι τὴν προῖκα, ταῦτ' ἤδη πειράσομαι διδάσκειν
ὑμᾶς. ἐγὼ γάρ, ὦ ἄνδρες δικασταί, τούτων ἕκαστον ἠρόμην 30

πολλῶν ἐναντίον μαρτύρων, Ὀνήτορα μὲν καὶ Τιμοκράτην,
εἴ τινες εἶεν μάρτυρες ὧν ἐναντίον τὴν προῖκ' ἀπέδοσαν,
αὐτὸν δ' Ἄφοβον, εἴ τινες παρῆσαν ὅτ' ἀπελάμβανεν. καί 20
μοι πάντες ἀπεκρίναντο καθ' ἕκαστον, ὅτι οὐδεὶς μάρτυς
5 παρείη, κομίζοιτο δὲ λαμβάνων καθ' ὁποσονοῦν δέοιτ' Ἄφοβος παρ' αὐτῶν. καίτοι τῷ τοῦθ' ὑμῶν πιστόν, ὡς ταλάντου
τῆς προικὸς οὔσης ἄνευ μαρτύρων Ὀνήτωρ καὶ Τιμοκράτης
Ἀφόβῳ τοσοῦτον ἀργύριον ἐνεχείρισαν; ᾧ μὴ ὅτι τοῦτον
τὸν τρόπον, ἀλλ' οὐδὲ μετὰ πολλῶν μαρτύρων ἀποδιδοὺς
10 εἰκῇ τις ἂν ἐπίστευσεν, ἵν' εἴ τις γίγνοιτο διαφορά, κομίσασθαι ῥᾳδίως παρ' ὑμῖν δύνηται. μὴ γὰρ ὅτι πρὸς τοῦτον 21
τοιοῦτον ὄντα, ἀλλ' οὐδὲ πρὸς ἄλλον οὐδ' ἂν εἰς οὐδένα
τοιοῦτον συνάλλαγμα ποιούμενος ἀμαρτύρως ἂν ἔπραξεν·
ἀλλὰ τῶν τοιούτων ἕνεκα καὶ γάμους ποιοῦμεν καὶ τοὺς
15 ἀναγκαιοτάτους παρακαλοῦμεν, ὅτι οὐ πάρεργον, ἀλλ' ἀδελ-
φῶν καὶ θυγατέρων βίους ἐγχειρίζομεν, ὑπὲρ ὧν τὰς ἀσφαλείας μάλιστα σκοποῦμεν. εἰκὸς τοίνυν καὶ τοῦτον, ὧνπερ 22
ἐναντίον ὀφείλειν ὡμολόγησεν καὶ τὸν τόκον οἴσειν, τῶν
αὐτῶν τούτων παρόντων διαλύσασθαι πρὸς Ἄφοβον, εἴπερ
20 ὡς ἀληθῶς ἀπεδίδου τὴν προῖκ' αὐτῷ. τοῦτον μὲν γὰρ τὸν
τρόπον πράξας, ὅλου τοῦ πράγματος ἀπηλλάττετο, μόνος
μόνῳ δ' ἀποδιδούς, τοὺς ἐπὶ ταῖς ὁμολογίαις παραγενομένους
ὡς κατ' ὀφείλοντος ἂν αὐτοῦ μάρτυρας ὑπελείπετο. νῦν 23
τοίνυν τοὺς μὲν ὄντας οἰκείους καὶ βελτίους αὐτῶν οὐκ
25 ἐδύναντο πεῖσαι τὴν προῖκ' ἀποδεδωκέναι σφᾶς μαρτυρεῖν,
ἑτέρους δ' εἰ παρέχοιντο μάρτυρας μηδὲν γένει προσήκοντας,
οὐκ ἂν ἡγοῦνθ' ὑμᾶς αὐτοῖς πιστεύειν. ἔτι δ' ἀθρόαν μὲν
φάσκοντες δεδωκέναι τὴν προῖκα, ᾔδεσαν ὅτι τοὺς ἀπενεγκόντας οἰκέτας ἐξαιτήσομεν, οὓς μὴ γεγενημένης τῆς δόσεως
30 παραδοῦναι μὴ 'θέλοντες ἠλέγχοντ' ἄν· εἰ δ' αὐτοὶ μόνοι
μόνῳ τοῦτον τὸν τρόπον ἀποδεδωκέναι λέγοιεν, ἐνόμιζον οὐκ
ἐλεγχθήσεσθαι. διὰ τοῦτο τοῦτον εἵλοντ' ἐξ ἀνάγκης ψεύ- 24
δεσθαι τὸν τρόπον. τοιαύταις τέχναις καὶ πανουργίαις, ὡς

ἁπλοῖ τινὲς εἶναι δόξοντες, ἡγοῦνται ῥᾳδίως ὑμᾶς ἐξαπατήσειν,
ἁπλῶς οὐδ᾽ ἂν μικρὸν ὑπὲρ τῶν διαφερόντων, ἀλλ᾽ ὡς οἷόν
τ᾽ ἀκριβέστατα πράξαντες. λαβὲ τὰς μαρτυρίας αὐτοῖς ὧν
ἐναντίον ἀπεκρίναντο, καὶ ἀνάγνωθι.

MAPTYPIAI.　5

25　Φέρε δή, ὦ ἄνδρες δικασταί, καὶ τὴν γυναῖχ᾽ ὑμῖν ἀποδείξω λόγῳ μὲν ἀπολελοιπυῖαν, ἔργῳ δὲ συνοικοῦσαν Ἀφόβῳ·
νομίζω γάρ, ἂν τοῦτ᾽ ἀκριβῶς μάθητε, μᾶλλον ὑμᾶς τούτοις
μὲν ἀπιστήσειν, ἐμοὶ δ᾽ ἀδικουμένῳ τὰ δίκαια βοηθήσειν.
μάρτυρας δὲ τῶν μὲν ὑμῖν παρέξομαι, τῶν δ᾽ ἐπιδείξω μεγάλα　10
26　τεκμήρια καὶ πίστεις ἱκανάς. ἐγὼ γάρ, ὦ ἄνδρες δικασταί,
μετὰ τὸ γεγράφθαι παρὰ τῷ ἄρχοντι ταύτην τὴν γυναῖκ᾽
ἀπολελοιπυῖαν καὶ τὸ φάσκειν Ὀνήτορ᾽ ἀντὶ τῆς προικὸς
ἀποτετιμῆσθαι τὸ χωρίον, ὁρῶν Ἄφοβον ὁμοίως ἔχοντα καὶ
γεωργοῦντα τὴν γῆν καὶ τῇ γυναικὶ συνοικοῦντα, σαφῶς　15
ᾔδειν ὅτι λόγος ταῦτα καὶ παραγωγὴ τοῦ πράγματός ἐστιν.
27　βουλόμενος δ᾽ ἐμφανῆ ποιῆσαι ταῦτα πᾶσιν ὑμῖν, ἐξελέγχειν
αὐτὸν ἠξίουν ἐναντίον μαρτύρων, εἰ μὴ φάσκοι ταῦθ᾽ οὕτως
ἔχειν, καὶ παρεδίδουν οἰκέτην εἰς βάσανον, ὃς συνῄδει πάντ᾽
ἀκριβῶς· ὃν ἔλαβον κατὰ τὴν ὑπερημερίαν ἐκ τῶν Ἀφόβου.　20
οὗτος δ᾽ ἐμοῦ ταῦτ᾽ ἀξιώσαντος, περὶ μὲν τοῦ συνοικεῖν
Ἀφόβῳ τὴν ἀδελφὴν ἔφυγε τὴν βάσανον· ὡς δ᾽ οὐκ ἐκεῖνος
ἐγεώργει τὴν γῆν, οὐκ ἐδύνατ᾽ ἀρνηθῆναι διὰ τὴν περιφάνειαν,
28　ἀλλὰ προσωμολόγησεν. οὐ μόνον δ᾽ ἐκ τούτων ἦν ῥᾴδιον
γνῶναι, ὅτι καὶ συνῴκει τῇ γυναικὶ καὶ τὸ χωρίον ἐκέκτητ᾽　25
ἔτι πρὶν γενέσθαι τὴν δίκην, ἀλλὰ καὶ ἐξ ὧν ὀφλὼν διε-
πράξατο περὶ αὐτῶν. ὡς γὰρ οὐκ ἀποτετιμηκώς, ἀλλ᾽ ἐμῶν
ἐσομένων κατὰ τὴν δίκην, ἃ μὲν οἷόν τ᾽ ἦν ἐξενεγκεῖν, ᾤχετο
λαβών, τοὺς καρποὺς καὶ τὰ σκεύη τὰ γεωργικὰ πάντα πλὴν
τῶν πιθακνῶν· ὃ δ᾽ οὐχ οἷόν τ᾽ ἦν ἀνελεῖν, ἐξ ἀνάγκης　30
ὑπέλιπεν, ὥστ᾽ ἐγγενέσθαι τούτῳ νῦν αὐτῆς τῆς γῆς ἀμφισ-
29　βητεῖν. καίτοι δεινὸν τὸν μὲν λέγειν ὡς ἀπετιμήσατο τὸ

χωρίον, τὸν δ᾽ ἀποτετιμηκότα φαίνεσθαι γεωργοῦντα, καὶ
φάσκειν μὲν ἀπολελοιπέναι τὴν ἀδελφήν, ὑπὲρ αὐτῶν δὲ
τούτων φανερὸν εἶναι φεύγοντα τοὺς ἐλέγχους, καὶ τὸν μὲν
οὐ συνοικοῦντα, ὡς οὗτός φησιν, καὶ τοὺς καρποὺς καὶ τὰ ἐκ
5 τῆς γεωργίας ἅπαντ᾽ ἐξενεγκεῖν, τὸν δ᾽ ὑπὲρ τῆς ἀπολελοι-
πυίας πράττοντα, ὑπὲρ ἧς ἀποτετιμῆσθαί φησι τὸ χωρίον,
φαίνεσθαι μηδ᾽ ὑπὲρ ἑνὸς τούτων ἀγανακτοῦντα, ἀλλ᾽ ἡσυχίαν
ἔχοντα. ταῦτ᾽ οὐ πολλὴ περιφάνει᾽ ἐστίν; ταῦτ᾽ οὐχ ὁμο- 30
λογουμένη προστασία; φήσειέ γ᾽ ἄν τις, εἰ διαλογίζοιτ᾽
10 ὀρθῶς ἕκαστ᾽ αὐτῶν. ὡς τοίνυν ὡμολόγει μὲν ἐκεῖνον
γεωργεῖν πρὶν γενέσθαι τὴν δίκην ἐμοὶ πρὸς αὐτόν, ὑπὲρ δὲ
τοῦ μὴ συνοικεῖν τὴν ἀδελφὴν οὐκ ἠθέλησεν ποιήσασθαι τὴν
βάσανον, ἡ δὲ γεωργία ἐξεσκευάσθη μετὰ τὴν δίκην πλὴν
τῶν ἐγγείων, λαβὲ ταύτας τὰς μαρτυρίας καὶ ἀνάγνωθι.

15   ΜΑΡΤΥΡΙΑΙ.

Ἐμοὶ τοίνυν τοσούτων ὑπαρχόντων τεκμηρίων, οὐχ 31
ἥκιστ᾽ αὐτὸς ἔδειξεν Ὀνήτωρ, ὅτι οὐκ ἀληθινὴν ἐποιήσατο
τὴν ἀπόλειψιν. ᾧ γὰρ προσῆκεν χαλεπῶς φέρειν, εἰ τὴν
προῖκα δούς, ὥς φησιν, ἀντ᾽ ἀργυρίου χωρίον ἀμφισβητού-
20 μενον ἀπελάμβανεν, οὗτος οὐχ ὡς διάφορος οὐδ᾽ ὡς
ἀδικούμενος, ἀλλ᾽ ὡς οἰκειότατος πάντων τὴν πρὸς ἐμὲ
δίκην αὐτῷ συνηγωνίζετο. κἀμὲ μὲν συναποστερῆσαι μετ᾽
ἐκείνου τῶν πατρῴων ἐπεχείρησεν, καθ᾽ ὅσον αὐτὸς οἷός τ᾽
ἦν, ὑφ᾽ οὗ κακὸν οὐδ᾽ ὁτιοῦν ἦν πεπονθώς· Ἀφόβῳ δ᾽, ὃν
25 ἀλλότριον εἶναι προσῆκε νομίζειν, εἴ τι τούτων ἀληθὲς ἦν
ὧν νῦν λέγουσιν, καὶ τἀμὰ πρὸς τοῖς ἐκείνου περιποιεῖν
ἐζήτησεν. καὶ οὐ μόνον ἐνταῦθα τοῦτ᾽ ἐποίησεν, ἀλλὰ καὶ 32
κατεγνωσμένης ἤδη τῆς δίκης, ἀναβὰς ἐπὶ τὸ δικαστήριον
ἐδεῖθ᾽ ἱκετεύων ὑπὲρ αὐτοῦ καὶ ἀντιβολῶν καὶ δάκρυσι
30 κλάων ταλάντου τιμῆσαι, καὶ τούτου αὐτὸς ἐγίγνετ᾽ ἐγγυη-
τής. καὶ ταῦθ᾽ ὁμολογούμενα μέν ἐστιν πολλαχόθεν (οἵ τε
γὰρ ἐν τῷ δικαστηρίῳ τότε δικάζοντες καὶ τῶν ἔξωθεν

παρόντων πολλοὶ συνίσασιν), ὅμως δὲ καὶ μάρτυρας ὑμῖν παρέξομαι. καί μοι λαβὲ ταύτην τὴν μαρτυρίαν.

MΑΡΤΥΡΙΑ.

33 Ἔτι τοίνυν, ὦ ἄνδρες δικασταί, καὶ τεκμηρίῳ μεγάλῳ γνῶναι ῥᾴδιον, ὅτι τῇ ἀληθείᾳ συνῴκει καὶ οὐδέπω καὶ 5 τήμερον ἀπολέλοιπεν. αὕτη γὰρ ἡ γυνή, πρὶν μὲν ὡς Ἄφοβον ἐλθεῖν, μίαν ἡμέραν οὐκ ἐχήρευσεν, ἀλλὰ παρὰ ζῶντος Τιμοκράτους ἐκείνῳ συνῴκησεν, νῦν δ' ἐν τρισὶν ἔτεσιν ἄλλῳ συνοικοῦσ' οὐδενὶ φαίνεται. καίτοι τῷ πιστόν, ὡς τότε μέν, ἵνα μὴ χηρεύσειεν, παρ' ἀνδρὸς ὡς ἄνδρ' 10 ἐβάδιζεν, νῦν δ', εἴπερ ὡς ἀληθῶς ἀπολέλοιπεν, τοσοῦτον ἂν χρόνον χηρεύουσ' ἠνείχετ' ἐξὸν ἄλλῳ συνοικεῖν, τοῦ τ' ἀδελφοῦ κεκτημένου τοσαύτην οὐσίαν, αὐτή τε ταύτην 34 ἔχουσα τὴν ἡλικίαν; οὐκ ἔχει ταῦτ' ἀλήθειαν, ὦ ἄνδρες δικασταί, πιθανήν, ἀλλὰ λόγοι ταῦτ' εἰσί, συνοικεῖ δ' ἡ 15 γυνὴ φανερῶς καὶ οὐκ ἐπικρύπτεται τὸ πρᾶγμα. παρέξομαι δ' ὑμῖν Πασιφῶντος μαρτυρίαν, ὃς ἀρρωστοῦσαν αὐτὴν θεραπεύων ἑώρα παρακαθήμενον Ἄφοβον ἐπὶ τούτου τοῦ ἄρχοντος, ἤδη τούτῳ ταυτησί τῆς δίκης εἰληγμένης. καί μοι λαβὲ τὴν Πασιφῶντος μαρτυρίαν.

20

ΜΑΡΤΥΡΙΑ.

35 Ἐγὼ τοίνυν εἰδώς, ὦ ἄνδρες δικασταί, καὶ μετὰ τὴν δίκην τοῦτον εὐθὺς ἀποδεδεγμένον τὰ ἐκ τῆς οἰκίας τῆς Ἀφόβου χρήματα, καὶ κύριον τῶν τ' ἐκείνου καὶ τῶν ἐμῶν ἁπάντων γεγενημένον, καὶ συνοικοῦσαν [αὐτῷ] τὴν γυναῖκα 25 σαφῶς ἐπιστάμενος, τρεῖς θεραπαίνας ἐξήτησ' αὐτόν, αἳ συνοικοῦσάν τε τὴν γυναῖκ' ᾔδεσαν καὶ τὰ χρήμαθ' ὅτι παρὰ τούτοις ἦν, ἵνα μὴ λόγοι μόνον, ἀλλὰ καὶ βάσανοι 36 περὶ αὐτῶν γίγνοιντο. οὗτος δ' ἐμοῦ προκαλεσαμένου ταῦτα, καὶ πάντων τῶν παρόντων δίκαια λέγειν μ' ἀποφηναμένων, 30 οὐκ ἠθέλησεν εἰς τοῦτο τἀκριβὲς καταφυγεῖν, ἀλλ' ὥσπερ

64

ἑτέρων τινῶν ὄντων περὶ τῶν τοιούτων σαφεστέρων ἐλέγχων
ἢ βασάνων καὶ μαρτυριῶν, οὔτε μάρτυρας παρεχόμενος τὴν
προῖχ' ὡς ἀπέδωκεν, οὔτ' εἰς βάσανον ἐκδιδοὺς τὰς συνειδυίας
περὶ τοῦ μὴ συνοικεῖν τὴν ἀδελφήν, ὅτι ταῦτ' ἠξίουν, ὑβρι-
5 στικῶς πάνυ καὶ προπηλακιστικῶς οὐκ εἴα μ' αὐτῷ δια-
λέγεσθαι. τούτου γένοιτ' ἄν τις σχετλιώτερος ἄνθρωπος,
ἢ μᾶλλον ἑκὼν τὰ δίκαι' ἀγνοεῖν προσποιούμενος; λαβὲ δ'
αὐτὴν τὴν πρόκλησιν καὶ ἀνάγνωθι.

ΠΡΟΚΛΗΣΙΣ.

10 Ὑμεῖς τοίνυν καὶ ἰδίᾳ καὶ δημοσίᾳ βάσανον ἀκριβεστάτην 37
πασῶν ⟨πίστεων⟩ νομίζετε, καὶ ὅπου ἂν δοῦλοι καὶ ἐλεύθεροι
παραγένωνται, δέῃ δ' εὑρεθῆναι τὸ ζητούμενον, οὐ χρῆσθε ταῖς
τῶν ἐλευθέρων μαρτυρίαις, ἀλλὰ τοὺς δούλους βασανίζοντες,
οὕτω ζητεῖτε τὴν ἀλήθειαν εὑρεῖν. εἰκότως, ὦ ἄνδρες δικασταί·
15 τῶν μὲν γὰρ μαρτυρησάντων ἤδη τινὲς οὐ τἀληθῆ μαρτυρῆσαι
ἔδοξαν· τῶν δὲ βασανισθέντων οὐδένες πώποτ' ἐξηλέγχθη-
σαν, ὡς οὐκ ἀληθῆ τὰ ἐκ τῆς βασάνου εἶπον. οὗτος δὲ 38
τηλικαῦτα δίκαια φυγὼν καὶ σαφεῖς οὕτω καὶ μεγάλους
ἐλέγχους παραλιπών, Ἄφοβον παρεχόμενος μάρτυρα καὶ
20 Τιμοκράτην, τὸν μὲν ὡς ἀπέδωκε τὴν προῖκα, τὸν δ' ὡς
ἀπείληφεν, ἀξιώσει πιστεύεσθαι παρ' ὑμῖν, ἀμάρτυρον τὴν
πρὸς τούτους πρᾶξιν γεγενῆσθαι προσποιούμενος· τοσαύτην
ὑμῶν εὐήθειαν κατέγνωκεν. ὅτι μὲν τοίνυν οὔτ' ἀληθῆ οὔτ' 39
ἀληθείᾳ ἐοικότα λέξουσιν, καὶ ἐκ τοῦ ἐξ ἀρχῆς αὐτοὺς
25 ὁμολογεῖν τὴν προῖκα μὴ δοῦναι, καὶ ἐκ τοῦ πάλιν ἄνευ
μαρτύρων ἀποδεδωκέναι φάσκειν, καὶ ἐκ τοῦ τὸν χρόνον μὴ
ἐγχωρεῖν ἀμφισβητουμένης ἤδη τῆς οὐσίας ἀποδοῦναι τἀργύριον, καὶ ἐκ τῶν ἄλλων ἁπάντων ἱκανῶς ἀποδεδεῖχθαι νομίζω.

XXXI

ΠΡΟΣ ΟΝΗΤΟΡΑ ΕΞΟΥΛΗΣ Β

Παραλελειμμένα τιν᾽ ἐν τῷ προτέρῳ λόγῳ διὰ τούτου προστίθησιν, ὡς καὶ αὐτὸς ἐπισημαίνεται, καὶ δὴ καὶ πρός τινας ἀντιρρήσεις ἵσταται.

Περὶ δὲ τῶν λόγων τούτων προειρήκαμεν ὅτι πολλοί φασιν   5
αὐτοὺς ὑπ᾽ Ἰσαίου συντεθῆναι, τοῦ ῥήτορος ἀπιστοῦντες εἶναι διὰ
τὴν ἡλικίαν, οἱ δέ γε, εἰ μὴ τοῦτο, διωρθῶσθαί γ᾽ ὑπὸ τοῦ Ἰσαίου·
ἐοίκασι γὰρ τοῖς ἐκείνου λόγοις. θαυμαστὸν δ᾽ οὐδέν, εἰ τὸν
διδάσκαλον ἐμιμήσατο, καὶ μηδέπω πρὸς τὸ τέλειον ἥκων [ἐπὶ]
τὸν ἐκείνου χαρακτῆρα μετῄει τέως.

Ὃ παρέλιπον ἐν τῷ προτέρῳ λόγῳ τεκμήριον, οὐδενὸς τῶν εἰρημένων ἔλαττον, τοῦ μὴ δεδωκέναι τὴν προῖκα τούτους Ἀφόβῳ, τοῦτο πρῶτον εἰπών, μετὰ τοῦτο καὶ περὶ ὧν οὗτος ἔψευσται πρὸς ὑμᾶς ἐξελέγχειν αὐτὸν πειράσομαι. οὗτος
5 γάρ, ὦ ἄνδρες δικασταί, τὸ πρῶτον ὅτε τῶν Ἀφόβου διενοεῖτ᾽ ἀμφισβητεῖν, οὐχὶ τάλαντον ἔφη τὴν προῖκα, ὥσπερ νυνί, ἀλλ᾽ ὀγδοήκοντα μνᾶς δεδωκέναι, καὶ τίθησιν ὅρους ἐπὶ μὲν τὴν οἰκίαν δισχιλίων, ἐπὶ δὲ τὸ χωρίον ταλάντου, βουλόμενος μὴ μόνον τοῦτο, ἀλλὰ κἀκείνην διασῴζειν αὐτῷ. γενομένης 2
10 δέ μοι τῆς δίκης πρὸς αὐτόν, ἰδὼν ὡς διάκεισθ᾽ ὑμεῖς πρὸς τοὺς λίαν ἀναιδῶς ἀδικοῦντας, ἔννους γίγνεται, καὶ δεινὰ πάσχειν ἡγήσατο δόξειν ἐμὲ τοσούτων χρημάτων ἀπεστερημένον, εἰ μηδ᾽ ὁτιοῦν ἔξοιμι τῶν Ἀφόβου λαβεῖν τοῦ τἄμ᾽ ἔχοντος, ἀλλ᾽ ὑπὸ τούτου κωλυόμενος φανερὸς γενήσομαι.
15 καὶ τί ποιεῖ; τοὺς ὅρους ἀπὸ τῆς οἰκίας ἀφαιρεῖ, καὶ τάλαντον 3 μόνον εἶναι τὴν προῖκά φησιν, ἐν ᾧ τὸ χωρίον ἀποτετιμῆσθαι. καίτοι δῆλον ὅτι τοὺς ἐπὶ τῆς οἰκίας ὅρους εἰ δικαίως ἔθηκεν καὶ ὄντως ἀληθεῖς, δικαίως καὶ τοὺς ἐπὶ τοῦ χωρίου τέθηκεν· εἰ δ᾽ εὐθὺς ἀδικεῖν βουλόμενος ψευδεῖς ἔθηκεν
20 ἐκείνους, εἰκὸς καὶ τούτους οὐκ ἀληθεῖς ὑπάρχειν. τοῦτο 4 τοίνυν οὐκ ἐξ ὧν ἐγὼ δεδήλωκα λόγων δεῖ σκοπεῖν, ἀλλ᾽ ἐξ ὧν αὐτὸς οὗτος διεπράξατο· οὐδ᾽ ὑφ᾽ ἑνὸς γὰρ ἀναγκασθεὶς ἀνθρώπων αὐτὸς ἀνεῖλεν τοὺς ὅρους, ἔργῳ φανερὸν ποιήσας ὅτι ψεύδεται. καὶ ταῦθ᾽ ὡς ἀληθῆ λέγω, τὸ μὲν χωρίον καὶ
25 νῦν οὗτός φησιν ἀποτετιμῆσθαι ταλάντου, τὴν δ᾽ οἰκίαν ὡς προσωρίσατο δισχιλίων καὶ πάλιν τοὺς ὅρους ἀνεῖλεν γενομένης τῆς δίκης, τοὺς εἰδότας ὑμῖν μάρτυρας παρέξομαι. καί μοι λαβὲ τὴν μαρτυρίαν.

MAΡΤΥΡΙΑ.

30 Δῆλον τοίνυν ὅτι δισχιλίων μὲν ὡρισμένος τὴν οἰκίαν, 5 ταλάντου δὲ τὸ χωρίον, ὡς ὀγδοήκοντα μνᾶς δεδωκὼς ἔμελλεν ἀμφισβητήσειν. μεῖζον οὖν ἄν τι γένοιτο τεκμήριον

ὑμῖν τοῦ μηδὲν ἀληθὲς νῦν λέγειν τοῦτον ἢ εἰ φανείη
μὴ ταὐτὰ λέγων τοῖς ἐξ ἀρχῆς περὶ τῶν αὐτῶν; ἐμοὶ μὲν
γὰρ οὐδὲν ἂν δοκεῖ τούτου μεῖζον εὑρεθῆναι.

6 Σκέψασθε τοίνυν τὴν ἀναίδειαν, ὃς ἐν ὑμῖν ἐτόλμησεν
εἰπεῖν, ὡς οὐκ ἀποστερεῖ μ᾽ ὅσῳ πλείονος ἄξιόν ἐστι 5
ταλάντου, καὶ ταῦτ᾽ αὐτὸς τιμήσας οὐκ ἄξιον εἶναι πλείονος.
τί γὰρ βουλόμενος δισχιλίων προσωρίσω τὴν οἰκίαν, ὅτε τὰς
ὀγδοήκοντα μνᾶς ἐνεκάλεις, εἴ γε τὸ χωρίον ἄξιον ἦν
7 πλείονος, ἀλλ᾽ οὐκ ἐπὶ τούτῳ καὶ τὰς δισχιλίας ἐτίθεις; ἢ
ὅταν μέν σοι δοκῇ πάντα τὰ Ἀφόβου διασῴζειν, τό τε 10
χωρίον ἔσται ταλάντου μόνον ἄξιον, καὶ τὴν οἰκίαν ἐν
δισχιλίαις προσέξεις, ἥ τε προῖξ ὀγδοήκοντα μναῖ γενή-
σονται, καὶ ἀξιώσεις ἔχειν ἀμφότερα· ὅταν δέ σοι μὴ
συμφέρῃ, τἀναντία πάλιν ἡ μὲν οἰκία ταλάντου, διότι νῦν
ἐγὼ ταύτην ἔχω, τοῦ δὲ χωρίου τὸ περιὸν οὐκ ἐλάττονος ἢ 15
δυοῖν ἄξιον, ἵν᾽ ἐγὼ δοκῶ βλάπτειν τοῦτον, οὐκ ἀποστερεῖ-
8 σθαι; ὁρᾷς ὡς ὑποκρίνει μὲν δεδωκέναι τὴν προῖκα, φαίνει
δὲ κατ᾽ οὐδ᾽ ὁντινοῦν τρόπον δεδωκώς; τὰ γὰρ ἀληθῆ καὶ
μὴ κακουργούμενα τῶν πραγμάτων ἁπλῶς, οἷ᾽ ἂν ἐξ ἀρχῆς
πραχθῇ, τοιαῦτ᾽ ἐστίν· σὺ δὲ τοὐναντίον ἐξελέγχει πράξας 20
εἰς τὴν καθ᾽ ἡμῶν ὑπηρεσίαν.

9 Ἄξιον τοίνυν καὶ τὸν ὅρκον, ὁποῖόν τιν᾽ ἂν ὤμοσεν,
εἴ τις ἔδωκεν, ἐκ τούτων ἰδεῖν. ὃς γὰρ ὀγδοήκοντα μνᾶς
ἔφη τὴν προῖκ᾽ εἶναι, εἰ τότ᾽ αὐτῷ τις ἔδωκεν, ὀμόσαντι
ταῦτ᾽ ἀληθῆ λέγειν, κομίσασθαι, τί ἐποίησεν ἄν; ἢ δῆλον 25
ὅτι ὤμοσεν; τί γὰρ καὶ λέγων οὐ φήσει τότ᾽ ἂν ὀμόσαι,
νῦν γε τοῦτ᾽ ἀξιῶν; οὐκοῦν ὅτι γ᾽ ἐπιώρκησεν ἄν, ἑαυτὸν
ἐξελέγχει· νῦν γὰρ οὐκ ὀγδοήκοντα μνᾶς, ἀλλὰ τάλαντον
δεδωκέναι φησίν. τί μᾶλλον ἂν οὖν εἰκότως τις αὐτὸν
ἐκεῖν᾽ ἐπιορκεῖν ἢ τάδ᾽ ἡγοῖτο; ἢ τίνα τις δικαίως ἂν ἔχοι 30
περὶ τούτου διάνοιαν, τοῦ ῥᾳδίως οὕτως αὐτὸν ἐξελέγχοντος
ὄντ᾽ ἐπίορκον;

10 Ἀλλὰ νὴ Δί᾽ ἴσως οὐχὶ πάντ᾽ αὐτῷ τοιαῦτα πέπρακται,

70

οὐδὲ πανταχόθεν δῆλός ἐστι τεχνάζων. ἀλλὰ καὶ τιμώμενος
φανερὸς γέγονεν ὑπὲρ Ἀφόβου ταλάντου, καὶ τοῦτ' αὐτὸς
ἡμῖν ἀποδώσειν ἐγγυώμενος. καίτοι σκέψασθ' ὅτι τοῦτ'
ἔστι τεκμήριον οὐ μόνον τοῦ τὴν γυναῖκα συνοικεῖν Ἀφόβῳ
5 καὶ τοῦτον οἰκείως ἔχειν, ἀλλὰ καὶ τοῦ μὴ δεδωκέναι τὴν
προῖκα. τίς γὰρ ἀνθρώπων ἠλίθιός ἐστιν οὕτως ὥστ' 11
ἀργύριον μὲν δοὺς τοσοῦτον, ἔπειθ' ἐν λαβὼν χωρίον
ἀμφισβητούμενον εἰς ἀποτίμησιν, σὺν οἷς πρότερον ἐζημίωτο,
τὸν ἀδικήσανθ' ὡς δίκαιόν τι ποιήσοντα καὶ τοῦ τῆς δίκης
10 ὀφλήματος προσεγγυήσασθαι; ἐγὼ μὲν οὐδέν' οἶμαι. καὶ
γὰρ οὐδὲ λόγον τὸ πρᾶγμ' ἔχον ἐστίν, τὸν αὐτὸν αὑτῷ
μὴ δυνάμενον κομίσασθαι τάλαντον, τοῦτον ἄλλῳ τινὶ
φάσκειν ἀποτείσειν καὶ ταῦτ' ἐγγυᾶσθαι. ἀλλὰ καὶ ἀπ'
αὐτῶν τούτων ἐστὶ δῆλον ὅτι τὴν μὲν προῖκ' οὐκ ἔδωκεν,
15 ἀντὶ δὲ πολλῶν χρημάτων τῶν ἐμῶν οἰκεῖος ὢν Ἀφόβῳ
ταῦτ' ἀπετιμᾶτο, κληρονόμον τὴν ἀδελφὴν τῶν ἐμῶν μετ'
ἐκείνου καταστῆσαι βουλόμενος. εἶτα νῦν παρακρούσασθαι 12
ζητεῖ καὶ φενακίζει, λέγων ὡς πρότερον τοὺς ὅρους ἔστησεν
ἢ 'κεῖνον τὴν δίκην ὀφλεῖν. οὐ πρότερόν γ' ἢ παρὰ σοί, νῦν
20 εἰ ἀληθῆ λέγεις. δῆλον γὰρ ὅτι καταγνοὺς ἀδικίαν αὐτοῦ
ταῦτ' ἐποίεις. εἶτα καὶ γελοῖον τοῦτο λέγειν, ὥσπερ οὐκ
εἰδότων ὑμῶν ὅτι πάντες οἱ τὰ τοιαῦτ' ἀδικοῦντες σκοποῦσι
τί λέξουσιν, καὶ οὐδεὶς πώποτ' ὤφλεν σιωπῶν οὐδ' ἀδικεῖν
ὁμολογῶν· ἀλλ' ἐπειδὰν οἶμαι μηδὲν ἀληθὲς λέγων ἐξε-
25 λεγχθῇ, τότε γιγνώσκεται ὁποῖός ἐστιν. ὅπερ καὶ οὗτος 13
ἔμοιγε δοκεῖ πάσχειν. ἐπεὶ φέρε, πῶς ἐστι δίκαιον, ἐὰν μὲν
ὀγδοήκοντα μνῶν θῆς ὅρους, ὀγδοήκοντα μνᾶς εἶναι τὴν
προῖκα, ἐὰν δὲ πλείονος πλέον, ἐὰν δ' ἐλάττονος ἔλαττον; ἢ
πῶς ἐστι δίκαιον, τῆς ἀδελφῆς τῆς σῆς μηδέπω καὶ τήμερον
30 ἄλλῳ συνοικούσης μηδ' ἀπηλλαγμένης Ἀφόβου, μηδὲ τὴν
προῖκα δεδωκότος σοῦ, μηδ' ὑπὲρ τούτων εἰς βάσανον μηδ'
εἰς ἄλλο δίκαιον μηδὲν καταφεύγειν ἐθέλοντος, ὅτι σὺ
στῆσαι φῂς ὅρους, σὸν εἶναι τὸ χωρίον; ἐγὼ μὲν οὐδαμῶς

οἶμαι· τὴν γὰρ ἀλήθειαν σκεπτέον, οὐχ ἅ τις αὐτῷ παρεσκεύασεν ἐξεπίτηδες εἰς τὸ λέγειν τι δοκεῖν, ὥσπερ ὑμεῖς.
14 ἔπειτα τὸ δεινότατον· εἰ καὶ δεδωκότες ἦθ' ὡς μάλιστα τὴν προῖκα, ἣν οὐ δεδώκατε, τίς ὁ τούτων αἴτιος; οὐχ ὑμεῖς, ἐπεὶ ⟨ἐπὶ⟩ τἄμ᾽ ἔδοτε; οὐχ ὅλοις ἔτεσιν πρότερον δέκα τἀμὰ λαβὼν 5 εἶχεν ἐκεῖνος ὧν ὦφλεν τὴν δίκην, ἢ κηδεστήν σοι γενέσθαι; ἢ σὲ μὲν δεῖ κομίσασθαι πάντα, τὸν δὲ καὶ καταδικασάμενον καὶ δι᾽ ὀρφανίαν ἠδικημένον καὶ προικὸς ἀληθινῆς ἀπεστερημένον, ὃν μόνον ἀνθρώπων οὐδὲ τῆς ἐπωβελίας ἄξιον ἦν κινδυνεύειν, ἠναγκάσθαι τοιαῦτα παθεῖν, κεκομισμένον μηδ᾽ ὁτιοῦν, 10 καὶ ταῦτ᾽ ἐθέλοντα ποιεῖν ⟨ἐφ᾽⟩ ὑμῖν αὐτοῖς, εἴ τι τῶν δεόντων ἐβούλεσθε πράττειν;

72

XXXVI

ΠΑΡΑΓΡΑΦΗ ΥΠΕΡ ΦΟΡΜΙΩΝΟΣ

Πασίων ὁ τραπεζίτης τελευτῶν ἐπὶ δύο παισὶν ἐξ Ἀρχίππης,
Ἀπολλοδώρῳ καὶ Πασικλεῖ, Φορμίων' οἰκέτην ἑαυτοῦ γενόμενον,
τετυχηκότα δ' ἔτι πρότερον ἐλευθερίας, ἐπίτροπον τοῦ νεωτέρου
τῶν παίδων Πασικλέους κατέλιπε, καὶ τὴν μητέρ' αὐτῶν, παλλα-   5
κὴν ἑαυτοῦ γενομένην, ἔδωκεν ἐπὶ προικὶ γυναῖκα. Ἀπολλόδωρος
οὖν νέμεται πρὸς τὸν ἀδελφὸν τὴν πατρῴαν οὐσίαν πλὴν τῆς
τραπέζης καὶ τοῦ ἀσπιδοπηγείου· ταῦτα γὰρ Φορμίων ἐμεμίσ-
θωτο παρὰ Πασίωνος εἰς ὡρισμένον χρόνον τινά. καὶ τέως μὲν
ἐλάμβανε τὸ ἥμισυ τῆς μισθώσεως ἑκάτερος, ὕστερον δὲ καὶ   10
αὐτὰ νέμονται, καὶ γίνεται τὸ μὲν ἀσπιδοπηγεῖον Ἀπολλοδώρου,
2 Πασικλέους δ' ἡ τράπεζα. ἀποθανούσης δὲ καὶ τῆς μητρὸς
ὕστερον, νειμάμενος καὶ τὴν ἐκείνης οὐσίαν ἐνεκάλει τῷ Φορμίωνι, ὡς πόλλ' ἔχοντι ἑαυτοῦ χρήματα. καθίσαντες οὖν αὐτοὺς
διαιτητάς, ὥς φησι Φορμίων, Ἀπολλοδώρῳ προσήκοντες, Νικίας   15
καὶ Δεινίας < καὶ Λυσῖνος > καὶ Ἀνδρομένης, ἔπεισαν Ἀπολλόδωρον
διαλύσασθαι πρὸς Φορμίωνα τὰ ἐγκλήματα λαβόντα πεντακισχιλίας. ὁ μὲν οὖν Ἀπολλόδωρος μετὰ ταῦτα πάλιν εἴληχε
δίκην Φορμίωνι, ἀφορμῆς (ἀφορμὴν δ' οἱ Ἀττικοὶ καλοῦσιν ὅπερ
3 ἡμεῖς ἐνθήκην)· ὁ δὲ Φορμίων παραγράφεται, νόμον παρεχόμενος   20
τὸν κελεύοντα περὶ ὧν ἂν ἅπαξ ἀφῇ τις καὶ διαλύσηται μηκέτ'
ἐξεῖναι δικάζεσθαι. ἅπτεται μέντοι καὶ τῆς εὐθείας ὁ ῥήτωρ,
δεικνὺς ὡς οὐκ εἶχεν ἡ τράπεζα χρήματ' ἴδια τοῦ Πασίωνος.
τοῦτο δὲ πεποίηκεν, ἵν' ἡ παραγραφὴ μᾶλλον ἰσχύῃ, τῆς εὐθείας
δεικνυμένης τῷ Ἀπολλοδώρῳ σαθρᾶς.   25

74

Τὴν μὲν ἀπειρίαν τοῦ λέγειν, καὶ ὡς ἀδυνάτως ἔχει Φορμίων, αὐτοὶ πάντες ὁρᾶτ᾽, ὦ ἄνδρες Ἀθηναῖοι· ἀνάγκη δ᾽ ἐστὶν τοῖς ἐπιτηδείοις ἡμῖν, ἃ σύνισμεν πολλάκις τούτου διεξιόντος ἀκηκοότες, λέγειν καὶ διδάσκειν ὑμᾶς, ἵν᾽ εἰδότες
5 καὶ μεμαθηκότες ὀρθῶς τὰ δίκαια παρ᾽ ἡμῶν, ἂν ᾖ δίκαια καὶ εὔορκα, ταῦτα ψηφίσησθε. τὴν μὲν οὖν παραγραφὴν 2 ἐποιησάμεθα τῆς δίκης, οὐχ ἵν᾽ ἐκκρούοντες χρόνους ἐμποιῶμεν, ἀλλ᾽ ἵνα τῶν πραγμάτων, ἐὰν ἐπιδείξῃ μηδ᾽ ὁτιοῦν ἀδικοῦνθ᾽ ἑαυτὸν οὑτοσί, ἀπαλλαγή τις αὐτῷ γένηται παρ᾽
10 ὑμῖν κυρία. ὅσα γὰρ παρὰ τοῖς ἄλλοις ἐστὶν ἀνθρώποις ἰσχυρὰ καὶ βέβαια ἄνευ τοῦ παρ᾽ ὑμῖν ἀγωνίσασθαι, ταῦτα πάντα πεποιηκὼς Φορμίων οὑτοσί, καὶ πολλὰ μὲν εὖ πεποιηκὼς Ἀπολλόδωρον τουτονί, πάντα δ᾽, ὅσων κύριος τῶν 3 τούτου κατελείφθη, διαλύσας καὶ παραδοὺς δικαίως, καὶ
15 πάντων ἀφεθεὶς μετὰ ταῦτα τῶν ἐγκλημάτων, ὅμως, ὡς ὁρᾶτε, ἐπειδὴ φέρειν τοῦτον οὐχ οἷός τ᾽ ἐστίν, δίκην ταλάντων εἴκοσι λαχὼν αὐτῷ ταύτην συκοφαντεῖ. ἐξ ἀρχῆς οὖν ἅπαντα τὰ πραχθέντα τούτῳ πρὸς Πασίωνα καὶ Ἀπολλόδωρον ὡς ἂν δύνωμαι διὰ βραχυτάτων εἰπεῖν πειράσομαι,
20 ἐξ ὧν εὖ οἶδ᾽ ὅτι ἥ τε τούτου συκοφαντία φανερὰ γενήσεται, καὶ ὡς οὐκ εἰσαγώγιμος ἡ δίκη γνώσεσθ᾽ ἅμα ταῦτ᾽ ἀκούσαντες.

Πρῶτον μὲν οὖν ὑμῖν ἀναγνώσεται τὰς συνθήκας, καθ᾽ ἃς 4 ἐμίσθωσε Πασίων τὴν τράπεζαν τούτῳ καὶ τὸ ἀσπιδοπηγεῖον.
25 καί μοι λαβὲ τὰς συνθήκας καὶ τὴν πρόκλησιν καὶ τὰς μαρτυρίας ταυτασί.

ΣΥΝΘΗΚΑΙ. ΠΡΟΚΛΗΣΙΣ. ΜΑΡΤΥΡΙΑΙ.

Αἱ μὲν οὖν συνθῆκαι, καθ᾽ ἃς ἐμίσθωσεν ὁ Πασίων τούτῳ τὴν τράπεζαν καὶ τὸ ἀσπιδοπηγεῖον ἤδη καθ᾽ ἑαυτὸν
30 ὄντι, αὗταί εἰσιν, ὦ ἄνδρες Ἀθηναῖοι· δεῖ δ᾽ ὑμᾶς ἀκοῦσαι καὶ μαθεῖν ἐκ τίνος τρόπου προσώφειλεν τὰ ἕνδεκα τάλανθ᾽ ὁ Πασίων ἐπὶ τὴν τράπεζαν. οὐ γὰρ δι᾽ ἀπορίαν ταῦτ᾽ 5

ὤφειλεν, ἀλλὰ διὰ φιλεργίαν. ἡ μὲν γὰρ ἔγγειος ἦν οὐσία
Πασίωνι μάλιστα ταλάντων εἴκοσιν, ἀργύριον δὲ πρὸς ταύτῃ
δεδανεισμένον [ἴδιον] πλέον ἢ πεντήκοντα τάλαντα. ἐν [οὖν]
τοῖς πεντήκοντα ταλάντοις τούτοις ἀπὸ τῶν παρακαταθηκῶν
6 τῶν τῆς τραπέζης ἕνδεκα τάλαντ' ἐνεργὰ ἦν. μισθούμενος 5
οὖν ὅδε τὴν ἐργασίαν αὐτὴν τῆς τραπέζης καὶ τὰς παρακαταθήκας [λαμβάνων], ὁρῶν ὅτι, μήπω τῆς πολιτείας αὐτῷ παρ'
ὑμῖν οὔσης, οὐχ οἷός τ' ἔσοιτ' εἰσπράττειν ὅσα Πασίων ἐπὶ
γῇ καὶ συνοικίαις δεδανεικὼς ἦν, εἵλετο μᾶλλον αὐτὸν τὸν
Πασίωνα χρήστην ἔχειν τούτων τῶν χρημάτων ἢ τοὺς ἄλλους 10
χρήστας, οἷς προείμενος ἦν. καὶ οὕτω διὰ ταῦτ' ἐγράφη εἰς
τὴν μίσθωσιν προσοφείλων ὁ Πασίων ἕνδεκα τάλαντα, ὥσπερ
καὶ μεμαρτύρηται ὑμῖν.
7   Ὃν μὲν τοίνυν τρόπον ἡ μίσθωσις ἐγένετο, μεμαρτύρηται
ὑμῖν ὑπ' αὐτοῦ τοῦ ἐπικαθημένου· ἐπιγενομένης δ' ἀρρωστίας 15
τῷ Πασίωνι μετὰ ταῦτα, σκέψασθ' ἃ διέθετο. λαβὲ τῆς
διαθήκης τὸ ἀντίγραφον καὶ τὴν πρόκλησιν ταυτηνὶ καὶ τὰς
μαρτυρίας ταυτασί[, παρ' οἷς αἱ διαθῆκαι κεῖνται].

ΔΙΑΘΗΚΗ. ΠΡΟΚΛΗΣΙΣ. ΜΑΡΤΥΡΙΑΙ.

8   Ἐπειδὴ τοίνυν ὁ Πασίων ἐτετελευτήκει ταῦτα διαθέμενος, 20
Φορμίων οὑτοσὶ τὴν μὲν γυναῖκα λαμβάνει κατὰ τὴν διαθήκην, τὸν δὲ παῖδ' ἐπετρόπευεν. ἁρπάζοντος δὲ τούτου καὶ
πόλλ' ἀπὸ κοινῶν ὄντων τῶν χρημάτων ἀναλίσκειν οἰομένου
δεῖν, λογιζόμενοι πρὸς ἑαυτοὺς οἱ ἐπίτροποι, ὅτι, εἰ δεήσει
κατὰ τὰς διαθήκας, ὅσ' ἂν οὗτος ἐκ κοινῶν τῶν χρημάτων 25
ἀναλώσῃ, τούτοις ἐξελόντας ἀντιμοιρεὶ τὰ λοιπὰ νέμειν, οὐδ'
ὁτιοῦν ἔσται περιόν, νείμασθαι τὰ ὄνθ' ὑπὲρ τοῦ παιδὸς
9 ἔγνωσαν. καὶ νέμονται τὴν ἄλλην οὐσίαν πλὴν ὧν ἐμε-
μίσθωθ' οὑτοσί· τούτων δὲ τῆς προσόδου τὴν ἡμίσειαν
τούτῳ ἀπεδίδοσαν. ἄχρι μὲν οὖν τούτου τοῦ χρόνου πῶς 30
ἔνεστ' ἐγκαλεῖν αὐτῷ μισθώσεως; οὐ γὰρ νῦν, ἀλλὰ τότ'
εὐθὺς ἔδει χαλεπαίνοντα φαίνεσθαι. καὶ μὴν οὐδὲ τὰς ἐπι-

γιγνομένας μισθώσεις ὡς οὐκ ἀπείληφεν ἔστ᾽ εἰπεῖν αὐτῷ.
οὐ γὰρ ἄν ποτ᾽, ἐπειδὴ δοκιμασθέντος Πασικλέους ἀπηλλάτ- 10
τετο τῆς μισθώσεως ὅδε, ἀφήκατ᾽ ἂν αὐτὸν ἁπάντων τῶν
ἐγκλημάτων, ἀλλὰ τότ᾽ ἂν παραχρῆμ᾽ ἀπῄτειτ᾽, εἴ τι προσώ-
5 φειλεν ὑμῖν. ὡς τοίνυν ταῦτ᾽ ἀληθῆ λέγω, καὶ ἐνείμαθ᾽
οὗτος πρὸς τὸν ἀδελφὸν παῖδ᾽ ὄντα, καὶ ἀφῆκαν τῆς μισθώσεως καὶ τῶν ἄλλων ἁπάντων ἐγκλημάτων, λαβὲ ταυτηνὶ
τὴν μαρτυρίαν.

ΜΑΡΤΥΡΙΑ.

10 Εὐθὺς τοίνυν, ὦ ἄνδρες Ἀθηναῖοι, ὡς ἀφεῖσαν τουτονὶ 11
τῆς μισθώσεως, νέμονται τὴν τράπεζαν καὶ τὸ ἀσπιδοπηγεῖον, καὶ λαβὼν αἵρεσιν Ἀπολλόδωρος αἱρεῖται τὸ ἀσπιδοπηγεῖον ἀντὶ τῆς τραπέζης. καίτοι εἰ ἦν ἰδία τις
ἀφορμὴ τούτῳ πρὸς τῇ τραπέζῃ, τί δή ποτ᾽ ἂν εἵλετο
15 τοῦτο μᾶλλον ἢ ᾽κείνην; οὔτε γὰρ ἡ πρόσοδος ἦν πλείων,
ἀλλ᾽ ἐλάττων (τὸ μὲν γὰρ τάλαντον, ἡ δ᾽ ἑκατὸν μνᾶς
ἔφερεν), οὔτε τὸ κτῆμ᾽ ἥδιον, εἰ προσῆν χρήματα τῇ τραπέζῃ ἴδια. ἀλλ᾽ οὐ προσῆν. διόπερ σωφρονῶν εἵλετο τὸ
ἀσπιδοπηγεῖον οὗτος· τὸ μὲν γὰρ κτῆμ᾽ ἀκίνδυνόν ἐστιν,
20 ἡ δ᾽ ἐργασία προσόδους ἔχουσ᾽ ἐπικινδύνους ἀπὸ χρημάτων
ἀλλοτρίων.

Πολλὰ δ᾽ ἄν τις ἔχοι λέγειν καὶ ἐπιδεικνύναι σημεῖα τοῦ 12
τοῦτον συκοφαντεῖν ἐγκαλοῦντ᾽ ἀφορμήν. ἀλλ᾽ οἶμαι μέγιστον μέν ἐστιν ἁπάντων τεκμήριον τοῦ μηδεμίαν λαβεῖν
25 ἀφορμὴν εἰς ταῦτα τουτονὶ τὸ ἐν τῇ μισθώσει γεγράφθαι
προσοφείλοντα τὸν Πασίων᾽ ἐπὶ τὴν τράπεζαν, οὐ δεδωκότ᾽
ἀφορμὴν τούτῳ, δεύτερον δὲ τὸ τοῦτον ἐν τῇ νομῇ μηδὲν
ἐγκαλοῦντα φαίνεσθαι, τρίτον δ᾽, ὅτι μισθῶν ἑτέροις ὕστερον
ταῦτὰ ταῦτα τοῦ ἴσου ἀργυρίου οὐ φανήσεται προσμεμισθωκὼς
30 ἰδίαν ἀφορμήν. καίτοι εἰ, ἣν ὁ πατὴρ παρέσχεν, ὑπὸ τοῦδ᾽ 13
ἀπεστερεῖτο, αὐτὸν νῦν προσῆκεν ἐκείνοις ἄλλοθεν πορίσαντα

77

δεδωκέναι. ὡς τοίνυν ταῦτ' ἀληθῆ λέγω, καὶ ἐμίσθωσεν ὕστερον Ξένωνι καὶ Εὐφραίῳ καὶ Εὔφρονι καὶ Καλλιστράτῳ, καὶ οὐδὲ τούτοις παρέδωκεν ἰδίαν ἀφορμήν, ἀλλὰ τὰς παρακαταθήκας καὶ τὴν ἀπὸ τούτων ἐργασίαν αὐτὴν ἐμισθώσαντο, λαβέ μοι τὴν τούτων μαρτυρίαν, καὶ ὡς τὸ ἀσπιδοπηγεῖον 5 εἵλετο.

MAPTYPIA.

14 Μεμαρτύρηται μὲν τοίνυν ὑμῖν, ὦ ἄνδρες Ἀθηναῖοι, ὅτι καὶ τούτοις ἐμίσθωσαν καὶ οὐ παρέδωκαν ἰδίαν ἀφορμὴν οὐδεμίαν, καὶ ἐλευθέρους ἀφεῖσαν ὡς μεγάλ' εὖ πεπονθότες, 10 καὶ οὐκ ἐδικάζοντ' οὔτ' ἐκείνοις τότ' οὔτε τούτῳ. ὃν μὲν τοίνυν χρόνον ἡ μήτηρ ἔζη, ἡ πάντ' ἀκριβῶς ταῦτ' εἰδυῖα, οὐδὲν ἔγκλημα πώποτ' ἐποιήσατο πρὸς τουτονὶ Φορμίων· Ἀπολλόδωρος· ὡς δ' ἐτελεύτησεν ἐκείνη, τρισχιλίας ἐγκαλέσας ἀργυρίου δραχμὰς πρὸς αἷς ἔδωκεν ἐκείνη δισχιλίαις 15 τοῖς τούτου παιδίοις, καὶ χιτωνίσκον τινὰ καὶ θεράπαιναν, 15 ἐσυκοφάντει. καὶ οὐδ' ἐνταῦθα τούτων οὐδὲν ὧν νῦν ἐγκαλεῖ λέγων φανήσεται. ἐπιτρέψας δὲ τῷ τε τῆς ἑαυτοῦ γυναικὸς πατρὶ καὶ τῷ συγκηδεστῇ τῷ αὑτοῦ καὶ Λυσίνῳ καὶ Ἀνδρομένει, πεισάντων τούτων Φορμίωνα τουτονὶ δοῦναι 20 δωρεὰν τὰς τρισχιλίας καὶ τὸ προσόν, καὶ φίλον μᾶλλον ἔχειν τοῦτον ἢ διὰ ταῦτ' ἐχθρὸν αὐτὸν εἶναι, λαβὼν τὸ σύμπαν πεντακισχιλίας, καὶ πάντων ἀφεὶς τῶν ἐγκλημάτων 16 τὸ δεύτερον εἰς τὸ ἱερὸν τῆς Ἀθηνᾶς ἐλθών, πάλιν, ὡς ὁρᾶτε, δικάζεται, πάσας αἰτίας συμπλάσας καὶ ἐγκλήματ' 25 ἐκ παντὸς τοῦ χρόνου τοῦ πρὸ τούτου (τοῦτο γάρ ἐστιν μέγιστον ἁπάντων), ἃ οὐδεπώποτ' ᾐτιάσατο. ὡς τοίνυν ταῦτ' ἀληθῆ λέγω, λαβέ μοι τὴν γνῶσιν τὴν γενομένην ἐν ἀκροπόλει, καὶ τὴν μαρτυρίαν τῶν παραγενομένων, ὅτ' ἀφίει τῶν ἐγκλημάτων ἁπάντων Ἀπολλόδωρος, λαμβάνων τοῦτο 30 τὸ ἀργύριον.

ΓΝΩΣΙΣ. ΜΑΡΤΥΡΙΑ.

Ἀκούετε τῆς γνώσεως, ἄνδρες δικασταί, ἣν ἔγνω Δεινίας, 17
οὗ τὴν θυγατέρ᾽ οὗτος ἔχει, καὶ Νικίας ὁ τὴν ἀδελφὴν τῆς
τούτου γυναικὸς ἔχων. ταῦτα τοίνυν λαβὼν καὶ ἀφεὶς
5 ἁπάντων τῶν ἐγκλημάτων, ὥσπερ ἢ πάντων τεθνεώτων τούτων ἢ τῆς ἀληθείας οὐ γενησομένης φανερᾶς, δίκην τοσούτων ταλάντων λαχὼν τολμᾷ δικάζεσθαι.

Τὰ μὲν οὖν πεπραγμένα καὶ γεγενημένα Φορμίωνι 18
πρὸς Ἀπολλόδωρον ἐξ ἀρχῆς ἅπαντ᾽ ἀκηκόατ᾽, ὦ ἄνδρες
10 Ἀθηναῖοι. οἶμαι δ᾽ Ἀπολλόδωρον τουτονί, οὐδὲν ἔχοντα
δίκαιον εἰπεῖν περὶ ὧν ἐγκαλεῖ, ἅπερ παρὰ τῷ διαιτητῇ
λέγειν ἐτόλμα, ταῦτ᾽ ἐρεῖν, ὡς τὰ γράμμαθ᾽ ἡ μήτηρ ἠφάνικε
πεισθεῖσ᾽ ὑπὸ τούτου, καὶ τούτων ἀπολωλότων οὐκ ἔχει τίνα
χρὴ τρόπον ταῦτ᾽ ἐξελέγχειν ἀκριβῶς. περὶ δὴ τούτων καὶ 19
15 ταύτης τῆς αἰτίας σκέψασθ᾽ ἡλίκ᾽ ἄν τις ἔχοι τεκμήρι᾽ εἰπεῖν
ὅτι ψεύδεται. πρῶτον μὲν γάρ, ὦ ἄνδρες Ἀθηναῖοι, τίς
ἂν ἐνείματο τὰ πατρῷα μὴ λαβὼν γράμματα, ἐξ ὧν ἔμελλεν
εἴσεσθαι τὴν καταλειφθεῖσαν οὐσίαν; οὐδὲ εἷς δήπου. καίτοι
δυοῖν δέοντ᾽ εἴκοσιν ἔτη ἐστὶν ἐξ ὅτου ἐνείμω, καὶ οὐκ ἂν
20 ἔχοις ἐπιδεῖξαι, ὡς ἐνεκάλεσας πώποθ᾽ ὑπὲρ τῶν γραμμάτων.
δεύτερον δέ, τίς οὐκ ἄν, ἡνίχ᾽ ὁ Πασικλῆς ἀνὴρ γεγονὼς 20
ἐκομίζετο τὸν λόγον τῆς ἐπιτροπῆς, εἰ δι᾽ αὐτοῦ τὰ γράμματ᾽
ὤκνει τὴν μητέρ᾽ αἰτιᾶσθαι διεφθαρκέναι, τούτῳ ταῦτ᾽ ἐδήλωσεν, ὅπως διὰ τούτου ταῦτ᾽ ἠλέγχθη; τρίτον δ᾽, ἐκ ποίων
25 γραμμάτων τὰς δίκας ἐλάγχανες; οὗτος γὰρ πολλοῖς τῶν
πολιτῶν δίκας λαγχάνων πολλὰ χρήματ᾽ εἰσπέπρακται,
γράφων εἰς τὰ ἐγκλήματα ῾ἔβλαψέ με ὁ δεῖνα οὐκ ἀποδιδοὺς
ἐμοὶ τὸ ἀργύριον, ὃ κατέλιπεν ὁ πατὴρ ὀφείλοντα αὐτὸν ἐν
τοῖς γράμμασιν᾽. καίτοι εἰ ἠφάνιστο τὰ γράμματα, ἐκ ποίων 21
30 γραμμάτων τὰς δίκας ἐλάγχανεν; ἀλλὰ μὴν ὅτι ταῦτ᾽ ἀληθῆ
λέγω, τὴν μὲν νομὴν ἀκηκόαθ᾽ ἣν ἐνείματο, καὶ μεμαρτύρηται
ὑμῖν· τῶν δὲ λήξεων τούτων ἀναγνώσεται ὑμῖν τὰς μαρτυρίας.
λαβὲ τὰς μαρτυρίας μοι.

ΜΑΡΤΥΡΙΑΙ.

Οὐκοῦν ἐν ταύταις ταῖς λήξεσιν ὡμολόγηκεν ἀπειληφέναι τὰ τοῦ πατρὸς γράμματα· οὐ γὰρ δὴ συκοφαντεῖν γε, οὐδ' ὧν οὐκ ὤφειλον οὗτοι δικάζεσθαι φήσειεν ἄν.

22 Νομίζω τοίνυν, ὦ ἄνδρες Ἀθηναῖοι, μεγάλων καὶ πολλῶν 5 ὄντων ἐξ ὧν ἔστιν ἰδεῖν οὐκ ἀδικοῦντα Φορμίωνα τουτονί, μέγιστον ἁπάντων εἶναι, ὅτι Πασικλῆς, ἀδελφὸς ὢν Ἀπολλοδώρου τουτουί, οὔτε δίκην εἴληχεν οὔτ' ἄλλ' οὐδὲν ὧν οὗτος ἐγκαλεῖ. καίτοι οὐ δήπου τὸν μὲν παῖδ' ὑπὸ τοῦ πατρὸς καταλειφθέντα, καὶ οὗ τῶν ὄντων κύριος ἦν, ἐπίτρο- 10 πος καταλελειμμένος, οὐκ ἂν ἠδίκει, σὲ δέ, ὃς ἀνὴρ κατελείφθης τέτταρα καὶ εἴκοσιν ἔτη γεγονώς, καὶ ὑπὲρ σαυτοῦ ῥᾳδίως ἂν τὰ δίκαι' ἐλάμβανες εὐθύς, εἴ τι ἠδικοῦ. οὐκ ἔστι ταῦτα. ὡς τοίνυν ταῦτ' ἀληθῆ λέγω καὶ ὁ Πασικλῆς οὐδὲν ἐγκαλεῖ, λαβέ μοι τὴν τούτου μαρτυρίαν. 15

ΜΑΡΤΥΡΙΑ.

23 Ἃ τοίνυν ἤδη περὶ αὐτοῦ τοῦ μὴ εἰσαγώγιμον εἶναι τὴν δίκην δεῖ σκοπεῖν ὑμᾶς, ταῦτ' ἀναμνήσθητ' ἐκ τῶν εἰρημένων. ἡμεῖς γάρ, ὦ ἄνδρες Ἀθηναῖοι, γεγενημένου μὲν διαλογισμοῦ καὶ ἀφέσεως τῆς τραπέζης καὶ τοῦ ἀσπιδοπηγείου τῆς μισθώ- 20 σεως, γεγενημένης δὲ διαίτης καὶ πάλιν πάντων ἀφέσεως, οὐκ ἐώντων τῶν νόμων δίκας ὧν ἂν ἀφῇ τις ἅπαξ λαγχάνειν, 24 συκοφαντοῦντος τούτου καὶ παρὰ τοὺς νόμους δικαζομένου παρεγραψάμεθ' ἐκ τῶν νόμων μὴ εἶναι τὴν δίκην εἰσαγώγιμον. ἵν' οὖν εἰδῆθ' ὑπὲρ οὗ τὴν ψῆφον οἴσετε, τόν τε νόμον ὑμῖν 25 τοῦτον ἀναγνώσεται καὶ τὰς μαρτυρίας ἐφεξῆς τῶν παρόντων, ὅτ' ἀφίει τῆς μισθώσεως καὶ τῶν ἄλλων ἁπάντων ἐγκλημάτων Ἀπολλόδωρος. λαβέ μοι τὰς μαρτυρίας ταυτασὶ καὶ τὸν νόμον.

ΜΑΡΤΥΡΙΑΙ. ΝΟΜΟΣ.   30

25 Ἀκούετε τοῦ νόμου λέγοντος, ὦ ἄνδρες Ἀθηναῖοι, τά τ'

ἀλλ' ὧν μὴ εἶναι δίκας, καὶ ὅσα τις ἀφῆκεν ἢ ἀπήλλαξεν.
εἰκότως· εἰ γάρ ἐστι δίκαιον, ὧν ἂν ἅπαξ γένηται δίκη,
μηκέτ' ἐξεῖναι δικάζεσθαι, πολὺ τῶν ἀφεθέντων δικαιότερον
μὴ εἶναι δίκας. ὁ μὲν γὰρ ἐν ὑμῖν ἡττηθεὶς τάχ' ἂν εἴποι
5 τοῦθ' ὡς ἐξηπατήθηθ' ὑμεῖς· ὁ δ' αὐτοῦ φανερῶς καταγνοὺς
καὶ ἀφεὶς καὶ ἀπαλλάξας, τίν' ἂν ἑαυτὸν αἰτίαν αἰτιασάμενος
τῶν αὐτῶν πάλιν εἰκότως δικάζοιτο; οὐδεμίαν δήπου. διόπερ
τοῦτο πρῶτον ἔγραψεν ὁ τὸν νόμον θεὶς ὧν μὴ εἶναι δίκας,
ὅσα τις ἀφῆκεν ἢ ἀπήλλαξεν. ἃ τῷδε γέγονεν ἀμφότερα·
10 καὶ γὰρ ἀφῆκεν καὶ ἀπήλλαξεν. ὡς δ' ἀληθῆ λέγω, μεμαρτύρηται ὑμῖν, ὦ ἄνδρες Ἀθηναῖοι.
Λαβὲ δή μοι καὶ τὸν τῆς προθεσμίας νόμον.

ΝΟΜΟΣ.

Ὁ μὲν τοίνυν νόμος, ὦ ἄνδρες Ἀθηναῖοι, σαφῶς οὑτωσὶ 26
15 τὸν χρόνον ὥρισεν· Ἀπολλόδωρος δ' οὑτοσὶ παρεληλυθότων
ἐτῶν πλέον ἢ εἴκοσιν τὴν ἑαυτοῦ συκοφαντίαν ἀξιοῖ περὶ
πλείονος ὑμᾶς ποιήσασθαι τῶν νόμων, καθ' οὓς ὀμωμοκότες
δικάζετε. καίτοι πᾶσι μὲν τοῖς νόμοις προσέχειν εἰκός ἐσθ'
ὑμᾶς, οὐχ ἥκιστα δὲ τούτῳ, ὦ ἄνδρες Ἀθηναῖοι. δοκεῖ γάρ 27
20 μοι καὶ ὁ Σόλων οὐδενὸς ἄλλου ἕνεκα θεῖναι αὐτὸν ἢ τοῦ μὴ
συκοφαντεῖσθαι ὑμᾶς. τοῖς μὲν γὰρ ἀδικουμένοις τὰ πέντ'
ἔτη ἱκανὸν ἡγήσατ' εἶναι εἰσπράξασθαι· κατὰ δὲ τῶν ψευ-
δομένων τὸν χρόνον ἐνόμισεν σαφέστατον ἔλεγχον ἔσεσθαι.
καὶ ἅμ' ἐπειδὴ ἀδύνατον ἔγνω ὂν τούς τε συμβάλλοντας καὶ
25 τοὺς μάρτυρας ἀεὶ ζῆν, τὸν νόμον ἀντὶ τούτων ἔθηκεν, ὅπως
μάρτυς εἴη τοῦ δικαίου τοῖς ἐρήμοις.

Θαυμάζω τοίνυν ἔγωγ', ὦ ἄνδρες δικασταί, τί ποτ' ἐστὶν ἃ 28
πρὸς ταῦτ' ἐπιχειρήσει λέγειν Ἀπολλόδωρος οὑτοσί. οὐ γὰρ
ἐκεῖνό γ' ὑπείληφεν, ὡς ὑμεῖς, μηδὲν ὁρῶντες εἰς χρήματα
30 τοῦτον ἠδικημένον, ὀργιεῖσθ' ὅτι τὴν μητέρ' ἔγημεν αὐτοῦ
Φορμίων. οὐ γὰρ ἀγνοεῖ τοῦτο, οὐδ' αὐτὸν λέληθεν, οὐδ'
ὑμῶν πολλούς, ὅτι Σωκράτης ὁ τραπεζίτης ἐκεῖνος, παρὰ τῶν

κυρίων ἀπαλλαγεὶς ὥσπερ ὁ τούτου πατήρ, ἔδωκε Σατύρῳ
29 τὴν ἑαυτοῦ γυναῖκα, ἑαυτοῦ ποτὲ γενομένῳ. ἕτερος Σωκλῆς
τραπεζιτεύσας ἔδωκε τὴν ἑαυτοῦ γυναῖκα Τιμοδήμῳ τῷ νῦν
ἔτ᾽ ὄντι καὶ ζῶντι, γενομένῳ ποθ᾽ αὑτοῦ. καὶ οὐ μόνον
ἐνθάδε ταῦτα ποιοῦσιν οἱ περὶ τὰς ἐργασίας ὄντες ταύτας, 5
ὦ ἄνδρες Ἀθηναῖοι, ἀλλ᾽ ἐν Αἰγίνῃ ἔδωκεν Στρυμόδωρος
Ἑρμαίῳ τῷ ἑαυτοῦ οἰκέτῃ τὴν γυναῖκα, καὶ τελευτησάσης
ἐκείνης ἔδωκε πάλιν τὴν θυγατέρα τὴν ἑαυτοῦ. καὶ πολλοὺς
30 ἂν ἔχοι τις εἰπεῖν τοιούτους. εἰκότως· ὑμῖν μὲν γάρ, ὦ
ἄνδρες Ἀθηναῖοι, τοῖς γένει πολίταις, οὐδὲ ἓν πλῆθος χρη- 10
μάτων ἀντὶ τοῦ γένους καλόν ἐστιν ἑλέσθαι· τοῖς δὲ τοῦτο
μὲν δωρεὰν ἢ παρ᾽ ὑμῶν ἢ παρ᾽ ἄλλων τινῶν λαβοῦσιν, τῇ
τύχῃ δ᾽ ἐξ ἀρχῆς ἀπὸ τοῦ χρηματίσασθαι καὶ ἑτέρων πλείω
κτήσασθαι καὶ αὐτῶν τούτων ἀξιωθεῖσιν, ταῦτ᾽ ἐστὶν φυλακτέα. διόπερ Πασίων ὁ πατὴρ ὁ σὸς οὐ πρῶτος οὐδὲ 15
μόνος, οὐδ᾽ αὑτὸν ὑβρίζων οὐδ᾽ ὑμᾶς τοὺς υἱεῖς, ἀλλὰ μόνην
ὁρῶν σωτηρίαν τοῖς ἑαυτοῦ πράγμασιν, εἰ τοῦτον ἀνάγκῃ
ποιήσειεν οἰκεῖον ὑμῖν, ἔδωκε τὴν ἑαυτοῦ γυναῖκα, μητέρα
31 δ᾽ ὑμετέραν τούτῳ. πρὸς μὲν οὖν τὰ συμφέροντ᾽ ἐὰν ἐξετάζῃς,
καλῶς βεβουλευμένον αὐτὸν εὑρήσεις· εἰ δὲ πρὸς γένους 20
δόξαν ἀναίνει Φορμίωνα κηδεστήν, ὅρα μὴ γελοῖον ᾖ σὲ
ταῦτα λέγειν. εἰ γάρ τις ἔροιτό σε, ποῖόν τιν᾽ ἡγεῖ τὸν
πατέρα τὸν σεαυτοῦ εἶναι, χρηστὸν εὖ οἶδ᾽ ὅτι φήσειας ἄν.
πότερον οὖν οἴει μᾶλλον ἐοικέναι τὸν τρόπον καὶ πάντα τὸν
βίον Πασίωνι σαυτὸν ἢ τουτονί; ἐγὼ μὲν εὖ οἶδ᾽ ὅτι τοῦτον. 25
εἶθ᾽ ὃς ἐστιν ὁμοιότερος σοῦ τῷ σῷ πατρί, τοῦτον, εἰ τὴν
32 μητέρα τὴν σὴν ἔγημεν, ἀναίνει; ἀλλὰ μὴν ὅτι γε δόντος
καὶ ἐπισκήψαντος τοῦ σοῦ πατρὸς ταῦτ᾽ ἐπράχθη, οὐ μόνον
ἐκ τῆς διαθήκης ἔστιν ἰδεῖν, ὦ ἄνδρες Ἀθηναῖοι, ἀλλὰ καὶ
σὺ μάρτυς αὐτὸς γέγονας. ὅτε γὰρ τὰ μητρῷα πρὸς μέρος 30
ἠξίους νέμεσθαι, ὄντων παίδων ἐκ τῆς γυναικὸς Φορμίωνι
τουτῳί, τόθ᾽ ὡμολόγεις κυρίως δόντος τοῦ πατρὸς τοῦ σοῦ
κατὰ τοὺς νόμους αὐτὴν γεγαμῆσθαι. εἰ γὰρ αὐτὴν εἶχε

λαβὼν ἀδίκως ὅδε μηδενὸς δόντος, οὐκ ἦσαν οἱ παῖδες κληρονόμοι, τοῖς δὲ μὴ κληρονόμοις οὐκ ἦν μετουσία τῶν ὄντων. ἀλλὰ μὴν ὅτι ταῦτ' ἀληθῆ λέγω, μεμαρτύρηται τὸ τέταρτον μέρος λαβεῖν καὶ ἀφεῖναι τῶν ἐγκλημάτων ἁπάντων.

5 Κατ' οὐδὲν τοίνυν, ὦ ἄνδρες Ἀθηναῖοι, δίκαιον οὐδὲν 33 ἔχων εἰπεῖν, ἀναιδεστάτους λόγους ἐτόλμα λέγειν πρὸς τῷ διαιτητῇ, περὶ ὧν προακηκοέναι βέλτιόν ἐσθ' ὑμᾶς, ἕνα μὲν τὸ παράπαν μὴ γενέσθαι διαθήκην, ἀλλ' εἶναι τοῦτο πλάσμα καὶ σκευώρημ' ὅλον, ἕτερον δ' ἕνεκα τούτου πάντα ταῦτα
10 συγχωρεῖν τὸν πρὸ τοῦ χρόνον καὶ οὐχὶ δικάζεσθαι, ὅτι μίσθωσιν ἤθελεν αὐτῷ φέρειν Φορμίων πολλὴν καὶ ὑπισχνεῖτ' οἴσειν· ἐπειδὴ δ' οὐ ποιεῖ ταῦτα, τηνικαῦτα, φησίν, δικάζομαι. ὅτι δὲ ταῦτ' ἀμφότερ', ἐὰν λέγῃ, ψεύσεται καὶ 34 τοῖς ὑφ' ἑαυτοῦ πεπραγμένοις ἐναντί' ἐρεῖ, σκοπεῖτ' ἐκ τωνδί.
15 ὅταν μὲν τοίνυν τὴν διαθήκην ἀρνῆται, ἐκ τίνος τρόπου πρεσβεῖα λαβὼν τὴν συνοικίαν κατὰ τὴν διαθήκην ἔχει, τοῦτ' ἐρωτᾶτ' αὐτόν. οὐ γὰρ ἐκεῖνό γ' ἐρεῖ, ὡς ἃ μὲν πλεονεκτεῖν τόνδ' ἔγραψεν ὁ πατήρ, κύρι' ἐστὶν τῆς διαθήκης, τὰ δ' ἄλλ' ἄκυρα. ὅταν δ' ὑπὸ τῶν τοῦδ' ὑποσχέσεων 35
20 ὑπάγεσθαι φῇ, μέμνησθ' ὅτι μάρτυρας ὑμῖν παρεσχήμεθα, οἳ χρόνον πολὺν τοῦδ' ἀπηλλαγμένου μισθωταὶ τούτοις ἐγίγνοντο τῆς τραπέζης καὶ τοῦ ἀσπιδοπηγείου. καίτοι τόθ', ὁπηνίκ' ἐμίσθωσεν ἐκείνοις, τῷδ' ἐγκαλεῖν παραχρῆμ' ἐχρῆν, εἴπερ ἀληθῆ ἦν ὑπὲρ ὧν τότ' ἀφεὶς νῦν τούτῳ δικάζεται.
25 ὡς τοίνυν ἀληθῆ λέγω, καὶ πρεσβεῖά τε τὴν συνοικίαν ἔλαβεν κατὰ τὴν διαθήκην, καὶ τῷδ' οὐχ ὅπως ἐγκαλεῖν ᾤετο δεῖν, ἀλλ' ἐπῄνει, λαβὲ τὴν μαρτυρίαν.

ΜΑΡΤΥΡΙΑ.

Ἵνα τοίνυν εἰδῆτ', ὦ ἄνδρες Ἀθηναῖοι, ὅσα χρήματ' ἔχων 36
30 ἐκ τῶν μισθώσεων καὶ ἐκ τῶν χρεῶν ὡς ἀπορῶν καὶ πάντ' ἀπολωλεκὼς ὀδύρεται, βραχέ' ἡμῶν ἀκούσατε. οὗτος γὰρ ἐκ μὲν τῶν χρεῶν ὁμοῦ τάλαντ' εἴκοσιν εἰσπέπρακται ἐκ

τῶν γραμμάτων ὧν ὁ πατὴρ κατέλιπεν, καὶ τούτων ἔχει
πλέον ἢ τὰ ἡμίσεα (πολλῶν γὰρ τὰ μέρη τὸν ἀδελφὸν ἀπο-
37 στερεῖ). ἐκ δὲ τῶν μισθώσεων, ὀκτὼ μὲν ἐτῶν ἃ Φορμίων
εἶχε τὴν τράπεζαν, ὀγδοήκοντα μνᾶς τοῦ ἐνιαυτοῦ ἑκάστου,
τὸ ἥμισυ τῆς ὅλης μισθώσεως· καὶ ταῦτ᾽ ἐστὶ δέκα τάλαντα 5
καὶ τετταράκοντα μναῖ· δέκα δὲ τῶν μετὰ ταῦτα, ὧν ἐμίσθωσαν ὕστερον Ξένωνι καὶ Εὐφραίῳ καὶ Εὔφρονι καὶ
38 Καλλιστράτῳ, τάλαντον τοῦ ἐνιαυτοῦ ἑκάστου. χωρὶς δὲ
τούτων, ἐτῶν ἴσως εἴκοσι τῆς ἐξ ἀρχῆς νεμηθείσης οὐσίας,
ἧς αὐτὸς ἐπεμελεῖτο, τὰς προσόδους, πλέον ἢ μνᾶς τριάκοντα. 10
ἐὰν δ᾽ ἅπαντα συνθῆτε, ὅσ᾽ ἐνείματο, ὅσ᾽ εἰσεπράξατο, ὅσ᾽
εἴληφε μίσθωσιν, πλέον ἢ τετταράκοντα τάλαντ᾽ εἰληφὼς
φανήσεται, χωρὶς ὧν οὗτος εὖ πεποίηκεν, καὶ τῶν μητρῴων,
καὶ ὧν ἀπὸ τῆς τραπέζης ἔχων οὐκ ἀποδίδωσι πένθ᾽ ἡμιτα-
39 λάντων καὶ ἑξακοσίων δραχμῶν. ἀλλὰ νὴ Δία ταῦθ᾽ ἡ 15
πόλις εἴληφεν, καὶ δεινὰ πέπονθας πολλὰ καταλελητουργη-
κώς. ἀλλ᾽ ἃ μὲν ἐκ κοινῶν ἐλῃτούργεις τῶν χρημάτων,
σὺ καὶ ἀδελφὸς ἀνηλώσατε· ἃ δ᾽ ὕστερον, οὐκ ἔστιν ἄξια
μὴ ὅτι δυοῖν ταλάντοιν προσόδου, ἀλλ᾽ οὐδ᾽ εἴκοσι μνῶν.
μηδὲν οὖν τὴν πόλιν αἰτιῶ, μηδ᾽ ἃ σὺ τῶν ὄντων αἰσχρῶς 20
40 καὶ κακῶς ἀνήλωκας, ὡς ἡ πόλις εἴληφεν, λέγε. ἵνα δ᾽ εἰδῆτ᾽,
ὦ ἄνδρες Ἀθηναῖοι, τό τε πλῆθος τῶν χρημάτων ὧν εἴληφε,
καὶ τὰς λῃτουργίας ἃς λελῃτούργηκεν, ἀναγνώσεται ὑμῖν
καθ᾽ ἓν ἕκαστον. λαβέ μοι τὸ βιβλίον τουτὶ καὶ τὴν πρόκλησιν ταυτηνὶ καὶ τὰς μαρτυρίας ταυτασί. 25

⟨ΒΙΒΛΙΟΝ.⟩ ΠΡΟΚΛΗΣΙΣ. ΜΑΡΤΥΡΙΑΙ.

41 Τοσαῦτα μὲν τοίνυν χρήματ᾽ εἰληφὼς καὶ χρέα πολλῶν
ταλάντων ἔχων, ὧν τὰ μὲν παρ᾽ ἑκόντων, τὰ δ᾽ ἐκ τῶν
δικῶν εἰσπράττει, ἃ τῆς μισθώσεως ἔξω τῆς τραπέζης καὶ
τῆς ἄλλης οὐσίας, ἣν κατέλιπεν Πασίων, ὠφείλετ᾽ ἐκείνῳ 30
καὶ νῦν παρειλήφασιν οὗτοι, καὶ τοσαῦτ᾽ ἀνηλωκὼς ὅσ᾽ ὑμεῖς
ἠκούσατε, οὐδὲ πολλοστὸν μέρος τῶν προσόδων, μὴ ὅτι τῶν

84

ἀρχαίων, εἰς τὰς λῃτουργίας, ὅμως ἀλαζονεύσεται καὶ τριηραρ-
χίας ἐρεῖ καὶ χορηγίας. ἐγὼ δ', ὡς μὲν οὐκ ἀληθῆ ταῦτ' 42
ἐρεῖ, ἐπέδειξα, οἶμαι μέντοι, κἂν εἰ ταῦτα πάντ' ἀληθῆ
λέγοι, κάλλιον εἶναι καὶ δικαιότερον τόνδ' ἀπὸ τῶν αὑτοῦ
5 λῃτουργεῖν ὑμῖν ἢ τούτῳ δόντας τὰ τούτου, μικρὰ τῶν πάντων αὐτοὺς μετασχόντας, τόνδε μὲν ἐν ταῖς ἐσχάταις
ἐνδείαις ὁρᾶν, τοῦτον δ' ὑβρίζοντα καὶ εἰς ἅπερ εἴωθεν
ἀναλίσκοντα. ἀλλὰ μὴν περί γε τῆς εὐπορίας, ὡς ἐκ τῶν 43
τοῦ πατρὸς τοῦ σοῦ κέκτηται, καὶ ὧν ἐρωτήσειν ἔφησθα,
10 πόθεν τὰ ὄντα κέκτηται Φορμίων, μόνῳ τῶν ὄντων ἀνθρώπων σοὶ τοῦτον οὐκ ἔνεστ' εἰπεῖν τὸν λόγον. οὐδὲ γὰρ
Πασίων ὁ σὸς πατὴρ ἐκτήσαθ' εὑρὼν οὐδὲ τοῦ πατρὸς αὐτῷ
παραδόντος, ἀλλὰ παρὰ τοῖς αὑτοῦ κυρίοις Ἀντισθένει καὶ
Ἀρχεστράτῳ τραπεζιτεύουσι πεῖραν δοὺς ὅτι χρηστός ἐστι
15 καὶ δίκαιος, ἐπιστεύθη. ἔστι δ' ἐν ἐμπορίῳ καὶ χρήμασιν 44
ἐργαζομένοις ἀνθρώποις φίλεργον δόξαι καὶ χρηστὸν εἶναι
τὸν αὐτὸν θαυμαστὸν ἡλίκον. οὔτ' οὖν ἐκείνῳ τοῦθ' οἱ
κύριοι παρέδωκαν, ἀλλ' αὐτὸς ἔφυ χρηστός, οὔτε τῷδ' ὁ σὸς
πατήρ· σὲ γὰρ ἂν πρότερον τοῦδε χρηστὸν ἐποίησεν, εἰ ἦν
20 ἐπ' ἐκείνῳ. εἰ δὲ τοῦτ' ἀγνοεῖς, ὅτι πίστις ἀφορμὴ πασῶν
ἐστι μεγίστη πρὸς χρηματισμόν, πᾶν ἂν ἀγνοήσειας. χωρὶς
δὲ τούτων πολλὰ καὶ τῷ σῷ πατρὶ καὶ σοὶ καὶ ὅλως τοῖς
ὑμετέροις πράγμασι Φορμίων γέγονε χρήσιμος. ἀλλ' οἶμαι
τῆς σῆς ἀπληστίας καὶ τοῦ σοῦ τρόπου τίς ἂν δύναιτ' ἐφι-
25 κέσθαι; καὶ δῆτα θαυμάζω πῶς οὐ λογίζει πρὸς σεαυτόν, 45
ὅτι ἔστιν Ἀρχεστράτῳ τῷ ποτὲ τὸν σὸν πατέρα κτησαμένῳ
υἱὸς ἐνθάδε, Ἀντίμαχος, πράττων οὐ κατ' ἀξίαν, ὃς οὐ
δικάζεταί σοι, οὐδὲ δεινά φησι πάσχειν, εἰ σὺ μὲν χλανίδα
φορεῖς, καὶ τὴν μὲν λέλυσαι, τὴν δ' ἐκδέδωκας ἑταίραν, καὶ
30 ταῦτα γυναῖκ' ἔχων ποιεῖς, καὶ τρεῖς παῖδας ἀκολούθους
περιάγει, καὶ ζῇς ἀσελγῶς ὥστε καὶ τοὺς ἀπαντῶντας αἰσθά-
νεσθαι, αὐτὸς δ' ἐκεῖνος πολλῶν ἐνδεής ἐστιν. οὐδὲ τὸν 46
Φορμίων' ἐκεῖνος οὐχ ὁρᾷ. καίτοι εἰ κατὰ τοῦτ' οἴει σοι

προσήκειν τῶν τούτου, ὅτι τοῦ πατρός ποτ' ἐγένετο τοῦ σοῦ,
ἐκείνῳ προσήκει μᾶλλον ἢ σοί· ὁ γὰρ αὖ σὸς πατὴρ ἐκείνων ἐγένετο, ὥστε καὶ σὺ καὶ οὗτος ἐκείνου γίγνεσθ' ἐκ
τούτου τοῦ λόγου. σὺ δ' εἰς τοῦθ' ἥκεις ἀγνωμοσύνης ὥσθ'
ἃ προσήκει σοι τοὺς λέγοντας ἐχθροὺς νομίζειν, ταῦτ' αὐτὸς 5
47 ποιεῖς ἀνάγκην εἶναι λέγειν, καὶ ὑβρίζεις μὲν σαυτὸν καὶ
τοὺς γονέας τεθνεῶτας, προπηλακίζεις δὲ τὴν πόλιν, καὶ ἃ
τῆς τουτωνὶ φιλανθρωπίας ἀπολαύσας ηὕρεθ' ὁ σὸς πατὴρ
καὶ μετὰ ταῦτα Φορμίων οὑτοσί, ταῦτ' ἀντὶ τοῦ κοσμεῖν καὶ
περιστέλλειν, ἵνα καὶ τοῖς δοῦσιν ὡς εὐσχημονέστατ' ἐφαί- 10
νετο καὶ τοῖς λαβοῦσιν ὑμῖν, ἄγεις εἰς μέσον, δεικνύεις,
ἐλέγχεις, μόνον οὐκ ὀνειδίζεις οἷον ὄντα σ' ἐποίησαντ'
48 Ἀθηναῖον. εἶτ' εἰς τοῦθ' ἥκεις μανίας (τί γὰρ ἂν ἄλλο τις
εἴποι;) ὥστ' οὐκ αἰσθάνει ὅτι καὶ νῦν ἡμεῖς μὲν ἀξιοῦντες,
ἐπειδήπερ ἀπηλλάγη Φορμίων, μηδὲν ὑπόλογον εἶναι εἴ ποτε 15
τοῦ σοῦ πατρὸς ἐγένετο, ὑπὲρ σοῦ λέγομεν, σὺ δὲ μηδέποτ'
ἐξ ἴσου σοι γενέσθαι τοῦτον ἀξιῶν κατὰ σαυτοῦ λέγεις· ἃ
γὰρ ἂν σὺ δίκαια σαυτῷ κατὰ τούτου τάξῃς, ταὐτὰ ταῦθ'
ἥξει κατὰ σοῦ παρὰ τῶν τὸν σὸν πατέρ' ἐξ ἀρχῆς κτησα-
μένων. ἀλλὰ μὴν ὅτι κἀκεῖνος ἦν τινῶν, εἶτ' ἀπηλλάγη 20
τὸν αὐτὸν τρόπον ὅνπερ οὗτος ἀφ' ὑμῶν, λαβέ μοι ταυτασὶ
τὰς μαρτυρίας, ὡς ἐγένετο Πασίων Ἀρχεστράτου.

MΑΡΤΥΡΙΑΙ.

49 Εἶτα τὸν σώσαντα μὲν ἐξ ἀρχῆς τὰ πράγματα καὶ πολλὰ
χρήσιμον αὐτὸν παρασχόντα τῷ πατρὶ τῷ τούτου, τοσαῦτα 25
δ' αὐτὸν τοῦτον ἀγάθ' εἰργασμένον, ὅσ' ὑμεῖς ἀκηκόατε,
τοῦτον οἴεται δεῖν ἑλὼν τηλικαύτην δίκην ἀδίκως ἐκβαλεῖν.
οὐ γὰρ ἄλλο γ' ἔχοις οὐδὲν ἂν ποιῆσαι. εἰς μὲν γὰρ τὰ
ὄντ' εἰ βλέπεις ἀκριβῶς, ταῦθ' εὑρήσεις ὧν ἔστιν, ἐάν, ὃ μὴ
50 γένοιτο, ἐξαπατηθῶσιν οὗτοι. ὁρᾷς τὸν Ἀριστόλοχον τὸν 30
Χαριδήμου· ποτ' εἶχεν ἀγρόν, εἶτά γε νῦν πολλοί· πολλοῖς
γὰρ ἐκεῖνος ὀφείλων αὐτὸν ἐκτήσατο. καὶ τὸν Σωσίνομον

καὶ τὸν Τιμόδημον καὶ τοὺς ἄλλους τραπεζίτας, οἴ, ἐπειδὴ
διαλύειν ἐδέησεν οἷς ὤφειλον, ἐξέστησαν ἅπαντες τῶν ὄντων.
σὺ δ' οὐδὲν οἴει δεῖν σκοπεῖν οὐδ' ὧν ὁ πατὴρ σοῦ πολλῷ
βελτίων ὢν καὶ ἄμεινον φρονῶν πρὸς ἅπαντ' ἐβουλεύσατο·
5 ὅς, ὦ Ζεῦ καὶ θεοί, τοσούτῳ τοῦτον ἡγεῖτο σοῦ πλείονος 51
ἄξιον εἶναι καὶ σοὶ καὶ ἑαυτῷ καὶ τοῖς ὑμετέροις πράγμασιν
ὥστ' ἀνδρὸς ὄντος σοῦ τοῦτον, οὐ σὲ τῶν ἡμίσεων κατέλιπεν
ἐπίτροπον καὶ τὴν γυναῖκ' ἔδωκεν καὶ ζῶν αὐτὸν ἐτίμα,
δικαίως, ὦ ἄνδρες Ἀθηναῖοι· οἱ μὲν γὰρ ἄλλοι τραπεζῖται
10 μίσθωσιν οὐ φέροντες, ἀλλ' αὐτοὶ ἑαυτοῖς ἐργαζόμενοι, πάντες ἀπώλοντο, οὗτος δὲ μίσθωσιν φέρων δύο τάλαντα καὶ
τετταράκοντα μνᾶς ὑμῖν ἔσωσε τὴν τράπεζαν. ὧν ἐκεῖνος 52
μὲν χάριν εἶχεν, σὺ δ' οὐδένα ποιεῖ λόγον, ἀλλ' ἐναντία τῇ
διαθήκῃ καὶ ταῖς ἀπ' ἐκείνης ἀραῖς, γραφείσαις ὑπὸ τοῦ σοῦ
15 πατρός, ἐλαύνεις συκοφαντεῖς διώκεις. ὦ βέλτιστ', εἰ οἷόν
τε σὲ τοῦτ' εἰπεῖν, οὐ παύσει, καὶ γνώσει τοῦθ', ὅτι πολλῶν
χρημάτων τὸ χρηστὸν εἶναι λυσιτελέστερόν ἐστιν; σοὶ γοῦν,
εἴπερ ἀληθῆ λέγεις, χρήματα μὲν τοσαῦτ' εἰληφότι πάντ'
ἀπόλωλεν, ὡς φής· εἰ δ' ἦσθ' ἐπιεικής, οὐκ ἄν ποτ' αὔτ'
20 ἀνήλωσας.

Ἀλλ' ἔγωγε μὰ τὸν Δία καὶ θεοὺς πανταχῇ σκοπῶν 53
οὐδὲν ὁρῶ, δι' ὅ τι ἂν σοὶ πεισθέντες τουδὶ καταψηφίσαιντο.
τί γάρ; ὅτι πλησίον ὄντων τῶν ἀδικημάτων ἐγκαλεῖς; ἀλλ'
ἔτεσι καὶ χρόνοις ὕστερον αἰτιᾷ. ἀλλ' ὅτι τοῦτον ἀπράγμων
25 ἦσθα τὸν χρόνον; καὶ τίς οὐκ οἶδεν ὅσα πράγματα πράττων
οὐ πέπαυσαι, οὐ μόνον δίκας ἰδίας διώκων οὐκ ἐλάττους
ταυτησί, ἀλλὰ δημοσίᾳ συκοφαντῶν καὶ κρίνων τίνας οὔ;
οὐχὶ Τιμομάχου κατηγόρεις; οὐχὶ Καλλίππου τοῦ νῦν ὄντος
ἐν Σικελίᾳ; οὐ πάλιν Μένωνος; οὐκ Αὐτοκλέους; οὐ Τι-
30 μοθέου; οὐκ ἄλλων πολλῶν; καίτοι πῶς ἔχει λόγον σέ, 54
Ἀπολλόδωρον ὄντα, πρότερον τῶν κοινῶν, ὧν μέρος ἠδικοῦ,
δίκην ἀξιοῦν λαμβάνειν, ἢ τῶν ἰδίων ὧν νῦν ἐγκαλεῖς,
ἄλλως τε καὶ τηλικούτων ὄντων, ὡς σὺ φής; τί ποτ' οὖν

87

ἐκείνων κατηγορῶν τόνδ' εἴας; οὐκ ἠδικοῦ, ἀλλ' οἶμαι
συκοφαντεῖς νῦν. ἡγοῦμαι τοίνυν, ὦ ἄνδρες Ἀθηναῖοι,
πάντων μάλιστ' εἰς τὸ πρᾶγμ' εἶναι τούτων μάρτυρας παρα-
σχέσθαι· τὸν γὰρ συκοφαντοῦντ' ἀεὶ τί χρὴ νομίζειν νῦν
55 ποιεῖν; καὶ νὴ Δί' ἔγωγ', ὦ ἄνδρες Ἀθηναῖοι, νομίζω πάνθ' 5
ὅσα τοῦ τρόπου τοῦ Φορμίωνός ἐστι σημεῖα καὶ τῆς τούτου
δικαιοσύνης καὶ φιλανθρωπίας, καὶ ταῦτ' εἰς τὸ πρᾶγμ' εἶναι
πρὸς ὑμᾶς εἰπεῖν. ὁ μὲν γὰρ περὶ πάντ' ἄδικος τάχ' ἄν, εἰ
τύχοι, καὶ τοῦτον ἠδίκει· ὁ δὲ μηδένα μηδὲν ἠδικηκώς,
πολλοὺς δ' εὖ πεποιηκὼς ἑκών, ἐκ τίνος εἰκότως ἂν τρόπου 10
τοῦτον μόνον ἠδίκει τῶν πάντων; τούτων τοίνυν τῶν
μαρτυριῶν ἀκούσαντες γνώσεσθε τὸν ἑκατέρου τρόπον.

MAPTYPIAI.

56 Ἴθι δὴ καὶ κατ' Ἀπολλοδώρου τῆς πονηρίας.

MAPTYPIAI. 15

Ἆρ' οὖν ὅμοιος οὑτοσί; σκοπεῖτε. λέγε.

MAPTYPIAI.

Ἀνάγνωθι δὴ καὶ ὅσα δημοσίᾳ χρήσιμος τῇ πόλει γέγονεν
οὑτοσί.

MAPTYPIAI. 20

57 Τοσαῦτα τοίνυν, ὦ ἄνδρες Ἀθηναῖοι, Φορμίων χρήσιμος
γεγονὼς καὶ τῇ πόλει καὶ πολλοῖς ὑμῶν, καὶ οὐδέν' οὔτ' ἰδίᾳ
οὔτε δημοσίᾳ κακὸν οὐδὲν εἰργασμένος, οὐδ' ἀδικῶν Ἀπολλόδωρον τουτονί, δεῖται καὶ ἱκετεύει καὶ ἀξιοῖ σωθῆναι, καὶ
ἡμεῖς συνδεόμεθ' οἱ ἐπιτήδειοι ταῦθ' ὑμῶν. ἐκεῖνο δ' ὑμᾶς 25
ἀκοῦσαι δεῖ. τοσαῦτα γάρ, ὦ ἄνδρες Ἀθηναῖοι, χρήμαθ' ὑμῖν
ἀνεγνώσθη προσηυπορηκώς, ὅσ' οὔθ' οὗτος οὔτ' ἄλλος οὐδεὶς
κέκτηται. πίστις μέντοι Φορμίωνι παρὰ τοῖς εἰδόσι καὶ
τοσούτων καὶ πολλῷ πλειόνων χρημάτων, δι' ἧς καὶ αὐτὸς

αὐτῷ καὶ ὑμῖν χρήσιμός ἐστιν. ἃ μὴ προῆσθε, μηδ' ἐπι- 58
τρέψητ' ἀνατρέψαι τῷ μιαρῷ τούτῳ ἀνθρώπῳ, μηδὲ ποιήσητ'
αἰσχρὸν παράδειγμα, ὡς τὰ τῶν ἐργαζομένων καὶ μετρίως
ἐθελόντων ζῆν τοῖς βδελυροῖς καὶ συκοφάνταις ὑπάρχει παρ'
5 ὑμῶν λαβεῖν· πολὺ γὰρ χρησιμώτερ' ὑμῖν παρὰ τῷδ' ὄνθ'
ὑπάρχει. ὁρᾶτε γὰρ αὐτοὶ καὶ ἀκούετε τῶν μαρτύρων, οἷον
ἑαυτὸν τοῖς δεηθεῖσι παρέχει. καὶ τούτων οὐδὲν εἵνεκα τοῦ 59
λυσιτελοῦντος εἰς χρήματα πεποίηκεν, ἀλλὰ φιλανθρωπίᾳ
καὶ τρόπου ἐπιεικείᾳ. οὔκουν ἄξιον, ὦ ἄνδρες Ἀθηναῖοι,
10 τὸν τοιοῦτον ἄνδρα προέσθαι τούτῳ οὐδὲ τηνικαῦτ' ἐλεεῖν
ὅτ' οὐδὲν ἔσται τούτῳ πλέον, ἀλλὰ νῦν ὅτε κύριοι καθέστατε
σῷσαι· οὐ γὰρ ἔγωγ' ὁρῶ καιρὸν ἐν τίνι ἂν μᾶλλον βοηθή-
σειέ τις αὐτῷ. τὰ μὲν οὖν πόλλ' ὧν Ἀπολλόδωρος ἐρεῖ, 60
νομίζετ' εἶναι λόγον καὶ συκοφαντίας, κελεύετε δ' αὐτὸν
15 ἐπιδεῖξαι, ἢ ὡς οὐ διέθετο ταῦθ' ὁ πατήρ, ἢ ὡς ἔστιν τις
ἄλλη μίσθωσις πλὴν ἧς ἡμεῖς δείκνυμεν, ἢ ὡς οὐκ ἀφῆκεν
αὐτὸν διαλογισάμενος τῶν ἐγκλημάτων ἁπάντων, ἃ ἔγνω
⟨θ'⟩ ὁ κηδεστὴς ὁ τούτου καὶ οὗτος αὐτὸς συνεχώρησεν, ἢ ὡς
διδόασιν οἱ νόμοι δικάζεσθαι τῶν οὕτω πραχθέντων, ἢ τῶν
20 τοιούτων τι δεικνύναι. ἐὰν δ' ἀπορῶν αἰτίας καὶ βλασφη- 61
μίας λέγῃ καὶ κακολογῇ, μὴ προσέχετε τὸν νοῦν, μηδ' ὑμᾶς
ἡ τούτου κραυγὴ καὶ ἀναίδει' ἐξαπατήσῃ, ἀλλὰ φυλάττετε
καὶ μέμνησθ' ὅσ' ἡμῶν ἀκηκόατε. κἂν ταῦτα ποιῆτε, αὐτοί
τ' εὐορκήσετε καὶ τοῦτον δικαίως σώσετε, ἄξιον ὄντα νὴ τὸν
25 Δία καὶ θεοὺς ἅπαντας.

Ἀνάγνωθι λαβὼν αὐτοῖς τὸν νόμον καὶ τὰς μαρτυρίας
τασδί.

ΝΟΜΟΣ. ΜΑΡΤΥΡΙΑΙ.

Οὐκ οἶδ' ὅ τι δεῖ πλείω λέγειν. οἶμαι γὰρ ὑμᾶς οὐδὲν
30 ἀγνοεῖν τῶν εἰρημένων. ἐξέρα τὸ ὕδωρ.

XXXII

ΠΡΟΣ ΖΗΝΟΘΕΜΙΝ ΠΑΡΑΓΡΑΦΗ

ΥΠΟΘΕΣΙΣ.

Δανεισάμενος παρὰ Δήμωνος, ἑνὸς τῶν Δημοσθένους συγγενῶν, ἔμπορός τις, Πρῶτος ὄνομα, ἐπρίατο τοῦ ἀργυρίου σῖτον
ἐν Συρακούσαις, καὶ τοῦτον ἐκόμισεν εἰς Ἀθήνας ἐπὶ νεὼς ἧς
Ἡγέστρατος ἐναυκλήρει. Ἡγέστρατος δὲ καὶ Ζηνόθεμις, πρὸς
ὅν ἐστιν ἡ παραγραφή, Μασσαλιῶται μὲν ἦσαν τὸ γένος, κα- 5
κούργημα δὲ τοιοῦτον ἐν Συρακούσαις ἐκακούργησαν, ὡς ὁ ῥήτωρ
φησίν. ἐδανείσαντο χρήματα, ταῦτα δ᾽ εἰς μὲν τὴν ναῦν οὐκ
ἐνέθεντο, λάθρᾳ δ᾽ εἰς τὴν Μασσαλίαν ἀπέστειλαν, ἀποστερῆσαι
2 τοὺς δανείσαντας βεβουλευμένοι. ἐπειδὴ γὰρ ἐγέγραπτ᾽ ἐν τῷ
συμβολαίῳ, εἰ πάθοι τι ἡ ναῦς, μὴ ἀπαιτεῖσθαι αὐτοὺς τὰ 10
χρήματα, ἐσκέψαντο καταδῦσαι τὴν ναῦν. νύκτωρ οὖν ἐν τῷ
πλῷ κατελθὼν ὁ Ἡγέστρατος διέκοπτε τοῦ πλοίου τὸ ἔδαφος.
φωραθεὶς δὲ καὶ φεύγων τοὺς ἐπιβάτας εἰς τὴν θάλασσαν εἰσπίπτει
καὶ παραχρῆμ᾽ ἀπόλλυται. ὁ τοίνυν Ζηνόθεμις, ὁ κοινωνός, ὥς
φησιν ὁ ῥήτωρ, τοῦ Ἡγεστράτου, μόλις σωθείσης εἰς Ἀθήνας 15
τῆς νεώς, ἠμφισβήτει τοῦ σίτου, λέγων εἶναι τὸν σῖτον Ἡγεστρά-
3 του, ἐκεῖνον δὲ παρ᾽ ἑαυτοῦ δεδανεῖσθαι χρήματα. ἐνστάντων δὲ
αὐτῷ τοῦ τε Πρώτου καὶ τοῦ Δήμωνος, ἀμφοτέροις ἔλαχε δίκην
ἐμπορικήν. καὶ τὸν Πρῶτον ἐξ ἐρήμης ἑλὼν ἑκόντα, ὥς φησι
Δημοσθένης, καὶ συγκακουργοῦντα, εἰσάγει καὶ τὸν Δήμωνα 20
δεύτερον εἰς τὸ δικαστήριον. ὁ δὲ παραγράφεται μὴ εἰσαγώγιμον
εἶναι τὴν δίκην, νόμον παρεχόμενος τὸν διδόντα τοῖς ἐμπόροις
τὰς δίκας εἶναι περὶ τῶν Ἀθήναζε καὶ τῶν Ἀθήνηθεν συμβολαίων·
4 Ζηνοθέμιδι δέ φησι μηδὲν συμβόλαιον εἶναι πρὸς αὐτόν. καὶ ὁ
μὲν ἀγών ἐστι παραγραφικός, ὁ δὲ λόγος, ὡς τῆς εὐθυδικίας τοῦ 25
πράγματος εἰσηγμένης, οὕτως εἴρηται περὶ τοῦ μὴ Ζηνοθέμιδος
εἶναι τὸν σῖτον, ἀλλὰ τοῦ Πρώτου, ᾧ ὁ Δήμων ἐδάνεισε τὸ
ἀργύριον. οὐ γὰρ βούλεται δοκεῖν ῥήματι τοῦ νόμου μόνον
ἰσχυρίζεσθαι κατὰ τὸ πρᾶγμ᾽ ἀδικῶν, ἀλλὰ δείκνυσιν ὡς θαρρεῖ
μὲν καὶ τῇ εὐθείᾳ, ἐκ περιουσίας δ᾽ αὐτῷ καὶ παραγραφὴν ὁ 30
νόμος δίδωσι.

Ἄνδρες δικασταί, βούλομαι παραγεγραμμένος μὴ εἰσαγώγιμον εἶναι τὴν δίκην, περὶ τῶν νόμων πρῶτον εἰπεῖν, καθ᾽
οὓς παρεγραψάμην. οἱ νόμοι κελεύουσιν, ὦ ἄνδρες δικασταί, τὰς δίκας εἶναι τοῖς ναυκλήροις καὶ τοῖς ἐμπόροις τῶν
5 Ἀθήναζε καὶ τῶν Ἀθήνηθεν συμβολαίων, καὶ περὶ ὧν ἂν
ὦσι συγγραφαί· ἂν δέ τις παρὰ ταῦτα δικάζηται, μὴ εἰσαγώγιμον εἶναι τὴν δίκην. τουτωὶ τοίνυν Ζηνοθέμιδι πρὸς μὲν 2
ἐμὲ ὅτι οὐδὲν ἦν συμβόλαιον οὐδὲ συγγραφή, καὐτὸς ὁμολογεῖ ἐν τῷ ἐγκλήματι· δανεῖσαι δέ φησιν Ἡγεστράτῳ ναυ-
10 κλήρῳ, τούτου δ᾽ ἀπολομένου ἐν τῷ πελάγει, ἡμᾶς τὸ ναῦλον
σφετερίσασθαι· τουτὶ τὸ ἔγκλημ᾽ ἐστίν. ἐκ δὴ τοῦ αὐτοῦ
λόγου τήν τε δίκην οὐκ εἰσαγώγιμον οὖσαν μαθήσεσθε, καὶ
τὴν ὅλην ἐπιβουλὴν καὶ πονηρίαν τουτουὶ τοῦ ἀνθρώπου
ὄψεσθε. δέομαι δ᾽ ὑμῶν πάντων, ὦ ἄνδρες δικασταί, εἴπερ 3
15 ἄλλῳ τινὶ πώποτε πράγματι τὸν νοῦν προσέσχετε, καὶ τούτῳ
προσέχειν· ἀκούσεσθε γὰρ ἀνθρώπου τόλμαν καὶ πονηρίαν
οὐ τὴν τυχοῦσαν, ἄνπερ ἐγὼ τὰ πεπραγμέν᾽ αὐτῷ πρὸς ὑμᾶς
πολλάκις εἰπεῖν δυνηθῶ. οἶμαι δέ.

Ζηνόθεμις γὰρ οὑτοσί, ὢν ὑπηρέτης Ἡγεστράτου τοῦ 4
20 ναυκλήρου, ὃν καὶ αὐτὸς ἔγραψεν ἐν τῷ ἐγκλήματι ὡς ἐν
τῷ πελάγει ἀπώλετο (πῶς δέ, οὐ προσέγραψεν, ἀλλ᾽ ἐγὼ
φράσω), ἀδίκημα τοιουτονὶ μετ᾽ ἐκείνου συνεσκευάσατο.
χρήματ᾽ ἐν ταῖς Συρακούσαις ἐδανείζεθ᾽ οὗτος κἀκεῖνος.
ὡμολόγει δ᾽ ἐκεῖνος μὲν πρὸς τοὺς τούτῳ δανείζοντας, εἴ τις
25 ἔροιτο, ἐνεῖναι σῖτον ἐν τῇ νηὶ τούτῳ πολύν, οὗτος δὲ πρὸς
τοὺς ἐκείνῳ τὸν γόμον οἰκεῖον ἔχειν αὐτὸν τῆς νεώς· ὢν δ᾽
ὁ μὲν ναύκληρος, ὁ δ᾽ ἐπιβάτης, ἐπιστεύοντ᾽ εἰκότως ἃ
περὶ ἀλλήλων ἔλεγον. λαμβάνοντες δὲ τὰ χρήματα, οἴκαδ᾽ 5
ἀπέστελλον εἰς τὴν Μασσαλίαν, καὶ οὐδὲν εἰς τὴν ναῦν
30 εἰσέφερον. οὐσῶν δὲ τῶν συγγραφῶν, ὥσπερ εἰώθασιν
ἅπασαι, σωθείσης τῆς νεὼς ἀποδοῦναι τὰ χρήματα, ἵν᾽ ἀποστερήσαιεν τοὺς δανείσαντας, τὴν ναῦν καταδῦσαι ἐβουλεύ-
σαντο. ὁ μὲν οὖν Ἡγέστρατος, ὡς ἀπὸ τῆς γῆς ἀπῆραν

93

δυοῖν ἢ τριῶν ἡμερῶν πλοῦν, καταβὰς τῆς νυκτὸς εἰς κοίλην
ναῦν διέκοπτε τοῦ πλοίου τὸ ἔδαφος. οὑτοσὶ δ', ὡς οὐδὲν
εἰδώς, ἄνω μετὰ τῶν ἄλλων ἐπιβατῶν διέτριβεν. ψόφου
δὲ γενομένου, αἰσθάνονται οἱ ἐν τῷ πλοίῳ ὅτι κακόν τι ἐν
6 κοίλῃ νηὶ γίγνεται, καὶ βοηθοῦσι κάτω. ὡς δ' ἡλίσκεθ' ὁ 5
Ἡγέστρατος καὶ δίκην δώσειν ὑπέλαβεν, φεύγει καὶ διω-
κόμενος ῥίπτει αὑτὸν εἰς τὴν θάλατταν, διαμαρτὼν δὲ τοῦ
λέμβου διὰ τὸ νύκτ' εἶναι, ἀπεπνίγη. ἐκεῖνος μὲν οὕτως,
ὥσπερ ἄξιος ἦν, κακὸς κακῶς ἀπώλετο, ἃ τοὺς ἄλλους ἐπε-
7 βούλευσε ποιῆσαι, ταῦτα παθὼν αὐτός. οὑτοσὶ δ' ὁ κοινω- 10
νὸς αὐτοῦ καὶ συνεργὸς τὸ μὲν πρῶτον εὐθὺς ἐν τῷ πλοίῳ
παρὰ τἀδικήματα, ὡς οὐδὲν εἰδώς, ἀλλ' ἐκπεπληγμένος καὶ
αὐτός, ἔπειθεν τὸν πρῳρέα καὶ τοὺς ναύτας εἰς τὸν λέμβον
ἐκβαίνειν καὶ ἐκλιπεῖν τὴν ναῦν τὴν ταχίστην, ὡς ἀνελπίστου
τῆς σωτηρίας οὔσης καὶ καταδυσομένης τῆς νεὼς αὐτίκα 15
μάλα, ἵν', ὅπερ διενοήθησαν, τοῦτ' ἐπιτελεσθείη καὶ ἡ ναῦς
8 ἀπόλοιτο καὶ τὰ συμβόλαι' ἀποστερήσαιεν. ἀποτυχὼν δὲ
τούτου, καὶ τοῦ παρ' ἡμῶν συμπλέοντος ἐναντιωθέντος καὶ
τοῖς ναύταις μισθούς, εἰ διασώσειαν τὴν ναῦν, μεγάλους
ἐπαγγειλαμένου, σωθείσης εἰς Κεφαλληνίαν τῆς νεὼς διὰ 20
τοὺς θεοὺς μάλιστά γε, εἶτα καὶ διὰ τὴν τῶν ναυτῶν ἀρετήν,
πάλιν μετὰ τῶν Μασσαλιωτῶν τῶν τοῦ Ἡγεστράτου πολιτῶν
μὴ καταπλεῖν Ἀθήναζε τὸ πλοῖον ἔπραττε, λέγων ὡς αὐτός
τε καὶ τὰ χρήματ' ἐκεῖθέν ἐστι, καὶ ὁ ναύκληρος εἴη καὶ οἱ
9 δεδανεικότες Μασσαλιῶται. ἀποτυχὼν δὲ καὶ τούτου, καὶ 25
τῶν ἀρχόντων τῶν ἐν τῇ Κεφαλληνίᾳ γνόντων Ἀθήναζε τὴν
ναῦν καταπλεῖν, ὅθενπερ ἀνήχθη, ὃν οὐδ' ἂν εἷς ἐλθεῖν ᾤετο
δεῦρο τολμῆσαι τοιαῦτά γ' ἐσκευωρημένον καὶ πεποιηκότα,
οὗτος, ὦ ἄνδρες Ἀθηναῖοι, τοσοῦτον ὑπερβέβληκεν ἀναιδείᾳ
καὶ τόλμῃ, ὥστ' οὐκ ἐλήλυθεν μόνον, ἀλλὰ καὶ τοῦ σίτου 30
τοῦ ἡμετέρου ἀμφισβητήσας ἡμῖν δίκην προσείληχεν.
10 Τί οὖν ποτ' ἐστὶν τὸ αἴτιον, καὶ τῷ ποτ' ἐπηρμένος οὗτος
καὶ ἐλήλυθεν καὶ τὴν δίκην εἴληχεν; ἐγὼ ὑμῖν ἐρῶ, ἄνδρες

δικασταί, ἀχθόμενος μὲν νὴ τὸν Δία καὶ θεούς, ἀναγκαζόμενος δέ. ἔστιν ἐργαστήρια μοχθηρῶν ἀνθρώπων συνεστηκότων ἐν τῷ Πειραιεῖ· οὓς οὐδ᾽ ὑμεῖς ἀγνοήσετ᾽ ἰδόντες. ἐκ 11
τούτων ἕνα, ἡνίχ᾽ οὗτος ἔπραττεν ὅπως ἡ ναῦς μὴ καταπλεύ-
5 σεται δεῦρο, πρεσβευτὴν ἐκ βουλῆς τινα λαμβάνομεν γνώριμον οὑτωσί, ὅ τι δ᾽ ἦν οὐκ εἰδότες, ἀτύχημ᾽ οὐδὲν ἔλαττον,
εἰ οἷόν τ᾽ εἰπεῖν, ἀτυχήσαντες ἢ τὸ ἐξ ἀρχῆς πονηροῖς ἀνθρώποις συμμεῖξαι. οὗτος ὁ πεμφθεὶς ὑφ᾽ ἡμῶν (Ἀριστοφῶν
ὄνομ᾽ αὐτῷ), ὃς καὶ τὰ τοῦ Μικκαλίωνος πράγματ᾽ ἐσκευώ-
10 ρηται (ταῦτα γὰρ νῦν ἀκούομεν), ἠργολάβηκεν αὐτὸς καὶ
κατεπήγγελται τουτῳί, καὶ ὅλως ἐστὶν ὁ πάντα πράττων
οὗτος· ὁδὶ δ᾽ ἄσμενος δέδεκται ταῦτα. ὡς γὰρ διήμαρτεν 12
τοῦ διαφθαρῆναι τὸ πλοῖον, οὐκ ἔχων ἀποδοῦναι τὰ χρήματα
τοῖς δανείσασιν (πῶς γάρ; ἅ γ᾽ ἐξ ἀρχῆς μὴ ἐνέθετο) ἀντι-
15 ποιεῖται τῶν ἡμετέρων, καί φησι τῷ Ἡγεστράτῳ ἐπὶ τούτῳ
τῷ σίτῳ δεδανεικέναι ὃν ὁ παρ᾽ ἡμῶν ἐπιπλέων ἐπρίατο.
οἱ δὲ δανεισταὶ τὸ ἐξ ἀρχῆς ἐξηπατημένοι, ὁρῶντες ἑαυτοῖς
ἀντὶ τῶν χρημάτων ἄνθρωπον πονηρὸν χρήστην, ἄλλο δ᾽
οὐδέν, ἐλπίδ᾽ ἔχοντες ὑπὸ τούτου παρακρουσθέντων ὑμῶν ἐκ
20 τῶν ἡμετέρων ἀπολήψεσθαι τὰ ἑαυτῶν, ὃν ἴσασιν ψευδόμενον ταῦτα καθ᾽ ἡμῶν, τούτῳ συνδικεῖν ἀναγκάζονται τοῦ
συμφέροντος εἵνεκα τοῦ ἑαυτῶν.

Τὸ μὲν οὖν πρᾶγμ᾽ ὑπὲρ οὗ τὴν ψῆφον οἴσετε, ὡς εἰπεῖν 13
ἐν κεφαλαίῳ, τοιοῦτόν ἐστιν. βούλομαι δὲ τοὺς μάρτυρας
25 ὧν λέγω πρῶτον ὑμῖν παρασχόμενος, μετὰ ταῦτ᾽ ἤδη καὶ
τἄλλα διδάσκειν. καί μοι λέγε τὰς μαρτυρίας.

ΜΑΡΤΥΡΙΑΙ.

Ἐπειδὴ τοίνυν ἀφίκετο δεῦρο τὸ πλοῖον, γνόντων τῶν 14
Κεφαλλήνων ἀντιπράττοντος τούτου, ὅθεν ἐξέπλευσε τὸ
30 πλοῖον, ἐνταῦθα καὶ καταπλεῖν αὐτό, τὴν μὲν ναῦν οἱ ἐπὶ τῇ
νηὶ δεδανεικότες ἐνθένδ᾽ εὐθέως εἶχον, τὸν δὲ σῖτον ὁ ἠγο-
ρακὼς εἶχεν· ἦν δ᾽ οὗτος ὁ ἡμῖν τὰ χρήματ᾽ ὀφείλων. μετὰ

ταῦθ' ἧκεν οὗτος ἔχων τὸν παρ' ἡμῶν πεμφθέντα πρεσβευτήν,
τὸν Ἀριστοφῶντα, καὶ ἠμφεσβήτει τοῦ σίτου, φάσκων
15 Ἡγεστράτῳ δεδανεικέναι. 'τί λέγεις, ἄνθρωπε;' εὐθέως ὁ
Πρῶτος (τοῦτο γὰρ ἦν τοὔνομα τῷ τὸν σῖτον εἰσαγαγόντι,
τῷ τὰ χρήμαθ' ἡμῖν ὀφείλοντι), 'σὺ χρήματα δέδωκας 5
Ἡγεστράτῳ, μεθ' οὗ τοὺς ἄλλους ἐξηπάτηκας, ὅπως δανεί-
σηται, καὶ σοὶ πολλάκις λέγοντος ὅτι τοῖς προϊεμένοις ἀπολεῖται τὰ χρήματα; σὺ οὖν ταῦτ' ἀκούων αὐτὸς ἂν προήκω;'
ἔφη καὶ ἀναιδὴς ἦν. 'οὐκοῦν εἰ τὰ μάλιστ' ἀληθῆ λέγεις,'
τῶν παρόντων τις ὑπέλαβεν, 'ὁ σὸς κοινωνὸς καὶ πολίτης, 10
ὁ Ἡγέστρατος, ὡς ἔοικεν, ἐξηπάτηκέν σε, καὶ ὑπὲρ τούτων
16 αὐτὸς αὑτῷ θανάτου τιμήσας ἀπόλωλεν.' 'καὶ ὅτι γ',' ἔφη
τις τῶν παρόντων, 'ἁπάντων ἐστὶ συνεργὸς οὗτος ἐκείνῳ,
σημεῖον ὑμῖν ἐρῶ· πρὸ γὰρ τοῦ διακόπτειν ἐπιχειρῆσαι τὴν
ναῦν, τίθενται πρός τινα τῶν συμπλεόντων οὗτος καὶ ὁ 15
Ἡγέστρατος συγγραφήν. καίτοι εἰ μὲν εἰς πίστιν ἔδωκας,
τί πρὸ τοῦ κακουργήματος ἂν τὰ βέβαι' ἐποιοῦ; εἰ δ' ἀπι-
στῶν ἐτύγχανες, τί οὐχ, ὥσπερ οἱ ἄλλοι, τὰ δίκαι' ἐλάμβανες
17 ἐν τῇ γῇ;' τί ἂν τὰ πολλὰ λέγοι τις; ἦν γὰρ οὐδ' ὁτιοῦν
πλέον ἡμῖν ταῦτα λέγουσιν, ἀλλ' εἴχετο τοῦ σίτου. ἐξῆγεν 20
αὐτὸν Πρῶτος καὶ ὁ κοινωνὸς τοῦ Πρώτου, Φέρτατος· οὑτοσὶ
δ' οὐκ ἐξήγετο, οὐδ' ἂν ἔφη διαρρήδην ὑπ' οὐδενὸς ἐξαχθῆναι,
18 εἰ μὴ αὐτὸν ἐγὼ ἐξάξω. μετὰ ταῦτα προὐκαλεῖθ' ὁ Πρῶτος
αὐτὸν καὶ ἡμεῖς ἐπὶ τὴν ἀρχὴν τὴν τῶν Συρακοσίων, κἂν μὲν
ἐωνημένος τὸν σῖτον ἐκεῖνος φαίνηται καὶ τὰ τέλη κείμεν' 25
ἐκείνῳ καὶ τὰς τιμὰς ὁ διαλύων ἐκεῖνος, τοῦτον πονηρὸν ὄντ'
ἀξιοῦμεν ζημιοῦσθαι, εἰ δὲ μή, καὶ τὰ διάφορ' ἀπολαβεῖν καὶ
τάλαντον προσλαβεῖν, καὶ τοῦ σίτου ἀφιστάμεθα. ταῦτ'
ἐκείνου προκαλουμένου καὶ λέγοντος καὶ ἡμῶν οὐδὲν ἦν
πλέον, ἀλλ' ἦν αἵρεσις ἢ τοῦτον ἐξάγειν ἢ ἀπολωλεκέναι 30
19 σωθέντα καὶ παρόντα τὰ ἡμέτερ' αὐτῶν. ὁ γὰρ αὖ Πρῶτος
διεμαρτύρετ' ἐξάγειν, βεβαιῶν ἀναπλεῖν ἐθέλειν εἰς τὴν
Σικελίαν· εἰ δὲ ταῦτ' ἐθέλοντος αὐτοῦ προησόμεθ' ἡμεῖς

τούτῳ τὸν σῖτον, οὐδὲν αὐτῷ μέλειν. καὶ ὅτι ταῦτ' ἀληθῆ
λέγω, καὶ οὔτ' ἂν ἐξαχθῆναι ἔφη, εἰ μὴ ὑπ' ἐμοῦ, οὔθ' ἃ
προὐκαλεῖτο περὶ τοῦ ἀναπλεῖν ἐδέχετο, ἔν τε τῷ πλῷ τὴν
συγγραφὴν ἔθετο, λέγε τὰς μαρτυρίας.

5   ΜΑΡΤΥΡΙΑΙ.

Ἐπειδὴ τοίνυν οὔτ' ἐξάγεσθαι ἤθελεν ὑπὸ τοῦ Πρώτου 20
οὔτ' εἰς τὴν Σικελίαν ἀναπλεῖν ἐπὶ τὰ δίκαια, προειδώς θ'
ἅπαντ' ἐφαίνετο, ἃ ὁ Ἡγέστρατος ἐκακούργει, λοιπὸν ἦν
ἡμῖν τοῖς ἐνθένδε μὲν πεποιημένοις τὸ συμβόλαιον, παρει-
10 ληφόσι δὲ τὸν σῖτον παρὰ τοῦ δικαίως ἐκεῖ πριαμένου, ἐξάγειν τοῦτον. τί γὰρ ἂν καὶ ἄλλ' ἐποιοῦμεν; οὔπω γὰρ 21
τοῦτό γ' οὐδεὶς ἡμῶν τῶν κοινωνῶν ὑπέλαβεν, ὡς ὑμεῖς
γνώσεσθέ ποτ' εἶναι τούτου τὸν σῖτον, ὃν καταλιπεῖν οὗτος
ἔπειθεν τοὺς ναύτας, ὅπως ἀπόλοιτο τοῦ πλοίου καταδύντος.
15 ὃ καὶ μέγιστόν ἐστι σημεῖον τοῦ μηδὲν προσήκειν αὐτῷ.
τίς γὰρ ἂν τὸν ἑαυτοῦ σῖτον ἔπειθε προέσθαι τοὺς σῴζειν
βουλομένους; ἢ τίς οὐκ ἂν ἔπλει δεξάμενος τὴν πρόκλησιν
εἰς τὴν Σικελίαν, οὗ ταῦτ' ἦν ἐλέγξαι καθαρῶς; καὶ μὴν 22
οὐδὲ τοῦτ' ἐμέλλομεν ὑμῶν καταγνώσεσθαι, ὡς εἰσαγώγιμον
20 ψηφιεῖσθε τούτῳ τὴν δίκην περὶ τούτων τῶν χρημάτων, ἃ
κατὰ πολλοὺς τρόπους οὗτος ἔπραττεν ὅπως μὴ εἰσαγώγιμα
δεῦρ' ἔσται, πρῶτον μὲν ὅτ' αὐτὰ καταλιπεῖν τοὺς ναύτας
ἔπειθεν, εἶθ' ὅτ' ἐν Κεφαλληνίᾳ μὴ δεῦρο πλεῖν τὴν ναῦν
ἔπραττεν. πῶς γὰρ οὐκ αἰσχρὸν καὶ δεινὸν ἂν γένοιτο, εἰ 23
25 Κεφαλλῆνες μέν, ὅπως τοῖς Ἀθηναίοις σωθῇ τὰ χρήματα,
δεῦρο πλεῖν τὴν ναῦν ἔκριναν, ὑμεῖς δ' ὄντες Ἀθηναῖοι τὰ
τῶν πολιτῶν τοῖς καταποντίσαι βουληθεῖσιν δοῦναι γνοίητε,
καὶ ἃ μὴ καταπλεῖν ὅλως οὗτος δεῦρ' ἔπραττεν, ταῦτ' εἰσαγώγιμα τούτῳ ψηφίσαισθε; μὴ δῆτ', ὦ Ζεῦ καὶ θεοί. λέγε
30 δή μοι τί παραγέγραμμαι.

                         ΠΑΡΑΓΡΑΦΗ.

Λέγε δή μοι τὸν νόμον.

ΝΟΜΟΣ.

24 "Οτι μὲν τοίνυν ἐκ τῶν νόμων παρεγραψάμην μὴ εἰσαγώγιμον εἶναι τὴν δίκην, ἱκανῶς οἴομαι δεδεῖχθαι· τέχνην δ' ἀκούσεσθε τοῦ σοφοῦ τοῦ ταῦτα πάντα συντεθηκότος, τοῦ Ἀριστοφῶντος. ὡς γὰρ ἐκ τῶν πραγμάτων ἁπλῶς οὐδὲν 5 ἑώρων δίκαιον ἑαυτοῖς ἐνόν, ἐπικηρυκεύονται τῷ Πρώτῳ καὶ πείθουσι τὸν ἄνθρωπον ἐνδοῦναι τὰ πράγμαθ' ἑαυτοῖς, πράττοντες μὲν ὡς ἔοικεν καὶ ἐξ ἀρχῆς τοῦτο, ὡς ἡμῖν νῦν φα-
25 νερὸν γέγονεν, οὐ δυνάμενοι δὲ πεῖσαι. ὁ γὰρ Πρῶτος, ἕως μὲν ᾤετο τὸν σῖτον κέρδος ἐλθόντα ποιήσειν, ἀντείχετο 10 τούτου, καὶ μᾶλλον ἡρεῖτ' αὐτός τε κερδᾶναι καὶ ἡμῖν τὰ δίκαι' ἀποδοῦναι, ἢ κατακοινωνήσας τούτοις τῆς μὲν ὠφελίας τούτους ποιῆσαι μερίτας, ἡμᾶς δ' ἀδικῆσαι· ὡς δὲ δεῦρ' ἥκοντος αὐτοῦ καὶ περὶ ταῦτα πραγματευομένου, ἐπανῆκεν ὁ
26 σῖτος, ἄλλην εὐθέως ἔλαβεν γνώμην. καὶ ἅμα (εἰρήσεται 15 γάρ, ἄνδρες Ἀθηναῖοι, πᾶσα πρὸς ὑμᾶς ἡ ἀλήθεια) καὶ ἡμεῖς οἱ δεδανεικότες προσεκρούομεν αὐτῷ καὶ πικρῶς εἴχομεν, τῆς τε ζημίας ἐφ' ἡμᾶς ἰούσης τῆς περὶ τὸν σῖτον καὶ συκοφάντην ἀντὶ χρημάτων αἰτιώμενοι τοῦτον ἡμῖν κεκομικέναι. ἐκ τούτων, οὐδὲ φύσει χρηστὸς ὢν ἄνθρωπος δῆλον ὅτι, ἐπὶ τούτους 20 ἀποκλίνει, καὶ συγχωρεῖ τὴν δίκην ἔρημον ὀφλεῖν, ἣν οὗτος
27 αὐτῷ λαγχάνει τότε, ὅτ' οὔπω ταῦτ' ἐφρόνουν. εἰ μὲν γὰρ ἀφῆκε τὸν Πρῶτον, ἐξελήλεγκτ' ἂν εὐθέως ἡμᾶς συκοφαντῶν· ὀφλεῖν δὲ παρὼν ἐκεῖνος οὐ συνεχώρει, ἵν' ἐὰν μὲν αὐτῷ ποιῶσιν ἃ ὡμολογήκασιν—, εἰ δὲ μή, τὴν ἔρημον ἀντιλάχῃ. 25 ἀλλὰ τί ταῦτα; εἰ μὲν γὰρ ἃ γέγραφεν οὗτος εἰς τὸ ἔγκλημ' ἐποίει, οὐκ ὀφλεῖν ἂν δίκην δικαίως, ἀλλ' ἀποθανεῖν Πρῶτος ἔμοιγε δοκεῖ. εἰ γὰρ ἐν κακοῖς καὶ χειμῶνι τοσοῦτον οἶνον ἔπινεν ὥσθ' ὅμοιον εἶναι μανία, τί οὐκ ἄξιός ἐστι παθεῖν;
28 ἢ εἰ γράμματ' ἔκλεπτεν; εἰ ὑπανέῳγεν; ἀλλὰ ταῦτα μὲν 30 αὐτοὶ πρὸς ἑαυτοὺς ὑμεῖς ὅπως ποτ' ἔχει διακρινεῖσθε· τῇ δ' ἐμῇ δίκῃ μηδὲν ἐκείνης πρόσαγε. εἴ τί σ' ἠδίκηκεν ὁ Πρῶτος ἢ λέγων ἢ ποιῶν, ἔχεις ὡς ἔοικε δίκην· οὐδεὶς ἡμῶν

ἐκώλυεν, οὐδὲ νῦν παραιτεῖται. εἰ σεσυκοφάντηκας, οὐ
περιεργαζόμεθα. νὴ Δί᾽, ἀλλ᾽ ἐκποδών ἐστιν ἄνθρωπος. 29
διά γ᾽ ὑμᾶς, ἵνα τάς τε μαρτυρίας τὰς ἡμετέρας λίπῃ, καὶ
νῦν ὑμεῖς ὅ τι ἂν βούλησθε λέγητε κατ᾽ αὐτοῦ. εἰ γὰρ μὴ
5 δι᾽ ὑμῶν ἔρημος ἐγίγνεθ᾽ ἡ δίκη, ἅμ᾽ ἂν αὐτὸν προσεκαλοῦ
καὶ κατηγγύας πρὸς τὸν πολέμαρχον, καὶ εἰ μὲν κατέστησέ
σοι τοὺς ἐγγυητάς, μένειν ἠναγκάζετ᾽ ἄν, ἢ σὺ παρ᾽ ὧν λήψει
δίκην ἑτοίμους εἶχες, εἰ δὲ μὴ κατέστησεν, εἰς τὸ οἴκημ᾽ ἂν
ᾔει. νῦν δὲ κοινωσάμενοι τὸ πρᾶγμα, ὁ μὲν διὰ σοῦ τὴν 30
10 γεγονυῖαν ἔκδειαν οὐκ ἀποδώσειν ἡμῖν οἴεται, σὺ δ᾽ ἐκείνου
κατηγορῶν τῶν ἡμετέρων κύριος γενήσεσθαι. τεκμήριον δέ·
ἐγὼ μὲν γὰρ αὐτὸν κλητεύσω, σὺ δ᾽ οὔτε κατηγγύησας οὔτε
νῦν κλητεύσεις.

Ἔτι τοίνυν ἑτέρα τις ἐστὶν ἐλπὶς αὐτοῖς τοῦ παρακρού- 31
15 σεσθαι καὶ φενακιεῖν ὑμᾶς. αἰτιάσονται Δημοσθένην, καὶ
ἐκείνῳ ἐμὲ πιστεύοντα φήσουσιν ἐξάγειν τουτονί, ὑπολαμ-
βάνοντες τῷ ῥήτορα καὶ γνώριμον εἶναι ἐκεῖνον πιθανὴν ἔχειν
τὴν αἰτίαν. ἐμοὶ δ᾽ ἐστὶ μέν, ὦ ἄνδρες Ἀθηναῖοι, Δημοσθένης οἰκεῖος γένει (καὶ πάντας ὑμῖν ὄμνυμι τοὺς θεοὺς ἦ μὴν
20 ἐρεῖν τἀληθῆ), προσελθόντος δ᾽ αὐτῷ μου καὶ παρεῖναι καὶ 32
βοηθεῖν ἀξιοῦντος εἴ τι ἔχοι, 'Δήμων,' ἔφη, 'ἐγὼ ποιήσω
μὲν ὡς ἂν σὺ κελεύῃς (καὶ γὰρ ἂν δεινὸν εἴη). δεῖ μέντοι
καὶ τὸ σαυτοῦ καὶ τοὐμὸν λογίσασθαι. ἐμοὶ συμβέβηκεν,
ἀφ᾽ οὗ περὶ τῶν κοινῶν λέγειν ἠρξάμην, μηδὲ πρὸς ἓν πρᾶγμ᾽
25 ἴδιον προσεληλυθέναι· ἀλλὰ καὶ τῆς πολιτείας αὐτῆς τὰ
τοιαῦτ᾽ ἐξέστηκα . . . . .

COMMENTARY

Note: *References to the Greek text are by section number—e.g.*
31.7 means Oration 31, section 7.   For points of grammar ref-
erences are given to the Greek Grammars of Smyth (revised by
Messing) and Goodwin-Gulick (GG.).

AGAINST APHOBUS I (27)

1. εἰ μὲν ἐβούλετ' Ἄφοβος, "if Aphobus were willing (which he is not)." The imperfect indicative in an if-clause always has this meaning, presenting a condition which is not fulfilled; the imperfect indicative with ἄν regularly follows with a "contrary to fact" apodosis, οὐδὲν ἂν ἔδει, "there would be no need." A plaintiff often begins in this style to show how unwillingly he has taken a case to court, that he would not have done so unless he had been forced into it, that he would gladly agree to a settlement if the other party were not so unreasonable. He wants to insist that he is not a συκοφάντης, a professional litigant who takes legal action on trifling grounds and depends on his skill as a speaker to get the better of an honest adversary. For parallels to this style of opening cf. 29.1, 34.2.

ὦ ἄνδρες δικασταί, "gentlemen of the jury." The Assembly (ἐκκλησία) and the large juries which sat in the trials for *On the Embassy* and *On the Crown* are addressed as ὦ ἄνδρες Ἀθηναῖοι.

τὰ δίκαια, "the right, proper, decent thing." Greek idiom uses neuter plural adjectives, where English prefers a singular or an abstract noun—thus τῶν δικαίων τυγχάνειν, "to obtain justice," at the end of this section. Cf. λέγειν τἀληθῆ, "to tell the truth." Neuter plurals of this kind will occur constantly in these speeches.

περὶ ὧν διεφερόμεθα, "concerning what matters we differed among ourselves" (cf. διαφορά, "quarrel, dispute" at end of this sentence). Again the neuter plural. English idiom prefers to insert a singular noun as antecedent, "the question on which we disagreed" or simply "the matter of our dispute." This style is very common in Greek prose—a clause beginning with a relative without any clear antecedent; the student should accustom himself to finding idiomatic English versions— περὶ ὧν λέγω, "the subject of my speech," ἐφ᾽ ᾧ ἠγανάκτησα, "the basis for my irritation," and so on.

τοῖς οἰκείοις, masculine, "relatives, members of the family."

ἐπιτρέπειν, "to entrust," hence ἐπίτροπος, "trustee." The Latin equivalent is *committere*. The direct object of the verb is περὶ ὧν διεφερόμεθα, "our dispute."

πραγμάτων. Again English may prefer a singular, "trouble, fuss" (in section 2 it means "business"). Cf. πράγματα παρέχειν, "to cause trouble."

ἀπέχρη γὰρ ἄν, "because in that case it would be enough, everyone would be content."

τοῖς ... γνωσθεῖσιν, neuter plural again, "the things decided by them" or "their decision."

ἐπειδὴ δ᾽, "but since in fact." The δέ marks the return to reality after the hypothetical μέν sentence.

τοὺς μὲν σαφῶς εἰδότας τὰ ἡμέτερα, a single phrase, "persons with definite knowledge of our affairs." It is best to avoid the wearisome "those who" translation of participles with the article. Where a noun does not readily suggest itself—like "speakers" for οἱ λέγοντες— "men" or "persons" is often preferable to "those."

ἔφυγε μηδὲν διαγνῶναι, a good example of what is sometimes called the redundant negative. What Aphobus has avoided is "informed persons making a decision," a complex verbal noun in accusative and infinitive, which would come naturally after a verb of wishing or allowing. The negative is used, it seems, because the infinitive is partly thought of in terms of the negative result—as though with ὥστε, "he shunned them so that they should not decide." Cf. Smyth, 2739–43; Goodwin-Gulick, 1618–19.

ἐλήλυθεν, perfect indicative, so that we are now in present time, and ἀνάγκη ἐστίν follows naturally.

ἐν ὑμῖν, "in your court." Cf. παρ' ὑμῖν (2), "in your presence."

τυγχάνειν, "to obtain," always with a genitive like its opposite ἁμαρτάνειν, "to fail to obtain," "fall short of," cf. 30.1. The reason for the genitive with the positive verb, which is strictly a partitive genitive, is clear if we think of τυγχάνειν meaning "to hit a target." No one hits all of a target but part of it; so one tastes of a dish or touches or holds on to a piece of the table, ἔχεσθαι τῆς τραπέζης. Cf. Smyth, 1341–50; GG. 1099–1103.

2. οἶδα . . . ὅτι. Elementary Greek books give the impression that οἶδα is always used with accusative and participle, but ὅτι is common in good Greek prose.

οἶδα μὲν οὖν, "I am well aware of course." For the force of the particles see Denniston, *Greek Particles*, pp. 470–80; Smyth, 2901.

πρὸς ἄνδρας, "in dealing with men." The preposition is used of any personal relationship—not only of hostility, which is meant here.

λέγειν ἱκανούς (like δεινοὺς λέγειν). It is well to remember that the infinitive is a noun, used here in the accusative of respect or limitation—"adequate as to speaking."

παρασκευάσασθαι. This very often means something like "contrive" rather than simply "arrange" or "make preparation."

χαλεπόν, not "difficult," but "troublesome, awkward, unpleasant."

εἰς ἀγῶνα καθίστασθαι, "to get put into competition, become involved in a contest." The verb is often used with εἰς πόλεμον.

τῶν ὄντων, neuter, "my property, all that I have."

ἄπειρον, accusative as qualifying the subject of the infinitive καθίστασθαι. It makes no difference whether it is "me" or "a person."

τεύξεσθαι, future infinitive of τυγχάνω, as demanded by the verb of hoping. So also ἀρκούντως ἐρεῖν, with αὐτός in nominative as subject of the infinitive.

μέχρι γε τοῦ . . . διεξελθεῖν, "to the point at least (γε) of describing (going right through) what happened."

ἀπολειφθῆναι τῶν πραγμάτων, "fall short of the facts"— another common meaning of πράγματα.

μηδὲ καθ' ἕν, "not even in a single detail."

περὶ ὧν, "the issue on which."

ψῆφον ἐνεγκεῖν, "cast your ballot." So ψηφίζεσθαι "to vote by ballot," as opposed to χειροτονεῖν, "vote by show of hands."

3. δέομαι δ' ὑμῶν. Note the genitive with verb of asking ("I beg of you") and also with ἀκοῦσαι.

βοηθῆσαί μοι τὰ δίκαια, "give me due assistance, the help to which I am entitled." Neuter plural adjective again; English generally prefers to make a noun out of the verb.

ὡς ἂν δύνωμαι διὰ βραχυτάτων, "however I can by the shortest method," "with the utmost possible brevity."

Again the neuter plural adjective, instead of the abstract. διά with genitive indicates the means.

ὅθεν . . . ἐντεῦθεν. The relative preceding its antecedent is common enough in modern English, but more common in the indefinite sense: "Where you look, there you shall find" or "Wherever you look you will find." The logic of this sentence may not be easy to grasp: "From what point (of observation or vantage) you will best be able to learn, from that point I shall start in trying to tell you." But ὅθεν besides the local meaning, "from which place," contains also the logical meaning "thanks to which, as a result of which," like ἐξ ὧν. The speaker wants to organize his narrative in such a way that everything will be clear, to choose the right starting point "as a result of which you will most easily learn." It is well to remember that Greek uses a relative adverb of place—like ἵνα, which means "where"—to indicate purpose, as well as an adverb of manner, ὅπως, "in what way."

For the narrator's insistence on choice of a starting point compare the opening of the *Iliad* and the *Odyssey*. Another orator might have wanted to begin earlier, saying something about his father's life and his plans for his children. Demosthenes decides to begin at his father's death.

Sections 1–3 constitute the introduction, the προοίμιον (Latin *exordium*). Its object is to make a good initial impression, to acquire the good will (εὔνοια) of the audience, put them in a certain frame of mind (sympathy or anger), and perhaps give some indication of one's own character. Aristotle insists on the importance that lies ἐν τῷ ἤθει τοῦ λέγοντος, ἐν τῷ τὸν ἀκροάτην διαθεῖναί πως (*Rhet.* 1.1356a), "in the character of the speaker, in putting the listener in a certain frame of mind" (διατιθέναι, "dispose").

In these opening sections Demosthenes has invited the jury to assume that his guardians have done their best to avoid any fair settlement and are relying on their skill and experience to get the better of him in court. He is trying to make the jury think (without saying so explicitly) that only a fool would venture to sue such scoundrels unless he had justice on his side, and that he lacks such talent as they have to tell a convincing series of falsehoods. All this is a way of establishing his own integrity, without insisting on it directly.

4. γάρ. γάρ really explains the choice of starting point— "I am starting at my father's death because . . ." The narrative (διήγησις) now begins.

ταλάντων. See note on Money, Introduction p. 18.

ἐπτ' ἐτῶν. A simple genitive of description, "a boy of seven."

εἰσενηνεγμένην, perfect participle middle of εἰσφέρω. She had "brought for herself" her dowry into the family or household (οἶκος). This is mentioned to show the economic scale and style of the household, definitely upper middle class. Plutarch describes the elder Demosthenes, with a partitive genitive, as τῶν καλῶν κἀγαθῶν (*Dem.* 4).

τουτῳί. The final -ι is deictic, the finger pointing at him, "this man here." οὗτος is the plaintiff's regular word for the defendant; in Cicero it is *iste*, and *hic* is "my client."

τούτοιν. It is good to be reminded that the dual is not obsolete—"these two being his nephews."

Παιανιεῖ. This shows the deme to which Therippides belongs. Demes are theoretically local divisions of Attica, but the family does not change its deme even if it has long since lived in a different area. This was the deme to which Demosthenes' family belonged; his full formal name is therefore: Δημοσθένης Δημοσθένους Παιανιεύς.

Without wasting words Demosthenes makes it clear that his father's choice of guardians was natural and reasonable—two close relatives and the other, though no relative, a lifelong friend (ἐκ παιδός—"since boyhood"). Nothing is said of their supposed character; there would be no point in insisting on his father's error of judgment about that.

5. κἀκείνῳ. According to the conventional rules of grammar this should not denote the man last mentioned, but it does, as becomes clear from what follows; it means Therippides.

ἔδωκεν . . . ἑβδομήκοντα μνᾶς καρπώσασθαι. If the speaker pauses after μνᾶς the meaning is: "Gave him 70 minas, to have the income (the fruit) from it," an epexegetic or explanatory infinitive, qualifying the "gift" to show that he is not given the capital outright; if he does not pause till καρπώσασθαι, the infinitive, with object accusative, is what he receives: "Gave him the right to receive the income from 70 minas." The second alternative is meant, as becomes clear from the last of a series of infinitive gifts made to the trustees: σκεύεσι χρῆσθαι τοῖς ἐμοῖς. It is useful to remember that infinitives, often accusatives and infinitives, can be grants or gifts. "A free trip to Paris" would be expressed by an accusative and infinitive in Greek, i.e. "they granted him to travel to Paris paying nothing."

ἕως . . . δοκιμασθείην. The father is presumed to have said: δίδωμι . . . ἕως ἂν δοκιμασθῇ. The optative is used to report his words in secondary sequence: "until I came of age (at eighteen.)" After formal recognition by the demesmen that he was eighteen and the legitimate son of citizen parents, a young man had to submit to further examination (δοκιμασία) by the Boule before he began his service as an Ephebe. This examination established him as a citizen with full rights; only then was Demosthenes entitled to bring suit. Cf. Aristot. *Resp. Ath.* 42; Lipsius, *Att. Recht*, pp. 282–83.

ὅπως ... διοικήσειεν. The purpose of the provision is explained. Therippides will have everything to gain by skilful handling of the money. This is the orator's comment, still justifying his father's arrangements, which nevertheless turned out so badly.

εὐθὺς ἔδωκεν ἔχειν. Demophon is to have the money and the little girl right away—the gift is outright. He will be expected either to marry the girl himself when she is old enough, or find a suitable husband for her, endowing her with the two talents. This is a larger dowry than the wife of the elder Demosthenes had brought with her, and enough to ensure finding her a husband of good standing. These arrangements are quite proper and conventional; it is a male relative, not the mother, who is held responsible for the girl's future.

αὐτῷ δὲ τούτῳ, "to this fellow, Aphobus himself." He is made responsible for the widow, either to marry her himself, with a dowry (προῖξ) substantially larger than she brought her first husband, or to make such arrangements as we shall be told subsequently. This also is in accordance with Attic custom.

τὴν οἰκίαν ⟨οἰκεῖν⟩. The infinitive is added by editors because it is in the text in 29.43, where the formal conditions of the will are given. It is understandable that

Aphobus does not receive the house outright, but the privilege of living in it and making use of its furniture; all this is to become the son's property when he is eighteen. The house is to stay in the family, and it is taken for granted that Aphobus will not live there unless he marries the widow. Demosthenes does not explain every detail, since the arrangements appear to be fairly conventional.

ἔτ' οἰκειοτέρους. If the provisions of the will are carried out, Aphobus and Demophon will become "closer relatives" of young Demosthenes, step-father and brother-in-law, as well as first cousins. The final genitive absolute is taken by some editors to be a pedantic addition by a copyist. But one can never be sure when Demosthenes will think it necessary to "dot every i."

οὐκ ἂν χεῖρόν μ' ἐπιτροπευθῆναι. "No worse" of course means "better"—this is not ironical, as it would sound in English, but regular Greek understatement (*meiosis*). It is unlucky that English lacks a transitive verb like "to guardian" or "to trustee" (Greek ἐπιτροπεύω).

6. λαβόντες δ' οὗτοι. Now we hear what they actually did, in contrast to what they were supposed to do.

ταῦτα, "these legacies."

σφίσιν αὐτοῖς. The dative shows how they looked after themselves.

διαχειρίσαντες. They got the capital in their hands and "handled" it for ten years. The implication is that, with any sort of good management, they should have increased it.

ἀπεστερήκασιν. The perfect tense shows that we are back in present time (cf. note on ἐλήλυθεν in 1).

μάλιστα, "just about, approximately," quite a common meaning.

σύμπαντα ταῦτ'. Not "They have given me all this," but "All this that they have handed over to me amounts to just about seventy minas." This is too low a valuation for what he received, as will appear when more detailed figures are given later, in 9–10. Though the values of house and slaves and furniture may have decreased, nothing is said about this.

7. κεφάλαιον, "total," "sum," "the gist of it."

ὡς ἂν συντομώτατ' εἴποι τις, "as one would put it most concisely" or "to put it in the briefest terms." The infinitive, ὡς συντομώτατ' εἰπεῖν, would also be good Greek.

αὐτοί, the emphasis is on this word, "themselves."

συμμορίαν, "symmory" or "payment-sharing group" (cf. μοῖρα, "share, portion"). In the fourth century, when Athens no longer financed wars with imperial tribute, it was necessary at intervals to levy a property tax on the assessed capital holdings of citizens. As a means of collecting this εἰσφορά, in the year 378–7 the 1200 citizens who were considered wealthiest were formed into twenty groups called "symmories," each group of sixty men being held responsible for one-twentieth of the total tax demanded, in any year. The details of organization are not clearly recorded, but it appears that each symmory was further subdivided into five groups (so that some historians speak of 100 symmories instead of 20) and it is likely that there were "leaders" in each group who were expected to pay in advance, as προεισφορά, what was due from the entire group, and then collect what was due to them from the other members. From what Demosthenes says here it looks as though wealthier men paid at a higher rate than others, but even this is not sure.

Twenty years later the same system was applied to sharing the costs of the trierarchy, so that groups instead of individuals became responsible for meeting the cost of keeping a ship at sea. In the first speech which Demosthenes made to the Assembly in 354 (Oration 14, *On the Symmories*), he proposed some modifications of the system.

For details consult the standard histories and for more extensive discussion of the knotty problems A. H. M. Jones, *Athenian Democracy*, pp. 23–30. A very important piece of evidence is a fragment of Philochorus—F. Jacoby, *Die Fragmente der griechischen Historiker*, III, B, 328 F. 41.

συνετάξαντο . . . εἰσφέρειν, "they assessed themselves to pay."

Τιμόθεος. This distinguished Athenian statesman and military leader, who was very active in the 370's and 60's, was not always so well provided with money, as we learn from the pseudo-Demosthenic oration 49.

τιμήματα. As with the English word "assessment" (which is a convenient translation) it is not always clear whether τίμημα means "assessed capital," "assessed tax," or "rate of tax." In this passage it scarcely matters which meaning is intended. The rate of tax appears to be 20%—500 drachmas in 2500, and the same percentage appears in 9—3 talents in 15. But the meaning of this 20% is not clear. It is quite impossible that any Athenian would have been even asked to pay up 20% of his capital, and there is no suggestion in the text that Aphobus paid any large sum.

ἐνεργά. Capital that produces income is said to be "put to work," whereas unproductive capital is "idle."

οὐδένες . . . διηρπάκασιν. Not "none plundered our

property more shamelessly," but "none have ever more shamelessly robbed a trust fund than these men have done in plundering our property."

8. συνετιμήσαντο, "they jointly assessed themselves this tax as due to the symmory on my behalf," an admirably orthodox use of the middle voice.

ἀναγίγνωσκε. Demosthenes addresses the clerk of the court, asking him to "take and proceed to read" (note the present imperative) the written deposition. μοι is ethical dative. Cf. Smyth, 1486; Goodwin-Gulick, 1171.

In some speeches texts of the documents which are submitted in evidence are given in the manuscripts, but in almost every case it can be shown that they are later fabrications, composed from indications in the text; an occasional error (legal or factual) on the part of the fabricator betrays him. No documents are given here, but the heading (μαρτυρία) is put in to show when the orator interrupts his speech.

9. τίμημα. Here is the 20% tax rate again; there is no suggestion that so much money was ever paid, and we can only guess what the significance of the figure is. Now Demosthenes drops the argument from the tax assessment, and explains how he arrives at the figure of nearly 15 talents for the estate.

ἐργαστήρια. "Workshops" or "businesses" rather than "factories," as there are no special premises and no machinery—only two gangs of slaves.

τέχνης οὐ μικρᾶς, a good descriptive genitive, "each a business on quite a large scale."

μαχαιροποιούς, makers of swords, daggers, knives— skilled cutlers and metal workers.

δύ’ ἢ τρεῖς, "two or three (of the thirty)." The comma
is rightly after τριάκοντα, not after τρεῖς.

ἀτελεῖς, "net." We need not believe it is literally true
that these thirty slaves, valued at about 100 minas,
regularly brought in a net income of 30 minas—a very
comfortable percentage on the capital. But it is useless
to speculate what the true figure would be.

κλινοποιούς, makers of beds, couches, and furniture
generally—carpenters and upholsterers.

ὑποκειμένους, "pledged to him as security for a loan of
40 minas." ὑποτιθέναι, literally "place under," means to
give as support (security) for a loan, and κεῖσθαι is the
regular passive of τιθέναι. Cf. ὑποθήκη, "mortgage."
In 25 we meet ὁ ὑποθείς, the man who pledged these
slaves as security, and the slaves are τὰ ὑποτεθέντα (28).

ἀργυρίου, partitive genitive, "a sum of money amount-
ing to about a talent."

ἐπὶ δραχμῇ δεδανεισμένου, "lent at the rate of one
drachma (per mina per month)," i.e. 1% per month or
12% per annum (the same rate that appears as normal in
Cicero's letters). Note δανείζειν, "lend," δανείζεσθαι,
"borrow"—the middle voice indicates one's immediate
advantage.

τόκος, "interest," literally "offspring," just as we can
still talk of money "bearing interest." 12% of 6000
drachmas is 720 drachmas.

10. τοῦ μὲν ἀρχαίου, (neuter) "the principal."

πεντακισχίλιαι (δραχμαί), i.e. five-sixths of a talent.
This total, 4⅚ talents, seems too large. The value of all
the slaves plus the talent in cash gives only about 3½
talents. How is the unexpectedly high figure to be explained? Is Demosthenes including stock or equipment?

For discussion see Schwahn, *Demosthenes gegen Aphobos*, 15–18.

τὸ δ' ἔργον. The "work" that the money does is the income or interest that it earns. The "idle" capital is now listed. First the stock on hand in the workshops ("the workmen" are readily understood as the subject of κατηργάζοντο); the ivory is for sword-hilts and knife-handles, the oak-gall (κηκίς) for staining woodwork, in which there could be decorative inlays of ivory.

ἑβδομήκοντα μνῶν. Genitive of price, which is no different from value or description, whereas in English we distinguish between buying an article *of* great value and *for* a high price.

τρισχιλίων, drachmas again; he might have said τριάκοντα, when it would clearly mean minas. The prices given here are valuable as showing comparative costs and values. The house is worth as much as fifteen slaves. But the low value of the house in proportion to its contents—furniture and other valuable articles—is remarkable.

τὸν κόσμον, her "trousseau," representing the dowry which she brought with her as a bride.

11. ναυτικά. Cf. Antonio in *The Merchant of Venice*, I i: "Thou know'st that all my fortunes are at sea."

ἔκδοσιν, a "loan" or "investment." Xuthus evidently used the money for financing trading ventures, and banks could also lend money for such purposes. We learn more of Pasion's bank in other speeches of Demosthenes, especially 36 (*For Phormio*). Cf. also T. R. Glover, *From Pericles to Philip* (London, 1917), chap. X, "The House of Pasion."

κατὰ διακοσίας, "and about one talent altogether invested in loans of 200 or 300 drachmas."

εὑρήσετε σκοποῦντες. The jury are invited to do their own arithmetic; they will find the exact sum is 13 talents 46 minas. The amount of money invested, in proportion to the value of the rest of the property, suggests that the elder Demosthenes had done well in his business.

Sections 9–11 have interrupted the narrative of events, so as to show the jury that a considerable sum of money is involved. They do not offer a precisely documented report with full accounting details; but the jury are presumed to be "simple men," who might be merely confused and irritated by too much detail.

12. ὅσα δ'αὐτῆς διακέκλεπται, "how much of it has been misappropriated." πρὸς ταὐτὸ ὕδωρ, "within the one time allowance," as measured by the flow of water in a water-timer, a κλεψύδρα, "water-stealer." This was a pot, varying in size according to the length of time allowed a speaker, which let water escape by a small hole in the base; this could be stopped when evidence was submitted; sometimes a speaker reminds the attendant to "stop the water" (45.8), when he asks the clerk to read a document, and it was stopped when evidence was given. See *Excavations of the Athenian Agora*, Picture Book No. 4, "The Athenian Citizen," (Princeton, 1960), pl. 25–26 for a photograph.

πρός. "In relation to" (cf. note on 2) means "in face of" in this context. Cf. 41.30 πρὸς ὀλίγον ὕδωρ ἀναγκαζόμενος λέγειν.

ἕκαστον διελεῖν, "to separate, take each one separately" (cf. diaeresis). Compounds with διά often imply division, e.g. διατιθέναι, "to distribute, make disposition in a will" (διαθήκη, cf. 13).

ἃ μὲν οὖν . . . ἔχουσιν, "as for the money that D. and T.

have." This money is neither subject or object of a verb, but in accusative of respect; it is perhaps easier to introduce it to us like this than to write περὶ ὧν ἔχουσι, περὶ τούτων.

τότ᾽ ἐξαρκέσει . . . ὅταν, literally "*then* will it suffice to speak, when . . ." Such heavy emphasis on τότε ("then and not before") is not idiomatic in English; it is better to say "it will be time enough to speak when . . ."

ὅταν. Relative and conditional clauses referring to the future commonly have ἄν and the subjunctive.

γραφάς. There is a formal distinction between δίκη, a civil suit, and γραφή, a prosecution in which some crime or misdemeanour is charged. The details of the cases against the other guardians are not known, and the use of the word γραφή does not actually prove that more serious charges were made against them than against Aphobus; but there is an implied threat in the use of the word.

ἐξελέγχουσιν, a strong word, "prove conclusively, show quite definitely." It balances οἶδα.

περὶ τούτων. English idiom needs a singular noun (cf. note on 1): "This will be the subject of my address to you." Likewise in the next sentence: "The first point that I shall make clear is that he has the dowry."

διὰ βραχυτάτων, see note on 3.

13. οὗτος γάρ, "yes, because *this* man." The narrative is now resumed, and the jury have been warned what conclusion it will lead to; each step shows Aphobus making sure of the money without a thought of his obligations.

ᾤκει, a good imperfect, "he proceeded to live, started living," the beginning of a continuous process, not a simple action. Then there is a shift to the historic present, "he starts taking."

χρυσία, presumably jewellery, since it is her personal property.

ταῦτα μέν.   One can almost see the orator holding up his hand, "here he had (this gave him) about fifty minas."

ἀνδραπόδων.   The grammatical reason for the genitive is not clear until we reach τὰς τιμάς, "the prices."   There might be various reasons for selling the slaves; some might be too old for the work, and replacements needed.   But Demosthenes is not concerned to discuss motives; what he wants the jury to see is that Aphobus acquired eighty minas in cash as soon as he could.   The completion of this process is shown by an aorist ἀνεπληρώσατο (middle, since it is definitely "for his advantage"), "he made up the full amount of the dowry."

14.   The basis for these statements now follows.   Aphobus was made trierarch (so that he must have been wealthy from other sources) and the other guardians wanted a statement from him, before he left, to certify that he had received what he was entitled to.

ἀπέγραψε . . . ἑαυτόν, "he declared himself (in a written statement to T.) in possession of this item."   The statement (aorist) was a momentary act; the admission (ὡμολόγει) was a more permanent state of mind, hence imperfect.

Λευκονοεύς, name of deme.   Cf. note on 4.

ὁ τὴν τηθίδα . . . ἔχων, "my aunt's husband."   Since he is not a blood relation it is not proper to call him θεῖος (uncle).

15.   σῖτον, "a living allowance."   One may suspect that she and the children were living in Demochares' house,

and dependent on him unless Aphobus made some provision.

τὸν οἶκον μισθοῦν, not "rent the house," but "farm out the estate," i.e. put all the income-producing property in the hands of a man or a group of men, who would give proper security, guarantee a fixed income from the property, and be entitled to keep any surplus income for themselves. It was one of the duties of the archon to supervise such arrangements for the property of orphans (Aristot. *Resp. Ath.* 56.7). It is emphasized later in the speech (58) that trouble would be saved by "farming out the property," but it was quite legitimate for guardians to take the responsibility of investing the money themselves. Cf. Lysias 32.23; Kennedy, *Orations of Demosthenes Translated*, vol. iv, Appendix 2; Lipsius, *Att. Recht*, pp. 346–49, 529.

ἠμφεσβήτησε μὴ ἔχειν, another "redundant" negative (see note on 1), "did not dispute that he had it, saying that he had not received it." Note the imperfect of ὡμολόγει as in 14.

διευκρινησάμενος, still part of what he said, "after settling this matter (of the χρυσιδία—the gold ornaments) he would take steps to satisfy me περὶ τῆς τροφῆς" ("maintenance"—his obligation to pay for my upbringing).

ὥστ' ἔχειν . . . καλῶς, "so as to satisfy me completely." ἔχει καλῶς means "it's all right."

16. εἰ φανήσεται . . . πάνθ' ὡμολογηκώς, "if he shall be shown having made these admissions." The use of φαίνομαι with a participle is common in argument—"be shown as having done something, be seen to have done something," not "appear to have done," like φαίνομαι with the infinitive.

ἐκ πάντων ὁμολογουμένου τοῦ πράγματος. There is a pause after πῶς οὐκ and the genitive absolute describes the situation: "With the facts admitted by all parties."

εὑρεθήσεται, used with a participle like φαίνομαι.

κεκομισμένος, a good use of a middle participle, "having acquired for himself."

μὴ λαβεῖν ἐξαρνούμενος. Cf. note on ἠμφεσβήτησεν in 15. We never learn exactly what Aphobus meant by saying he had not received the dowry; it is represented as a lie which insults the jury's intelligence; they can see that he received and still has it!

17. μὴ γήμαντος. μή shows that this is a conditional participle, equivalent to ἐὰν μὴ γαμῇ. Since Aphobus is presumed to have the dowry and not to have married the widow, he is considered liable for the interest on the sum over a period of ten years. ἐπ᾽ ἐννέ᾽ ὀβολοῖς, "at the rate of 9 obols (1½ drachmas)" per mina per month; i.e. 18% per annum. Magnanimously Demosthenes agrees to reckon at the lower rate of 12%.

μάλιστα τρία τάλαντα. Again the jury are left to do their own arithmetic. 80 minas plus ten years' simple interest at 12% will result in 176 minas, just 4 minas short of 3 talents.

18. ταῦτα μέν, "*these* amounts," with the implication that there will be more to come.

λαβόντα . . . ὁμολογήσαντα, the participles are more vivid than infinitives; not "I have proved to you that he received," but "I have shown him to you in receipt of these sums, admitting that he had them."

ἄλλας τοίνυν, as ταῦτα μέν had led us to expect.

τὴν πρόσοδον, "the income," because it is assumed that

the workshop brought in an income; as the next sentence explains, this income was part of the inheritance left to Demosthenes by his father.

ἀναισχυντότατ' ἀνθρώπων, "most shamelessly of all men," i.e. in the most shameless manner possible.

ἀποστερεῖν. A translator has to supply "me": "deprive me of this money." Cf. μ' ἀποστεροῦσι in 24.

The assumption that the workshop should produce a fixed income, and half as much with half as many men working, may seem unrealistic, but a prosecutor will not do the work of the defence for them by offering reasons for a decline in income or suggesting that there were years when business was bad.

19. ἀπέφηνε, "showed, declared an income of 11 minas." Cf. ἀποφαίνουσιν in 24 and ἀποδείκνυσιν in the next sentence. This may be a correct return of income, but Demosthenes will not concede anything of the kind; and when Aphobus appears to have given different explanations at different times, this is easily made to appear suspicious.

ἐπίτροπος, not "trustee" this time, but someone "entrusted" with the business, a manager or concessionaire. As in Pasion's bank (cf. Oration 36) this is a former slave.

20. ἀπενήνοχεν, "he has rendered an account." An English translation has to say: "If he says the workshop was idle, that is a lie, because he has himself rendered an account of expenses."

ἐπισκευάς, a vague word; "fixtures" or "attachments" might be a fair modern equivalent.

ὡς ἐργαζομένων, introducing a comparison, not neces-

122

sarily "as if," but "as he would do when they were working."

Θηριππίδῃ, dative, as would appear in the account book, "paid to Therippides."

μισθόν, "wages."

λογίζεται, "enters into the account." It was normal procedure for a man to hire out his slaves—like renting out equipment.

μὴ γενομένης, i.e. εἰ μὴ ἐγένετο.

21. γενέσθαι. Since this echoes γενομένης ἐργασίας there is no need to write ἐργασίαν.

ἔργων ἀπρασίαν, "no sale of the products."

ἀποδεδωκότα μοι φαίνεσθαι, "he ought surely to have shown himself as having returned the products to me." In better English: "should have proved that he returned the products to me (which he cannot do, since he didn't)." The active ἀποδιδόναι must be distinguished from the middle ἀποδίδοσθαι, "sell," i.e. "give away for one's own advantage." Cf. note on δανείζειν in 9.

ὧν ἐναντίον, "persons in whose presence he returned them produce as witnesses," i.e. "produce witnesses who were present when he returned them."

πῶς οὐκ ἔχει, "he *must* have in his possession."

ἔργων, the word can mean equally "work" or "product," and a Greek speaker need not make the distinction.

22. λῆμμα, "receipt" as opposed to "expenditure." It does indeed seem a piece of "pure shamelessness" to count the expenses himself and attribute the receipts to Milyas, and it is hard to believe that this is in fact what Aphobus did; but we never hear his account of the matter.

ἂν γενέσθαι, "would have happened." The infinitive represents ἂν ἐγένετο not ἂν γένοιτο.

εἰ καὶ . . . ἐπεμελεῖτο, "if in fact Milyas had been looking after the business." The imperfect in the conditional clause represents what would have been an imperfect in a statement; Demosthenes might have added in parenthesis: ἀλλ' οὐκ ἐπεμελεῖτο.

ἀναλῶσαι, λαβεῖν. ἄν could have been repeated with these infinitives, but it is not necessary.

τεκμαίρεσθαι, "draw any conclusion having regard (πρός) to his general style of behaviour," i.e. if we are to use his general behaviour as an indication (τεκμήριον) of what he is likely to do in this matter. Greek rhetorical theory recognized the value of such τεκμήρια in argument, and Athenian courts were not as particular as our courts are supposed to be in distinguishing them from evidence. Demosthenes is suggesting to the court how they should interpret evidence before it is actually presented to them.

23. ταύτας τοίνυν ἔχει, "he has therefore . . ." The inference from the evidence is presented as beyond all doubt. The 30 minas represents the income of the workshop in two years.

ἔργον, "interest on this amount" (cf. 10), 12% per annum as usual, so that the sum could have doubled itself into a talent in the interval.

τέτταρα τάλαντα, the dowry, interest plus principal amounted to 3 talents (cf. 17).

διήρπακεν, quite an offensive word, "grabbed, plundered." Cf. 7.

ὅσ' ἔνια, "the quantity that, some of it," i.e. "amounts which in some instances he argues were not even left in the estate at all."

24. ἀφανίζουσιν, "make them disappear, eliminate from

their accounting." What is meant will soon become clear.

ὑποκειμένους, cf. 9.

οἴκοι. This shows that there was no separate factory and that the work was done in the house. Cf. the scene described in Lysias, *Against Eratosthenes* 8.

δώδεκα μνᾶς, cf. 9.

οὐδέν . . . ἀλλ' οὐδὲ μικρόν, "nothing—no, not even a small amount." Thus Aphobus is made to appear worse than Therippides, who at least declared some income, even though "less than he should" (19).

ὀλίγου δεῖν, "only a little short of, almost." Cf. Smyth, 1399, 2012d; GG 1116, 1538.

εἰς τοῦτ' ἀναιδείας, cf. Smyth, 1325; GG. 1088.

25. κενότατον, "most absurd, totally lacking in substance."

ὁ ὑποθείς, cf. note on 9. His name is Moeriades (cf. 27).

ἐράνους, loans made by a group of persons, as a friendly act, on which interest would not be payable.

λέλοιπεν, "has left unpaid."

ὑπέρχρεως, "heavily in debt." The inference is that the guardians said they had surrendered the slaves to meet the other obligations of Moeriades and that his other creditors had a prior claim—and that Moeriades had no business to borrow from the elder Demosthenes if the slaves were already pledged elsewhere. But Demosthenes is not explicit about any of this, and contrives to make their story seem more suspicious by giving so few details; he insists that they gave none of the details which might make their story credible.

πρός τίνα δίκην, "in face of what lawsuit they have been defeated in respect of them," i.e. "how they lost them in a lawsuit."

οὐκ ἔχουσιν εἰπεῖν, "they cannot explain," because (so Demosthenes argues) there is not a word of truth in their story—"no health in it."

26. τούτων ἂν ἀντελαμβάνοντο, "they would have held on to the slaves." Their apparent willingness to let the slaves go so easily is indeed suspicious, and demands an explanation. The next section shows that Demosthenes does not believe Moeriades is a rogue at all; thus he can rightly say here that his bad character is no concern of his.

νῦν δέ, "but the fact is . . ." Thus we are brought back to immediate reality, in contrast to what might have happened and what the defendants say took place—their behaviour is "utterly heartless," without a thought for their unfortunate ward.

καρπώσαντες, "having enjoyed the fruits (i.e. the earning powers) of these men."

27. ἄπορος, "insolvent," but this is an ambiguous word meaning either "one who has no way or means" (poor, helpless) or "one who offers no way of attack" (unassailable), as a bankrupt might be.

συμβόλαιον, a general word for a contract, here a contract of loan. Demosthenes naturally resents the suggestion that his father had made a contract "like a fool" with a rogue, who could not repay the loan.

τὸ ἐργαστήριον, "the team of workers," who constitute the "workshop."

εἰς ταῦτα συμβαλεῖν, "make a contract of loan, using these slaves as security," i.e. grant a loan accepting these slaves as security, though they are already pledged to the estate; the active verb is used of lending, cf. τῷ εἰς τὰ ἡμέτερα δανείσαντι in 28.

A second loan on the same security, like a second mortgage on a house in our own time, is legitimate if the first creditor makes no objection. In the next paragraph Demosthenes speaks as though he, and not the estate, were the first creditor; but if the trustees of the estate are willing, there is nothing illegal about the transaction, though we may agree with Demosthenes that it is scarcely proper "for a trustee at least" (ἐπίτροπόν γ' ὄντα) to use trust funds for his own purposes.

28. ἡμῖν μέν . . . οἳ πρότερον συνεβάλομεν, "to us who put up the first loan." As his father's heir Demosthenes regards himself as the creditor, as though it were he who had lent Moeriades the money.

εἰ . . . πρὸς τῷ λῆμμ' ἀπ' αὐτῶν μηδὲν γεγονέναι, "if in addition to getting no income from them we also lose the slaves themselves who were pledged to us as security."

τῷ δέ . . . δανείσαντι καί . . . πράξαντι, "the man who lent the money accepting our property as security and recovered his due over the years." πράττειν means to obtain or exact money, equally the principal or the interest on a loan. Demosthenes presumably wants the jury to think that Aphobus got interest on this second loan in addition to the money which the slaves earned.

29. The evidence showed that an annual income of 12 minas was actually obtained from the slaves' work.

παρὰ τοὺς κλινοποιούς, "in respect of." Cf. Thuc. 1, 141.7, παρὰ τὴν ἑαυτοῦ ἀμέλειαν, "in consequence of his own carelessness."

ἐξ ἀφανοῦς ποθεν "to be looked for in (literally 'from') some obscure corner."

παραλογίσασθαι, "to overlook in reckoning." Compounds with παρα- often indicate error or oversight, cf. παραβαίνω, παροράω.

φανερῶς οὑτωσί, "perfectly clearly," cf. γνώριμον οὑτωσί, "quite well known," in 32.11.

μικροῦ δεῖν, "almost," cf. note on ὀλίγου δεῖν in 24. More exactly 2⅔ talents; but this is more than Demosthenes can claim, since slaves as they grow older will decline in capital value, and the decline in ten years will have been considerable. Cf. Introduction, p. 19.

30. οὐδὲ γὰρ ταῦτα, "for not even these items," better "even these items they fail to report in their accounts."

κεκτημένον, "a man who possessed," i.e. the elder Demosthenes.

οὐχ οἷόν τε μὴ οὐχί, a strong double negative, "it is impossible that he didn't."

ταῦτά γ', an *ergasterion* can exist without machinery or buildings, but it must have material as well as workmen.

31. δυοῖν τέχναιν, "two industries." The point is that the elder Demosthenes was not only wealthy, but experienced in business; he would not allow the stock of material to run out and leave his workmen idle. The sentence is carefully put together; the situation of the proprietor with his two active workshops is presented first: "Look at the kind of man he was; they say he left no material for the work and expect us to believe them."

32. ἐκ τούτων αὐτῶν, masculine not neuter, "these men themselves."

τῷ βουλομένῳ πρὸς ὠνεῖσθαι τῶν ἄλλων, "for anyone else also who wanted to buy." πρός is adverb, like χωρίς in 33.

ἐκεῖθεν, points forward, "from the following point."

αὐτός τ᾽ ἐπώλει. An interesting detail about the business. Note the various words for selling in this and the next section: ἀποδίδοσθαι, πιπράσκειν, πωλεῖν.

33. τὸν καταλειφθέντα, i.e. ἐλέφαντα καὶ σίδηρον.

φαίνηται . . . ἐξαρκῶν, "is found to have been enough for such large working parties."

πλείω τῶν ἐγκεκλημένων (from ἐγκαλέω). It is time for Demosthenes to make it clear once again that he is really claiming less than he could if he insisted on every detail. Cf. 17.

34. παρὰ τὸν λόγον, "in accordance with," not "contrary to."

ἐξ ὧν . . . ὁμολογοῦσιν, "from their own admissions of what they received."

τούτων πλείω τιθείς, "reckoning their expenses higher than they do."

χωρίς is adverbial and does not govern τούτων.

ἀπέδοσαν, "active, gave back, restored to me." Cf. 21.

ἀφαιρῶν, "subtracting."

οὐ μικρᾶς ἀναιδείας, descriptive genitive, "undertakings of no small shamelessness," i.e. "fantastically impudent."

35. χωρὶς ὧν . . . ἐπιδείξω, "apart from what I shall show." Here χωρίς is used like a preposition with the genitive, not as in 33 and 34 where it stands by itself.

οὐχ ἄθρουν, "not all at once," "not in a lump sum." The income, naturally, came in gradually over the years, while the capital came into their hands εὐθύς.

36. τροφήν, "the cost of my upbringing."

129

λογιστέον "one must count, include in the account." The figures come early in each sentence, so that the hearers have time to do the arithmetic before the next sentence starts. The reckoning alternates between minas and drachmas, e.g. 700 drachmas instead of 7 minas.

τὸ περιόν, "what is left over, the balance."

τούτων πλείω, the same kind of concession as before, cf. 34.

δοκιμασθέντι, "when I came of age." See note on 5.

ὅσον . . . εἰσενηνόχασιν, "the amount of *eisphora* that they paid." See note on 7.

τοῦ προσόντος, "the additional amount." "8 talents plus" is what is meant.

37. εἰσφοράς. It is interesting to see how little they actually paid in tax over ten years.

ὑπερβαλὼν τοῦτο, "going one better in this detail also," another concession. The literal meaning of *hyperbole* is "overshooting."

τὸ τάλαντον, 30 plus 31 minas; the odd mina is ignored.

τὰ λειπόμενα, "the remainder."

ἀναγκαῖον, "they *must* have it, there is no escaping it."

ἐκ τῶν ἐμῶν, not "taken this out of my property," but "acquired this amount in income out of my property." This is income earned by the estate, and does not belong to them.

38. νῦν δέ, "but in fact."

καὶ πρός, "in addition actually." Cf. note on 32.

περιφανὴς ἀναισχυντία, "flagrant and outrageous defiance."

τηλικαύτας ὑπερβολὰς ἔχοντα, "behaviour which shows such extremes of dishonesty," "far beyond the mark." Cf. note on 37.

τὸ δεινόν, "monstrous behaviour, villainy."

39. τὸ καθ' αὑτόν, "for his own part, as an individual."

ὀκτὼ καὶ ἑκατόν. This figure is not explained, but evidently occurred in the documents read out in evidence. And since the interest is less than 12 %, there will have been a detailed accounting of that also.

ὡς ἀληθῆ λέγω, "to show that this account is true."

ἅπαν ἀνηλωκέναι. Demosthenes does not say for what purpose they said they had spent all the income, or even consider whether such expenses might have been legitimate; that is left for the defence to argue.

40. τὰς διαθήκας. Now we (and the jury) learn for the first time that Demosthenes has never seen the text of his father's will, and that his knowledge of the details comes from what his mother told him.

ἃ κατέλιπε, "all the items which he left in his estate."

ἐξ ὧν ἔδει τούτους, "from what sources they were to obtain the money for their legacies."

ἅπως μισθώσουσι, "instructions for farming out the estate" (cf. note on 15).

41. οὐ βουλόμενοι. This is confidently stated as the true reason for not producing the will; in their own defence they will have to explain why they kept Demosthenes from seeing it.

ἵνα μὴ δοκῶσιν ἔχειν, "so as to make it appear that they never received the gifts made to them."

ὥσπερ οὐκ ... ἐξελεγχθησόμενοι. ὡς with a participle introduces a comparison, "acting like people who would not be exposed and disproved." But since it is contended that "the facts" have disproved their contentions, "as

131

though they would not be" reproduces the sense of contempt that is implied for men who are as naive as they are dishonest.

ὧν ἐναντίον, "evidence of people before whom they answered our questions." Cf. 21.

αὐτοῖς is ethical dative again. See note on 8.

42. οὗτος picks up where the document which has been read in evidence leaves off: "Here is a man who says." It is not Aphobus (who is τούτῳ later in the sentence), but Therippides, who denies receiving his particular legacy.

ἃς Θ. ἔλαβεν, "which in fact he received," as stated in 5. It is a strong point in Demosthenes' favour when he shows each trustee giving the version of the will that suits his own purpose best and the apparent lack of honour among thieves.

43. οὗτος αὖ. This time it is Aphobus, and ἐκεῖνος is Therippides.

ἵνα μὴ δοκῇ, cf. 41. The infinitive λαβεῖν can be taken equally with δοκῇ and ὁμολογῆσαι.

οὐδ' οὗτος, "he also fails to reveal the total value of the estate."

τὸ μισθοῦν, "the order to farm it out." An infinitive can report a command as well as a statement.

προσομολογῆσαι. The προς- compounds in these sections deserve attention; translation demands a word like "add" or "include."

44. The total amount of the estate is revealed indirectly because each trustee mentions the considerable sums left to the others, though denying that he received anything himself; thus the truth is revealed "despite their efforts to

conceal and minimize my inheritance" (καίπερ ἀφανιζόντων τούτων τὴν οὐσίαν).

ἐκ τεττάρων ταλάντων, "a man who used 4½ talents to give so much in dowries etc." The sentence will be understood more easily if the Greek word order is carefully observed: "It was no small estate from which such sums were set aside—it must have been more than twice as much, the legacy that he intended for me, if he set these sums aside for them."

45. In this section Demosthenes tries to present the same argument in terms of his father's presumed intentions; his generosity to Therippides and Demophon can be explained only by the size of the legacy intended for his son and by his determination to ensure that they were faithful trustees or at least had no excuse for being otherwise.

ἕνεκα, "because of, in view of, in consideration of," not "for the sake of," which is the commoner meaning.

ἵνα διαπράξαιτο. Cf. the account of his father's intentions in 5.

εἰ τοιούτων ἀξιωθέντες τοιαῦτ' εἰς ἡμᾶς ἐξαμαρτάνοιεν, "if entrusted with such large responsibilities (as he gave them) they behaved in such a shameful way (as I have described)."

46. τὰ ἑαυτοῦ πράττειν φησίν, "says that this is his own business (and that we have no right to meddle with it)."

αἰσχροκερδίας, "contemptible meanness." Thus Aphobus is presented as a rich man who dodges taxes and refuses to pay teachers' fees. This devastating detail is postponed until now, when it will have its maximum effect on the jury.

47. ἀπεσχημένον, "that he did not keep his hands away even from small things."

ὁμολογήσαντα. The participles continue, describing the various things that Aphobus is shown as "having done."

ἀπογράψαντα, cf. 14.

48. τὰς τιμάς, "the prices received for them."
παρά, "according to," see note on 34.
διῳκηκότα, "administered."

49. ἐτόλμα, "he had the effrontery."

πρὸς τῷ διαιτητῇ, "before the arbitrator." See Introduction, p. 8. Except for the opening sentences of the speech we hear only in these sections about what happened before the arbitrator.

οὔτε γὰρ ὡς ὀφείλοντά με κατέλιπεν, "neither with respect to his statement that my father left me in debt did he offer documentary proof (in the accounts), nor with respect to the persons to whom he said he paid the money has he provided witnesses." As always, it is difficult for English to follow the Greek order of words in sentences which begin with relative adverbs or pronouns.

ἐπανέφερεν, "entered to the credit of his fellow trustees."

50. ἐρωτηθείς. The arbitrator questioned Aphobus in detail, and formed a low opinion of him. The words that begin the clauses show the emphasis in his questions: τὴν οὐσίαν τὴν αὐτοῦ, "what about your *own* property? how did you manage it?" And πότερον ἐπιτροπευθείς, "if *you* had been in the care of a guardian, would you have accepted this story?" The participle ἐπιτροπευθείς has conditional force (for the verb cf. note on 5). As we

learn in the following section, the arbitrator gave judgment against Aphobus; but there was no compulsion to accept such a decision, and the jury might disregard it.

προὐκαλεῖτο. Instead of answering the arbitrator's awkward questions Aphobus issued a πρόκλησις. "Challenge" is the usual non-technical translation, but a *proklesis* can take the form of a demand or invitation issued to one's opponent—to produce a document or witness for examination, to swear an oath, or submit to some procedure—or it may be an offer to do the same on one's own part. Often a *proklesis* is made to look like a concession, a pledge of good faith, so that, if it is refused, the other party will appear in a bad light, though in fact it may be an illusory or irrelevant concession or a quite unreasonable demand. In this instance Aphobus undertakes to prove that the sum due was no more than ten talents and has been paid in full, challenges Demosthenes to prove the contrary, and offers to make good any unpaid deficit if it can be proved. Demosthenes accepts the offer, and then complains that Aphobus offers no proof at all.

ἐπιδεῖξαι . . . οὖσαν, "to prove that the estate consisted of ten talents." But Aphobus also claimed that the amount had been paid in full, as subsequent argument shows.

51. οὐδ' ὥς . . . . "nor did he show that his co-trustees had paid; if he had, the arbitrator would not have given judgment against him." γάρ, as so often, means "for otherwise." The reference to the arbitrator's judgment is deliberately casual; it was useless to insist upon it, since the jury might not pay any attention to it.

μαρτυρίαν δ' ἐνεβάλετο, "he presented a statement by a

witness to this effect." This is the usual verb for sub-
mitting a document—"throwing it into" the *echinus*, the
container in which papers to be exhibited at the trial were
kept under seal. Demosthenes prefers to wait and see
whether this statement will be produced in court before
he offers any comment on it.

καὶ νῦν, "now too," i.e. just as he did before the arbitrator.

τίνος παραδόντος, a question in the form of a genitive
absolute, "because who paid it to me?" A translator
had better say: "Ask him from whom I got it."

καθ' ἕκαστον, "witnesses for each of the three trustees."

52. εἶναί μοι, i.e. ἔχειν ἐμέ.

διπλασίοις ἐλάττω, "too little by double," i.e. only one
third of the proper sum, falling short of the right sum by
twice its own amount: "If he claims that I have been
paid, by reckoning as paid to me what is in the hands of
each of the others, he will of course be talking (φανήσεται
λέγων) of a sum only one third of the right amount."

ἔχοντα, the emphatic word: "And he still won't prove
that I *have* the money." Suppose I admit, says Demosthenes, that he has paid his share; that is only one third
of the whole amount; he doesn't make me any richer by
saying that the others have paid their shares.

ὥστ' οὐ . . . λεκτέον: "Instead of presenting calculations
which show that I have the money if all three have paid
up, he ought to show that either he or his co-trustees *did*
pay up." Demosthenes talks like a plain man to plain
men who are always baffled by accounting: "Nicely
balanced statements don't prove anything; the fact is he
hasn't paid, and his *proklesis* is a worthless piece of
bravado which you should disregard; he cannot prove that
I have been paid."

53.   Another side of Aphobus' character is now presented;
not only is he dishonest, but he must think the jury very
naive if he expects them to believe this story of a cache in
the house.   It is represented as his final desperate attempt
to save his case, when he found himself "thoroughly
baffled" (πολλὰ ἀπορηθείς) before the arbitrator.

δεινότατον, a "very strange" and "very shocking" lie.

κυρίαν ἐποίησεν, "gave her control of it."

καὶ νῦν, cf. note on 51.   One purpose, Demosthenes
argues, in making such a fantastic statement was to make
me waste time (διατρίβειν) in court, when I ought (δέον) to
be dealing with more serious charges.   In fact, of course,
Demosthenes welcomes the opportunity to talk about
it.   ὡς οὐ ῥηθησομένων, a genitive absolute, with the statement (ταῦτα) as subject: "If, on the assumption that it
would not be mentioned, I left it out."   εἴποι, after ἵνα
like διατρίβοιμι.   This is Aphobus' purpose.   ἧττον . . .
ἐλεοίμην.   Demosthenes will of course have a weaker case
if he cannot claim sympathy or pity (ἔλεος) as a poor
man.

54.   ἐνεβάλετο, cf. 51.

δι' ἐκείνων, "by that means," but Blass reads εἰκῇ,
"wildly, without reason," an attractive conjecture since
in 28.5 εἰκῇ πιστεύεσθαι is used for "being believed on the
strength of a bare statement," without supporting
evidence.

χρέα.   We hear no details of these supposed "debts"
until the second speech; Aphobus maintained that
Demosthenes' grandfather owed money to the state
treasury (εἶπεν γὰρ ὡς ὁ πάππος ὤφειλε τῷ δημοσίῳ, 28.1).
For the present they are treated as part of the fiction that
Aphobus has concocted.   They are introduced at this
point only to suggest that this story is not even consistent

with itself, that he cannot make up his mind whether Demosthenes is really rich or poor.

55. Demosthenes is not satisfied with merely ridiculing the story of the cache; but since he cannot disprove it by evidence, he has to show that the behaviour attributed to his father is so improbable (contrary to τὸ εἰκός) as to be unbelievable. Aphobus apparently claimed that the elder Demosthenes told him of the cache, an unlikely thing for a man to do if he distrusted the guardians. Three possible combinations of circumstances, all equally unlikely, are set forth for the jury to consider:

(a) A man refuses to let the guardians have control over the major part of the property (since he distrusts them), and then tells them about the cache; only a madman would do that (μανία γὰρ δεινή).

(b) A man gives the guardians control over the major part of the property, but hides some of it (since he distrusts them)—and then tells them about it (δῆλον ὅτι οὐκ ἄν . . .).

(c) A man trusts the guardians, gives them control of most of the property, but keeps some of it out of their control—why, if he trusts them? (εἰ δ' ἐπίστευεν, οὐκ ἂν δήπου . . .).

To a modern reader this may seem the more natural order in which to consider the alternatives, but Demosthenes puts them in the order (b) (a) (c). It is the last to which he devotes most attention, since he does not doubt his father's trust in the guardians.

οὐκ ἂν δήπου. What he "surely would not do" is the μέν . . . δέ combination. Cf. Denniston, *Greek Particles*, p. 371. When μέν follows a negative, it is the μέν . . . δέ combination of events that is negatived, not the μέν clause by itself—as is very clear in this instance.

At first sight, this combination of behaviour does not seem so improbable. But with οὐδ' ἂν τῇ μέν we have another μέν . . . δέ combination negatived—"giving my mother control of the cache and then arranging for one of the guardians to marry her; that does not make sense (οὐ γὰρ ἔχει λόγον), to make her κυρία of the cache and then make one of the guardians κύριος of her and the money" (as would be the effect in Attic law, if he married her).

56. But how very strange, in such a situation, that he did not in fact marry her! That is incredible, no matter which alternative you consider (εἴ τι τούτων ἦν ἀληθές, "if any one of these alternatives were true," which they are not).

ὅς, "this man who." Here we are back to Aphobus and the admitted facts. He received the dowry, and then married someone else.

τοῦ Μελιτέως, "of the deme of Melite."

ἔνδον, "in the house,"

οὐκ ἂν ἡγεῖσθ' αὐτὸν κἂν ἐπιδραμεῖν, "don't you think he would simply jump at the chance." The first ἄν shows that an infinitive with conditional force is coming, then ἄν is repeated, as frequently—the "iterated ἄν." See Smyth, 1765; GG. 1312.

57. φανερὰν οὐσίαν, "the recognizable estate," which was identifiable and indisguisable, unlike a sum in cash "about which the jury would never know anything" (ὧν οὐκ ἐμέλλετ' ὑμεῖς ἔσεσθαι μάρτυρες).

ἀπέσχετ' ἄν. The ἄν is important: "would he have kept his hands away from it?" The accusative absolute ἐξὸν αὐτῷ supplies the "if" clause, "if the opportunity had been given him."

πάντα. The word gains in importance by being postponed.

ἵν' ἧττον ἐλεηθῶ, cf. 53. Since it is easy to supply a motive for Aphobus to invent this story, Demosthenes sees no need to spend more time on it.

58. πολλά . . . καὶ ἄλλα. It is regular Greek idiom to put in the καί, while English is content with "many other."

ἕν . . . κεφάλαιον, "one fundamental charge under which all complaints can be grouped." The κεφάλαιον is like a heading, which covers and applies to all the charges; one failure explains all the other failures. If there is no defence against this, there is no defence against any of the detailed charges.

μισθώσαντι, cf. note on 15. The participle is conditional, "if he had farmed out the estate." Demosthenes has overstated his case in the previous sentence, since there was no legal compulsion to take this step. But by quoting an example, in which the result was a remarkable increase in capital value, he invites the jury to conclude that it was an almost criminal error not to follow this method of administering the estate. We need not believe that it was always so successful, as it was for Antidorus (of whom nothing is known beyond this sentence).

Προβαλίσιος, of the deme Probalinthos.

ὁ μισθωσάμενος, "the man to whom the property was leased, the man who held the lease." This is the regular meaning of the middle voice. Cf. note on δανείζεσθαι in 9.

It is useless to speculate about the details of this transaction, since we are told nothing. But the implication is that Demosthenes expects this kind of investment to earn 12% per annum, since that is what Antidorus got.

ἐν τῇ ἀγορᾷ. This must mean that the settlement was witnessed and that the transaction was public.

59. ἐμοὶ δ', in contrast to Ἀντιδώρῳ μέν. "My experience" is compared, point for point, with that of Antidorus.

πρὸς τὸν χρόνον, "in comparison with the time in his case."

προσῆκον γενέσθαι, accusative absolute, "though the result ought to have been, reasonably (κατὰ τὸ εἰκός), a tripling of the capital." This was hardly a "reasonable" expectation. But it was neither "right nor reasonable" that the capital should dwindle to nothing—and so (at the end of this section) Demosthenes wants to know "how it is right or fitting (πῶς . . . προσήκει) to accept their account."

οἱ μέν, the two others, ὁ δέ, Aphobus.

πρός, adverb, "in addition, besides." Cf. 38 and note on 32.

ἀπέγραψεν, cf. 14, where the word is used of a statement about a man's financial position: "he formally declared that I was in debt to him."

60. As in the previous section, Demosthenes takes for granted that an investment can and will bring in the return that it "ought to bring in."

τοῦ τρίτου μέρους . . . φερούσης. This is not really a fact at all—it is what "a third of the capital" (i.e. Aphobus' share) "ought to produce." And it is, as before, an extremely optimistic expectation.

τῶν προσιόντων (neuter), i.e. προσόδων, "income."

ἐῶντας, "leaving things alone, in place as they were," without displaying any great business ability. Despite the dative τούτοις the accusative is quite proper as subject of the infinitive.

τρέφειν could mean "pay for our upbringing," but since his mother is involved as well as his sister, it perhaps means simply "take care of us, maintain us."

τὰ πρὸς τὴν πόλιν διοικεῖν, a very vague expression, but in the context it means "meet his obligations towards the city," i.e. taxes and services.

περιεγίγνετο, the imperfect is important, "the surpluses that were available each year."

προσπεριποιεῖν. περιποιεῖν is used of capital acquisition, cf. 30.31 τὰ ἐμὰ πρὸς τοῖς ἐκείνου περιποιεῖν ἐζήτησεν. So the meaning here is "add these sums to the capital."

61. τὴν δ' ἄλλην οὐσίαν "the rest of the estate," i.e. the other two-thirds, since the income from one third would have been enough to meet current needs.

ἐνεργὸν ποιήσασιν, "making it productive, putting it to work." The dative of the participle is used, quite correctly after ἐξὸν τούτοις, but with the first set of infinitives an accusative participle had been used, equally correctly (cf. note on ἐῶντας in 60).

αὐτοῖς τε . . . μέτρι' ἐξ αὐτῶν λαβεῖν. After taking a "modest amount" for themselves (in return for their services) they should have used the rest of the income to increase the οἶκος (the capital).

ἀφανίσαντες, cf. 24.

ἐμοῦ μέν, in the genitive this time (in contrast to ἐμοί earlier in the section and σφίσιν αὐτοῖς which follows) to show what "they took away from me."

καὶ τὴν ὑπάρχουσαν πρόσοδον, "even the existing income," not to mention the income they should have obtained if they had handled the estate properly.

κατεσκευάσαντο, "contrived, organized for themselves."

62. λαβόντες, "after getting into their own hands."

μηδὲ καταλειφθῆναι, "they argue that it was not even left by my father, that it never existed." ἀμφισβητεῖν means "dispute," but as with "denying" a negative is often used with the infinitive, to emphasize that the statement is a negative one. Cf. 15 and note.

ἀπενηνόχασιν, perfect of ἀποφέρω, "they base their accounts on an estate of *that* size," i.e. as though it were worth only five talents.

οὐ πρόσοδον μέν. The negative affects the μέν ... δέ combination (see note on 55 above). Instead of "showing no income, but keeping the capital intact" (which would have been a lesser offence), they made "the bare-faced claim" that the actual capital had been spent.

63. ἐπετροπεύθην. For this passive use of the verb cf. 5 and 50.

οὐκ ἂν ἔχοιεν εἰπεῖν, because even with more time and greater ingenuity they could hardly have treated me worse; and they would not care to give the answer which Demosthenes now offers.

ὅπου, "whereas."

παρὰ μὲν τῶν ... τῷ δέ, "the other two" and "Aphobus."

πῶς οὐκ ἄξιον διαγανακτεῖν. Since this seems a rather feeble complaint, editors since Blass are inclined to reject it as the addition of a scribe who did not understand the grammar of the sentence. If the phrase is omitted and δῆλον δή read instead of δῆλον δέ, a more forceful argument is presented: "Since this happened to me in ten years, it's perfectly obvious what would have happened if the period has been longer—if I had been left as a child one year old (ἐνιαύσιος), I should not have recovered even this small amount."

ὀρθῶς. For the moment the jury are invited to suppose that the accounting is correct.

ἐξήρκεσεν, from ἐξαρκέω, "suffice." So as to make sure of not losing the jury's sympathy, he reminds them again of the threat of real poverty which he has faced.

παρ' αὑτῶν, "out of their own pockets."

περιεῖδον, "allowed." The verb means to look all around something without seeing it, and so to let something happen without interfering ("to overlook").

64. ὥστ' ἀξιοῦσθαι λειτουργεῖν, "so as to be thought fit (or called upon) to perform liturgies," like the trierarchy or choregia.

μηδὲ μικράς, "not even small payments."

ἀναισχυντίας. The translator soon wearies of "shamelessness," and the plurals of abstract nouns have concrete meaning—"acts which show a complete lack of decent feeling."

τίνας ... ὑπερβολάς, "what chance to exaggerate have they left us in description of their behaviour?"

τὴν διαθήκην ἠφανίκασιν, "they have kept the will out of sight." It now becomes clear that Demosthenes has no copy of the will to present in court, and is dependent on witnesses.

ὡς λήσοντες, "thinking that they will escape detection." If no copy of the will is produced, they presume no one can prove that they have failed to carry out its provisions; but this expectation that "they will get away with it" is a good point against them; it suggests sheer contempt for the jury's intelligence. This section is designed to characterize the defendants, by insisting on their intentions and attitudes—they do not care what happens to me or my property, so long as they feather their own nests. Even the order of words in this last sentence shows that their predominant interest is in their property, not mine.

ὥσπερ . . . ἀδικηθέντες, "as though they had suffered an injury at my hands." If they had, the jury might be disposed to sympathize with their vindictiveness—but not with the sheer inhumanity which the next section attributes to them.

65. οὐδὲ τῶν εἰς ὑμᾶς ἁμαρτανόντων, "not even in the case of persons who commit offences against you," i.e. against Athens, since the jury represents the state. The reason for the genitive does not appear until ἀφείλεσθε, "you took away from them." Aorists are used in this sentence to describe what juries generally do and have done—a gnomic use. Cf. Smyth, 1931-32; GG. 1293-94.

ἐλεήσαντες. Thus juries show humanity towards the families of convicted criminals, but Aphobus and his colleagues, who have been well treated, show *hybris* in return.

οὐδ᾽ ἠσχύνθησαν . . ., "they felt no shame at my sister's misfortune, if . . ."

ἀξιωθεῖσα, "thought worthy of." This was the dowry which had been set aside for her, cf. 5. If deprived of her dowry she had little chance of finding a suitable husband. The special sort of meanness described in this paragraph has been postponed until the end of the speech, as a final indication of the defendants' character.

66. πρὸς ἀμφότερ᾽ ἀπορῶ, "I am at a loss in face of these

two problems," to find a husband for my sister and manage the rest of the family affairs.

προσεπικεῖται, "is on my neck besides, demanding taxes".

67. Demosthenes is now busy seeking sympathy from the jury, showing how his problems have mounted up. His attempt to recover his property is a perilous affair.

ὃ μὴ γένοιτο, "which Heaven forbid," the King James version of St. Paul, when he uses the phrase, will serve well to show that this is a prayer as well as a wish.

ἐπωβελίαν. The penalty to which a plaintiff was liable, in certain suits, if judgment went against him, and less than one-fifth of the votes were in his favour: an obol in each drachma or one-sixth of the sum which he was claiming; 100 minas is one-sixth of ten talents. Fear of the penalty was supposed to deter purely vexatious prosecutions (sycophantia).

τιμητόν, "an estimate of the sum due has to be made." In a τιμητὸς ἀγών the jury not only decides between plaintiff and defendant but has the additional responsibility of "estimating" the penalty or the damages (in an ἀτίμητος ἀγών these matters would be established by law). As readers of Plato's *Apology* will remember, the jury had to accept the defendant's or the plaintiff's proposal; no compromise between them was allowed, and most defendants (unlike Socrates) were prudent in making suggestions that the jury might reasonably adopt. Demosthenes here is making the point that, even if he wins the case against Aphobus, it does not follow that then he will be awarded the sum which he claims, since Aphobus will suggest a smaller amount—and it will be no hardship for him to pay a fraction of what he owes out of money that does not belong to him!

146

ἐμοὶ δ' ἀτίμητον, since Demosthenes will get nothing at all if he loses his case—and may even have to pay the epobelia.

οὐ μόνον . . . ἀλλὰ καὶ πρὸς ἠτιμωμένος, "punished with *atimia* in addition," i.e. deprived of all civic rights, disenfranchised. This does not mean that the losing plaintiff is punished in this way, and Demosthenes seems to be exaggerating the danger that he faces. An unsuccessful plaintiff in a criminal case who incurred *epobelia* might be deprived of some legal rights (as was Aeschines, when he received less than one-fifth of the votes in the case *On the Crown*) and an Athenian condemned to pay a fine to the state which was beyond his powers to pay might prefer to go into exile, taking with him whatever cash he could gather together. But the *epobelia* to which Demosthenes would be liable was not a sum of such dimensions, and it is difficult to see how he was seriously threatened with *atimia* at all.

68. δέομαι, the final emotional plea to the jury.

μνησθέντας, aorist participle, because it corresponds to an aorist imperative, "remind yourselves."

οὓς ὀμόσαντες δικάζετε, "which having sworn you sit in judgment," i.e. "which you swore before taking your place on the jury." Orators frequently remind the jurors of the oath by which they are bound. In *Against Timocrates* (24.148) Demosthenes has the oath read out to them. The authenticity of the document, which is preserved in our texts at this point, is doubtful (as with all documents given in our manuscripts), but it is certainly correct in many details. See the note at this point in the Budé edition (ed. Navarre and Orsini); Lipsius, *Att. Recht*, pp. 151–52; Bonner & Smith, *The Administration of Justice from Homer to Aristotle*, II, pp. 152–56. Among other things the juror had sworn to listen to both sides and give his verdict in accordance with the laws.

τὰ δίκαια, "give me the assistance to which I am entitled." Cf. 3 and note.

περὶ πλείονος . . . ποιήσασθαι, "to consider of greater importance," a very common expression in the orators, with or without περί.

δίκαιοι δ' ἔστε, not "you are entitled to," which is sometimes the meaning, but "you are obliged to," "justice demands that." The context generally makes it clear which meaning is intended, since the infinitive shows what "you will be right in doing."

τἀλλότρια, "other people's property."

ὧν, genitive because of στερομένους, "deprived of what our father left us."

ἀτιμίας, cf. note on preceding section.

69. μέγα . . . στενάξαι. "Turn in his grave" would be the natural modern equivalent. The jury would be reminded of Homeric passages like *Iliad* 7.125: ἦ κε μέγ' οἰμώξειε γέρων ἱππηλάτα Πηλεύς.

τῶν προικῶν. The reason for the genitive becomes clear with ὑπὲρ τούτων, "if he saw that in the case of the dowries . . . in fighting for them his son was running the risk of *epobelia*."

κινδυνεύοντα is equal to ἐν κινδύνῳ ὄντα and so needs a genitive to define the danger.

ἄλλους . . . τῶν πολιτῶν. The voice pauses here; the genitives which follow are not in agreement with πολιτῶν. The phrase οὐ μόνον συγγενῶν . . . ἀπορούντων looks like a genitive absolute, and may well be so regarded by a translator: "when not only relatives but friends are hard up for money." But it is justified grammatically by θυγατέρας παρὰ σφῶν αὐτῶν ἐκδόντας, "had contributed money out of their pockets to arrange marriages for the daughters of friends as well as relatives who were in need." The obligation to help was of course stronger within the family, but a man of decent feeling would be glad to help his friends.

ἐκδόντας, the regular word for "giving in marriage," which implies a dowry; the word is contrasted with ἀποδοῦναι, "to give back."

καὶ ταῦτ' ἔτει δεκάτῳ, "and that too in the tenth year," i.e. after more than nine years. He has presumably enjoyed the interest on the money all this time, so that he should not be out of pocket.

The speech ends by insisting on the meanness and selfishness of Aphobus, so that he will now find himself facing a hostile jury.

AGAINST APHOBUS II (28)

This is the prosecutor's reply to the defendant's speech; a final speech by the defendant would follow. It reveals something of the tactics of the defence; but since only a short time is allowed for it, Demosthenes does not go into much detail about "all the lies that Aphobus has told;" he concentrates his attack on one or two details of the story, and begins by taking up a point which Aphobus is reserving for his final speech.

1. τῶν ῥηθέντων, "of all the things he said."

τῷ δημοσίῳ, "to the state, the public treasury." Sons and grandsons could be held responsible for a man's public debts (such as unpaid taxes or fines); they might be liable to disenfranchisement (*atimia*) if the debts remained unpaid, and their property might be seized. But since, as will appear in 3, this is Demosthenes' maternal grandfather, it is doubtful if he was in fact liable at all for his debts. In any case, the argument was clearly one that Aphobus would use only if he thought everything else had failed; its only purpose would be to maintain that, if he was going to lose the property, Demosthenes had no more right to it than he had.

μισθωθῆναι. Cf. 27.15 and note.

ἵνα μὴ κινδυνεύσῃ. It is not specified exactly what risk

they would run by farming out the estate, except that they would draw attention to it and perhaps invite an attempt by the state to take possession of it. But there was not in any case any secrecy about the estate, as Demosthenes had already pointed out (27.7–9).

πρόφασιν. The failure to farm out the estate needed an excuse or explanation.

ὡς ὤφλεν, "that he once owed money, had been in debt." This is not at all the same thing as showing that "he was in debt," ὡς ὀφείλει (cf. the next section), or that he died in debt (ὀφείλων).

ἐνεβάλετο. Cf. 27.51 and note. By waiting until the last moment before producing the document he left no time for Demosthenes to collect evidence that could counter it.

ταύτην, i.e. τὴν μαρτυρίαν, object of ἐνεβάλετο.

εἰς τὸν ὕστερον λόγον, "until his second speech." Whether he even mentioned the supposed debt in his earlier speech is not quite clear, though he presumably spoke of it before the arbitrator.

διαβαλεῖν, "prejudice." διαβολή, "slander," is always an underhand weapon, which one accuses one's adversary of using.

2. ἐφ' ᾧ φρονεῖ μάλιστα, which corresponds to ἐφ' ᾧ μάλιστ' ἠγανάκτησα. μέγα φρονεῖν, "to be proud, pride oneself."

εἰ . . . ἐξεγένετο, "if it had been possible."

τῷ χρόνῳ τοῦτ' ἐνηδρεύθημεν. ἐνεδρεύειν means "to sit waiting in a trap" for someone (Latin *insidere*), "to trap," and the cognate accusative τοῦτο needs a noun in translation, "if we had not had this trap set for us." It is "the time-element" (χρόνος) which constituted the trap.

τὰ πρὸς τὴν πόλιν, a noun is needed in translation, "his obligations towards the city."

τεκμηρίοις. The contrast between such "indications" and actual evidence is common in the orators; since Demosthenes has no statements by witnesses ready, he must be content with showing that the story of the debt is highly unlikely. Cf. note on 27.22.

φανερά, English would prefer an adverb, "openly."

3. This section helps us to complete the family tree; evidently it is Gylon who is supposed to have been the debtor. It is interesting to see that this side of the family is also reasonably wealthy.

τέτταρα τάλαντα . . .. For these figures see 27.5. This was actual cash.

4. For the taxes paid by the guardians on behalf of the estate see 27.7 and 37.

τούτων, "these statements" about the debt.

ηὐλαβήθη, transitive; the aorist middle of this verb is not used.

5. λέγοντας. It does not matter whether one takes the subject to be Aphobus and the others, or simply "persons."

ἐξ ἧς ἦν εἰδέναι. Although they did not produce the will, this was the place "from which knowledge was to be obtained." Greek idiom regularly uses an indicative in this kind of statement, although English often prefers "would have been," as χαλεπὸν ἦν εἰδέναι, "it would have been hard to distinguish."

εἰκῇ, cf. note on 27.54, "without any basis."

παρασημήνασθαι, "seal up," cf. Latin obsignare.

ἦν. In order to express the purpose of what "could,

would or should" have been done (as here, "they should
have given orders to seal"), ἵνα is used with a past tense
of the indicative, "so that it would have been possible."
Cf. Smyth, 2185c; GG. 1381.

ἐπανελθεῖν, "go back to" or "refer."

The failure of the guardians to produce the will is
naturally a point that tells very heavily against them; the
jury will inevitably assume that they have suppressed
it, because it would bear out what Demosthenes says;
Demosthenes does not point out what must seem obvious.

6. πολλὰ . . . οὐκ ἐγέγραπτο, "many items were not
mentioned," since these were not complete lists but
ὑπομνήματα, "notes, memoranda."

κύριοι, "masters of, in control."

τοῦ μὴ μισθοῦν . . . etc., "released from the blame for
not . . ."

ταύτην δέ. The δέ is not co-ordinate, but is used like
δή to underline the word it follows, "*this* they did not seal
up." Cf. Smyth, 2837; GG. 1432.

ἄξιόν γε πιστεύειν, "a likely story!" γε shows the
scornful tone.

7. ὅ τι τοῦτ᾽ ἔστιν. "This" is the statement that follows, which might be printed in quotation marks: "I
don't know what they mean when they say: 'Father
would not let them . . .'"

ἐμοί, with ἐμφανῆ.

ἀφανῆ, a sour little play on words. In the previous
speech much was said about "causing property to
disappear," ἀφανίζειν (27.24,26.). Cf. Section 10 below.

ἐξ ὧν τιμησάμενοι . . . εἰσεφέρετε. For the property
taxes paid by the guardians on behalf of the estate and the

inference that these taxes permitted about the size of the estate, cf. 27.7–8. Now Demosthenes complains that they do not produce or account for the capital property on the basis of which they estimated and paid the tax. By paying the tax, they admitted that this large sum was in the estate. What has happened to it?

8. For the figures see 27.5. The tax paid by the estate cannot have been based on these sums which were bequeathed to the guardians; "these sums were yours." The feminine plural is because of οὐσίαι. Nor does the small amount of property that they now produce explain why such a large tax was due.

συνετάξασθε, "assessed yourselves" or "agreed to pay." Cf. 27.8 and note.

σύνταξις, "contribution" (a less offensive word than φόρος), was the name for the money paid by members of the Fourth Century Athenian confederacy.

9. ἅ, object of διηρπάκατε, "which that you stole being convicted." English idiom will not tolerate this use of the relative pronoun; the meaning is: "after being clearly found guilty of stealing it."

ἀναφέρετε, "refer;" "support one another" is a more likely meaning than "pass the responsibility." For the varying accounts of what each guardian received cf. 27.41–49. And for the "heavy expenses" (debts supposedly owed by Demosthenes senior) cf. 27.49.

10. As in the previous speech, Demosthenes continues to insist that there is no honour among these thieves. The contrast between joint and individual action (κοινῇ, ἰδίᾳ), and public and private affairs (δημοσίᾳ, ἰδίᾳ, cf. 30.37) is very common.

ἦν εἰδέναι, cf. note on 5.

αὐτοῖς, the jury.

The following five sections recall details from the narrative, each confirmed by formal evidence. The story is summarized so as to remind the jury of matters which the defendants have not explained satisfactorily.

11. πρός. The preposition denotes the relation between the tax declaration and the property on which it is based, "appropriate to, in keeping with." πρός can be used of any relationship, cf. note on 27.2. συνετιμήσαντο. Cf. note on 27.8.

τὴν οὐσίαν. The article is important; not "they left me a property," but "the property that they left me is worth . . ."

τρεῖς ὄντες, at the end, has an effect something like "this precious trio." In 15 below it is more like "all three of them."

καταμαρτυροῦσιν. The compound shows that it is evidence *against* him.

τὸν σῖτον, "the living allowance." Cf. 27.15.

12. τὸ ἔργον, "the interest." Cf. 27.23 and the narrative in preceding sections.

ὑποτεθέντα, "pledged as security," cf. 27.24–25 and note on ὑποκειμένους in 27.9.

ἀνάλωμα. The slaves were an expensive liability if they were not employed. Were they perhaps getting old and not in the best of health? Demosthenes never denies it explicitly.

13. ἐλέφαντα. Cf. 27.30–33.

μάλιστα, "about," commonly used with numbers to show that a round figure is being given.

ἐπὶ δραχμῇ, cf. 27.17 and note on 27.9.

14. The narrative that follows, with its new details, is introduced at this point to remind the jury how serious a breach of trust there has been—a trust for which the guardians formally accepted responsibility (though Aphobus may deny it).

ὁμολογῆσαι. In the earlier narrative (27.4) we were told only that Demosthenes senior made these arrangements in his will, not that he secured verbal agreement from the guardians to the provisions he was making.

καὶ προσεισεληλυθώς, "though he went in also" (note the double compound). This and the following participle are not part of what he said, but what Demosthenes says took place in fact.

γράψας κατέλιπεν, "provisions that he left in written form in his will." A contrast between verbal and written arrangement is intended. Demosthenes has no text of the will, but claims to have proved all the provisions in his previous speech.

15. τρεῖς ὄντας, cf. note on 11 above.

συμπαρακαθισάμενος, a triple compound, "putting Demon to sit down together with them beside them." The presence of Uncle Demon as a witness is of course very important for Demosthenes. But he seems not to have been called to give evidence, either because he was dead (though we are not told of his death) or because he was unwilling to testify against his son, Demophon. In the third speech against Aphobus (29.56) he is mentioned as a fourth member of the group of guardians, a puzzling discrepancy from the account here, which has led critics to doubt the authenticity of the third speech.

τὰ σώμαθ' ἡμῶν. The choice of words must be deliberate. It seems that in the symbolism of this act the
children are thought of as "parcels" entrusted to the care
of the guardians; by putting the children in their arms,
the father puts their safety and future happiness in their
hands. He refers to them as a παρακαταθήκη, "a
deposit," a regular banking term.

διδοὺς εὐθύς, not "giving him on the spot;" it is the
language of the will that Demosthenes is trying to recall
(cf. 27.5), but the present participle should mean "offering," as though Demophon is being invited to give his
consent to the terms of the will.

ἐπισκήπτων, a strong word for legal instructions, which
translators like to render by "enjoin" or "conjure." It
must originally have been connected with the imagery of
the sceptre, with which a king tapped a man when
requiring his obedience, but the sceptre has disappeared
from Greek legal symbolism, though it plays quite a part
in Roman law—the *vindicta* with which a man claimed his
property, animate as well as inanimate.

16. ἐπὶ ταῖς ὀγδοήκοντα μναῖς. ἐπί with the dative
regularly indicates the condition or basis on which an
agreement rests—here the basis of the marriage agreement
is the dowry of 80 minas.

ἐπὶ τούτοις, "on these terms," as described in 27.5.
ἐλεεῖσθαι, passive, not middle.
τρίτος αὐτός, "himself the third," i.e. with the two others.
καὶ τούτοις, "even these 70 minas."

17. τὰς δίκας . . . εἰσιέναι, "enter upon this litigation."
ἀντίδοσιν, "exchange." A citizen who was called upon
to undertake a liturgy, like the trierarchy or choregia,

might challenge another citizen to an *antidosis*—forcing him to choose between undertaking the liturgy in his place or effecting a complete exchange of property with him. The intention was to protect the less wealthy from financial burdens that were too heavy for them; but it is not hard to believe that the procedure was misused by people who could well afford the expense of a liturgy. In the story as told here, the guardians "contrived" (παρεσκεύασαν, cf. note on 27.2) an *antidosis* for Demosthenes, using Thrasylochus who "did them the favour" (ὑπηρέτησεν, in next sentence) of co-operating. Thrasylochus challenges Demosthenes to accept the trierarchy or exchange property with him. The object is that εἰ μὲν ἀντιδοίην ("if I consented to give my property in exchange"), I should no longer be able to sue them, "on the principle that these lawsuits also became part of the property of the challenger" (ὁ ἀντιδιδούς is the man who offers or challenges, ὁ ἀντιδούς the one who agrees to the exchange). There is no evidence elsewhere that lawsuits were considered part of a man's property for the purposes of *antidosis*, but we have no direct reason to doubt it. In the speech *Against Meidias* 78–79 Demosthenes gives a more vivid account of what happened—it was the first occasion on which he crossed the path of Meidias:

μελλουσῶν εἰσιέναι τῶν δικῶν εἰς ἡμέραν ὡσπερεὶ τετάρτην ἢ πέμπτην εἰσεπήδησαν ἀδελφὸς ὁ τούτου καὶ οὗτος (i.e. Meidias, not Aphobus) εἰς τὴν οἰκίαν ἀντιδιδόντες τριηραρχ-ίαν. τοὔνομα μὲν δὴ παρέσχεν ἐκεῖνος, καὶ ἦν ὁ ἀντιδιδοὺς Θρασύλοχος, τὰ δ' ἔργα πάντ' ἦν καὶ τὰ πραττόμενα ὑπὸ τούτου. καὶ πρῶτον μὲν κατέσχισαν τὰς θύρας τῶν οἰκημάτων, ὡς αὐτῶν ἤδη γιγνομένας κατὰ τὴν ἀντίδοσιν· εἶτα τῆς ἀδελφῆς, ἔτ' ἔνδον τότε καὶ παιδὸς οὔσης κόρης,

ἐναντίον ἐφθέγγοντο αἰσχρὰ καὶ τοιαῦθ' οἶ' ἂν ἄνθρωποι
τοιοῦτοι φθέγξαιντο (οὐ γὰρ ἔγωγε προαχθείην ἂν εἰπεῖν πρὸς
ὑμᾶς τῶν τότε ῥηθέντων οὐδέν), καὶ τὴν μητέρα κἀμὲ καὶ
πάντας ἡμᾶς ῥητὰ καὶ ἄρρητα κακὰ ἐξεῖπον. ὃ δ' οὖν
δεινότατον καὶ οὐ λόγος ἀλλ' ἔργον ἤδη, τὰς δίκας ὡς αὐτῶν
οὔσας ἀφίεσαν τοῖς ἐπιτρόποις.

Meidias and his brother Thrasylochus were acting on
the assumption that Demosthenes had agreed to the
exchange of property, and assuming that the lawsuits
became their property, "they proposed to let them drop"
(ἀφίεσαν, imperfect). In fact the exchange was not
carried through, although at first the alternative ("being
ruined if I performed a liturgy with inadequate resources")
seemed worse; and when Thrasylochus "did this service
for them" (τοῦτ' αὐτοῖς ὑπηρέτησε), ἀντέδωκα μέν,
ἀπέκλεισα δ' ὡς διαδικασίας τευξόμενος. This must mean
"I consented to the exchange, but shut them out (i.e.
refused to admit them on to the property), expecting to
obtain a judicial hearing." The precise meaning is not
certain—did the *diadikasia* decide who was to perform the
liturgy (by determining which of them was the wealthier?)
or merely determine the precise extent of each party's
property? In any case, for whatever reason, Demosthenes did not "obtain this hearing" (οὐ τυχὼν δὲ ταύτης),
and since the date of the trial was very close, borrowed
money to pay the cost of the liturgy. Cf. *Meidias* 80:
δίδωμι εἴκοσι μνᾶς τούτοις, ὅσου τὴν τριηραρχίαν ἦσαν
μεμισθωκότες. They had been able to "farm out" the
trierarchy, finding someone who was willing to carry it
out for twenty minas—a smaller sum than one might have
expected; and so Demosthenes, though twenty minas
poorer, was still able to take his suit to court.

The details of *antidosis* are not as clear as one would like them to be. For further discussion see the introduction in the Budé edition to Oration 42 (*Against Phaenippus*); W. A. Goligher, "Studies in Attic Law, II," *Hermathena* 14 (1907), pp. 481–515; Lipsius, *Att. Recht*, 590–99.

18. Demosthenes now asks the jury to have some pity for his sorry plight.

δικαίως, not "justly," since envy has nothing to do with justice, but "reasonably."

τῷ μέν, Aphobus.

παραδοθείσῃ, "handed down to him," by his father presumably.

τῶν νῦν παραδοθέντων. The *antidosis* trick is represented as a device to rob him even of the 70 minas that they now are proposing to hand over to him. It is taken for granted that the property of Thrasylochus, which he was supposed to get in exchange, was not worth much. There is a careful rhetorical contrast between the good fortune of Aphobus, who gets his inheritance and a very substantial subsequent windfall, and Demosthenes, robbed of his inheritance and not even allowed to have what is finally being offered to him.

τι ἄλλο, "other than the right verdict."

τὰ ὑποκείμενα, cf. note on 27.9. The middle, τῶν ὑποθεμένων, is used of the persons who accept security, "who arrange security for their own advantage." Cf. δανείζω in the active meaning "lend," while the middle means "borrow."

τὰ περιόντα, "what is left." But everything was mortgaged, to raise money to pay for the trierarchy, according to the story in 17.

τούτου, "his property," possessive genitive.

ἐπωβελίαν. Cf. 27.67 and note.

19. μηδαμῶς, often used in entreaty, stronger than simple μή. περιίδητε is like English "overlook"—followed by a participial phrase. Cf. 27.63 and note.

ἐπὶ ταύταις ταῖς ἐλπίσιν. The "expectations" were the basis on which they relied; so "relying on" is a fair translation; and the two talents of dowry constitute the condition on which the marriage should rest.

σχετλιωτάτῳ. The adjective is from the same root as ἔχω, "holding fast, enduring," but generally in the sense of "relentless, cruel."

διάδοχον, "successor." Cf. the verb διαδέχομαι. With a fine show of public spirit, Demosthenes points out that he should "inherit" the liturgies which his father had carried out; but he cannot do it unless the court saves him from poverty.

20. In his final plea, Demosthenes reminds the jury that they will be furthering the cause of justice (τὸ δίκαιον) and their own interests as well. A plea is always stronger if justice and interest appear to coincide. The imperatives are aorist; a favourable verdict is a momentary act.

συγγενεῖς ὄντες. Relatives should have shown pity; since they did not, the court must take their place.

πρὸς παίδων . . . . etc. πρός with genitive means "from the point of view of," but in entreaties English idiom prefers "for the sake of."

ἀγαθῶν, neuter, "blessings"—picked up by the following οὕτως ὄναισθε τούτων, "so may you have joy of them." A prayer for good fortune or divine aid is often accompanied by conditions: "God bless you, if you help me," and "so" means "on these conditions." When a witness says: "I swear to tell the truth, so help me God" (*ita me Deus adiuvet*), he means: "May God help me only on this condition, if I tell the truth; if I do not, may he damn me." Sometimes, as here, the condition is denoted by a second imperative: μὴ περιίδητέ με, "So may good fortune be yours, do not let me perish." This use of "so" has become obsolete in English; a witness who says "so help me God" often does not understand what he is saying.

μηδὲ ποιήσητε. The rest of the sentence must be spoken in one breath, so that the infinitive παθεῖν will be recognized as dependent on ποιήσητε. "Make her suffer" is good Greek, as well as good English.

21. A plea for his mother, waiting at home, confident of a favourable verdict. Note that the emphasis ·is on τυχόντα rather than on the infinitive ὑποδέξεσθαι: "it will be as a successful son that she will welcome me."

ἐκδώσειν, "give in marriage;" and without money to provide an adequate dowry, it will be difficult to find a good husband for her.

ἄλλο τι, cf. 18 above and note.

ὃ μὴ γένοιτο, ἠτιμωμένον, see notes on 27.67. τῶν προσηκόντων, one of the "proper things" being a suitable marriage.

22. Demosthenes now contrasts his worth and promise as a good citizen with the worthlessness of Aphobus, who has shown no sign of any *philotimia*, being more interested in stealing other people's property than in using his wealth for the public good. Thus it cannot be in the public interest to give judgment in such a man's favour. Such a plea may not seem strictly legitimate, but it may help to turn the scale.

23. μνησθέντες, "remembering," the passive form is normally used in the aorist. πίστεις. For these different kinds of proof cf. Introduction pp. 16–17.

ἐξ ὧν, explains εἰκότων: "that which is likely, as result of what they say—if we are to judge by their statement." And their statement is made to appear a patent falsehood, when compared with the participles ὁμολογοῦντες, οὐκ ἀνηλωκότες, ἔχοντες.

24. ἐνθυμουμένους. The subject is either "you" or simply "people." Cf. 5 above, λέγοντας.

κομισάμενος, conditional participle, "if I recover." For the meaning of this verb in the middle voice cf. 27.67.

εἰκότως, not "probably" but "reasonably," while δικαίως here means "justly;" I should properly show gratitude for a just verdict.

ὑπὲρ ὧν. The neuter plural refers to property, "on behalf of which, thanks to which" he should be performing public services.

ἀποκρύψεσθαι, a shrewd underhand accusation to finish with and a return to the theme with which this speech started—concealment of property to avoid meeting obligations, a device to make an unjust action seem just.

AGAINST ONETOR I and II
ORATIONS 30 and 31

Demosthenes won his case against Aphobus. The court awarded him ten talents, but Aphobus had no intention of making it easy for him to collect this sum. He continued the struggle in the courts by suing one of the witnesses on a charge of giving false evidence, and we have the text of a third speech (Oration 29) which purports to be Demosthenes' defence of this witness; but there are a number of reasons which make it difficult to believe that the speech was delivered or intended to be delivered in this form.

We do not know all the devices that Aphobus used to prevent parts of his property from falling into Demosthenes' hands, but the case against Onetor gives us one example of his methods. When Demosthenes tried to take possession of a farm property in part payment of Aphobus' debt to him, Onetor ejected him forcibly, maintaining that he was the legal owner and that it had been transferred to him by Aphobus as a security to cover the amount of a dowry. This sum (a talent or more), according to his story, had been paid to Aphobus as the dowry of Onetor's sister when she became Aphobus' wife; but their marriage ended in divorce, the dowry was therefore due to be returned, and the farm was transferred to Onetor as security for the amount. In order to gain possession of this property, Demosthenes sues Onetor on a charge of wrongful ejectment ($\delta i\kappa\eta$ $\dot{\epsilon}\xi o\acute{u}\lambda\eta s$) maintaining that Onetor has no legal title at all to the place, that he has been working in close co-operation with Aphobus in an effort to keep his property away from his creditors, that the dowry was never paid in the first place and could not therefore be returned, and that the so-called divorce was a pure fraud and the lady (whose name we never learn) had not left her husband at all.

It is not so easy for Demosthenes to prove his case, because his adversaries have taken pains to prevent documentary evidence falling into his hands. His task is to make this strange story of conspiracy convincing and to show how every detail is designed to meet their special needs. It will be necessary to convince the jury from the beginning that they are a pair of scoundrels, and circumstantial detail is cleverly used to achieve this effect. The date of this trial seems to be more than two years later than the trial of Aphobus, and Demosthenes has acquired experience and confidence in the interval. Since Onetor is not one of his guardians, he cannot moralize on his failure to meet his obligations or his cruelty in robbing helpless orphans; the tone is more worldly and there is no place for appeals to the jury's emotions. It is also interesting to notice that Demosthenes says hardly anything about himself, does not even offer any detail of the manner in which Onetor threw him off the property—except that it was done with extreme *hybris*! Since his concern is to prove that the property still belongs legally to Aphobus, rather than to recover damages for injury to his feelings, he makes no specific effort to prove a formal case of unlawful ejectment—it is after all Aphobus, not Onetor,

166

who is really still his adversary.   But it is a little surprising that he never tells the jury what verdict he is asking them to give—is it really within their power to authorize him to take possession of the property? The suppression of any clear statement about his own immediate needs and the absence of any explanation of the court's powers in the case create a difficulty in the legal interpretation of the speech.   But the argument and the narrative are easy to follow, and the speech offers great opportunities in its delivery for a good speaker with a turn of dry humour and a scornful touch when necessary.

AGAINST ONETOR I (30)

1. περὶ πολλοῦ ποιούμενος, "while thinking it of great importance, valuing it very highly." Cf. περὶ πλείονος ποιήσασθαι in 27.68. Demosthenes is the subject of the sentence himself; though this is not made clear grammatically until we reach the finite verb, it will be clear to the audience at once when they see what it is that he thinks so important: μὴ συμβῆναι τὴν διαφοράν, "the non-happening of the quarrel." But the quarrel with Aphobus and with Onetor *did* take place, so what he means is: "While I would have given the world to prevent the quarrel happening."

τουτονί, the deictic form, "this man here in court."

κηδεστήν, in general a relation by marriage, here "brother-in-law."

προκαλεσάμενος. See note on προὐκαλεῖτο in 27.50. Here the meaning is "offer," the thing offered and the person approached being both in the accusative. "Making many fair offers to both of them" is a better rendering than "offering many and fair things."

τυχεῖν τῶν μετρίων, cf. τῶν δικαίων τυγχάνειν in 3 and also 27.1 and note. Demosthenes might have been satisfied with what was "fair and reasonable" even if he could not get what was "just"—i.e. his full due. But he fails to get any of his demands. The style of introduction

169

is very similar to that of 27. Onetor will not listen to reason, he is even more impossible than Aphobus, and there is no alternative except to sue him.

2. τὸν μέν, Aphobus, in contrast to "this man here in court."

διαδικάσασθαι, "reach a settlement" by accepting the verdict of friends. Cf. the opening sentence of 27. Making a settlement out of court will avoid the risk (πεῖρα, κίνδυνος) of facing a jury; so Onetor is asked "to be his own jury."

λόγου τυχεῖν, cf. τυχεῖν τῶν μετρίων in 1. This could mean "receive consideration" (since λόγος is a word of wide range), but the meaning here is "I was not thought worthy even to receive speech," i.e., "he would not even talk to me."

ὅτ' ὠφλίσκανε, "at the time when he lost the suit." The imperfect is used because it describes the situation of Aphobus; he was in debt to Demosthenes for ten talents, and property in his possession could be claimed as part of the payment if cash was not forthcoming.

ἐξεβλήθην. The word is deliberately left to the end—the situation described first; the land was not the legal property of Onetor, he showed *hybris* in an extreme form—"and threw me out!"

3. συναποστερεῖ . . . κηδεστῇ, "joins his brother-in-law in robbing me." As with all συν- compounds the ally or partner is in the dative case. Likewise πιστεύων which follows needs a noun in the dative. By putting τῷ ἑαυτοῦ κηδεστῇ and ταῖς ἑαυτοῦ παρασκευαῖς in parallel phrases, Demosthenes suggests that his "schemes" are just as crooked as those of Aphobus, whom the courts

have condemned. παρασκευαί commonly denote the "schemes" of a crafty litigant, as in the next sentence where they are "tricks of argument." Cf. παρασκευάσασθαι in 27.2.

ἐν ὑμῖν, cf. 27.1.

οἶδα μὲν οὖν, cf. 27.2 and note.

μαρτυρήσοντας, future participle; they have not testified yet.

διοίσειν, from διαφέρω, which often means "differ for the better," i.e. "be superior."

4. εἰ καί τις ... ἡγεῖτο ... γνώσεσθαι. The MSS. read γνώσεσθε or γνώσεται, "even if in the past one of you thought, you (or he) will learn ...," a protasis in the past followed by an apodosis in the future indicative. Editors have preferred to read the infinitive γνώσεσθαι as demanded by οἶμαι.

τῶν ... πεπραγμένων, "the things he did to me," i.e. "his behaviour." τὸν ἄλλον χρόνον, "the rest of the time until now," i.e. in the past. ἐλάνθανεν αὐτόν. Onetor is the subject, αὐτόν the member of the jury ("someone of you").

ἀποδείξω. This sentence is puzzling to a reader who has not yet been told the story of Onetor's behaviour. A plaintiff often insists on the lies and dishonesty of a defendant before giving details; Demosthenes does not want to delay attacking Onetor's character, even though some of the jury may not be familiar with the story. In due time we shall learn that Onetor arranged for his sister to marry Aphobus, and claimed to have paid a dowry over to him; that subsequently she was supposed to have separated from him, so that the dowry would have to be returned; the farm was then supposed to have been transferred to Onetor by Aphobus as a pledge to cover the amount of the dowry. But Demosthenes denies that Onetor ever paid the dowry in the first place.

ἧς φησι νῦν ἀποτετιμῆσθαι, "in return for which he says that the farm is pledged to him." ἀποτιμάω is used in a way very similar to ὑποτίθημι. Cf. 26 below, ἀντὶ τῆς προικὸς ἀποτετιμῆσθαι. This is the property from which Demosthenes was ejected, when he claimed it as Aphobus' property in part payment of the debt of ten talents.

ἀπολελοιπυῖαν, "left her husband" or "was divorced." Divorce by mutual consent was legally valid without any court proceedings. We shall learn in time why Demosthenes believes that she and Aphobus had not parted company and that the whole scheme is a device to keep the farm out of his hands.

ὑπὲρ ἧς, "on whose behalf," because the farm represents her dowry.

ἐξήγαγε, "ejected," but a politer word than ἐκβάλλω.

5. προιστάμενον . . . Ἀφόβου, "standing in front of Apho-bus," i.e. shielding him or acting as his agent; ἐπί with the dative shows the purpose. The Greek does not mean "shielding Aphobus and facing this litigation," but "it is as the agent of Aphobus that he faces this trial also," just as from the beginning he had planned the attack on my property. The list of what is to be proved is now closed— it is to be established with the strongest of proofs!

The sentence would have been difficult to declaim; no pause or drop in the voice could be allowed, since it has to be clear that οὕτω μεγάλοις τεκμηρίοις modifies ἀποδείξω, the first word in the sentence. What Demosthenes says he will prove is: Onetor never paid the dowry in return for which he says the farm was transferred to him, but from the beginning he was helping Aphobus to keep the property out of my hands, just as he is doing now; and the divorce is just as much a fiction as the payment of the dowry. It is a clear enough statement of what is to be proved, but Demosthenes never says what precise offence he will prove Onetor to have committed, never says he will establish his own right to the property or tells the jury what verdict he will ask them to pass. His immediate object evidently is to show how Onetor is involved in a conspiracy to prevent him from recovering what is due to him. This is what he wants to be established firmly in the minds of the jurors before he starts the narrative.

In other respects these introductory sections (1–5) follow the same pattern as in the prosecution of Aphobus: "I am in court against my will, and efforts to achieve an equitable settlement have been baffled by the defendant's monstrous arrogance; I know that I am facing an ingenious opponent in court, but I am sure that I can make the justice of my case plain; I shall tell the story in such a way that you will understand all the details." He does not refer to his success against Aphobus, says nothing about his youth and inexperience, and makes no special plea for a favourable hearing. It is a more confident opening than in his first speech.

6. οὐκ ἐλάνθανον, in literal translation "I did not escape the notice of Athenians (many others besides Onetor) being badly treated by my guardians." Better: "There were many Athenians (including Onetor) who were well aware that I was being badly treated . . ." The use of λανθάνω with a personal subject and the preference for

negative expression are in contrast with English idiom. πολλούς τ' ἄλλους . . . καί has the force of "many others and in particular . . ."

ἦν καταφανής, still the personal subject, where English idiom would prefer "it was perfectly clear that . . ."

τῷ ἄρχοντι. Legal issues were regularly presented to members of the board of nine archons (cf. Introduction p. 8), and "the archon" (the so-called eponymous member of the board, who gave his name to the year) was responsible for matters concerning orphans. See Aristotle, *Resp. Ath.*, 56. There is, however, no other mention in these speeches of any hearing before the archon, so that the statement here is puzzling.

τῶν καταλειφθέντων, cf. 27.4 and 12.

ἀμίσθωτον, cf. 27.15 and note.

καρποῖντο, δοκιμασθείην, cf. 27.5 and note.

Demosthenes talks as though his personal affairs were common knowledge and excited great interest; we need not believe that this was so, but since he obtained a judgment in his favour against Aphobus, it might be unwise for the defendant to contradict him.

7. Τιμοκράτης, divorced first husband of Onetor's sister, as we learn at the end of this section. Though not formally accused of complicity in Onetor's schemes, he is likely to have known what was going on. But he is kept in the background so as not to distract attention from Onetor.

προέσθαι, "let the dowry go." προίημι regularly means "throw away, abandon,"—"for one's disadvantage" in the middle voice. Onetor had provided a dowry when she married Timocrates; when their marriage broke up, it should have been returned.

ὥσπερ εἰ ... νομίζων, "as though he supposed that the property of trustees was recognized as a pledge (or security) given to wards."

καθεστάναι, "be established," "be set down," is something like "be tied up." If Onetor had really thought this, it would have been a proper reason for not putting this money in Aphobus' hands; Demosthenes means that he did not really think so (because this was not the law), but was afraid that the courts might condemn Aphobus to pay a large sum to Demosthenes, which would force him to surrender the dowry as part payment; the object of this paragraph is to establish that Onetor was well aware of Aphobus' dishonesty, and so was co-operating with him. If he was as innocent as he claimed to be, there was no reason why he should not have handed over the cash to Aphobus. The matter is argued in more detail later.

ἐπὶ πέντ' ὀβολοῖς. Timocrates, therefore, instead of returning the dowry to Onetor, when he and his wife separated, recognized his debt and paid five obols interest per mina per month—a low rate of interest (10% per annum); the regular rate, as we learn from 27.17, would have been nine obols (18% per annum).

ὀφειλήσειν, future infinitive, "that he would remain in debt."

8. διαλύειν, "reconcile us," i.e. "arrange a financial settlement between us."

κύριος, not exactly "in possession of," since Timocrates retained the principal, but "in control."

ὡς, with participle, "as though," i.e. "maintaining that." The objects of the verbs are easily supplied, as they have been mentioned before.

ἀποτιμήσασθαι, middle, "receive as a pledge." Cf.

δανείζεσθαι, "borrow," although the active means "lend" (note on 27.9).

κειμένων, equivalent to τεθέντων, "established," "existing."

9. τὰ μὲν γενόμενα. For the moment this is all the narrative that is offered, enough to show "the basis of the action."

ἀπεδίδου, imperfect, "was paying." Here is the evidence that Timocrates is involved—he is paying the interest to Aphobus directly instead of to Onetor; it would be interesting to see what form this evidence took, and whether it really proved, as is claimed, that Aphobus never received the dowry, but only the interest on it.

10. ἐκ τῶν εἰκότων. There is no logical certainty that this was the reason for not paying the dowry in cash, but argument from τὸ εἰκός (the "probable" or "likely" thing) can be very convincing. Cf. the argument in 22 and 39 below.

μέλλουσαν, "going to be endangered," if it became part of Aphobus' property.

ἀπορίαν, "poverty, financial difficulty," is the meaning in this context. οὐ διὰ τοῦτό γ', "not on *this* account" (the γε underlines).

11. οὔτε . . . μέν . . . δέ. As always, with μέν following οὐ, it is the entire combination of clauses that is negatived. It is best to think of it as: "Nor can you say that. . . ." Cf. 27.55 and note.

ἀργύριον . . . παρόν, "cash available."

ἠπείχθησαν, from ἐπείγω, "they were hurried, pushed into it."

δανείζουσιν. The force of the present tense is shown by

saying: "We find them lending money," so that they cannot be short of cash.

συνοικοῦσαν . . . ἐξέδοσαν. It is the participles, not the finite verb, that carry the emphasis. It is the state of the woman at the time of her second marriage that is important—she was not a widow, but still living with a husband when they married her to another husband, from the first husband's house. Later on (33) it will be made clear that she was not "without a husband" for a single day.

12. The story of these very "odd" arrangements for a marriage settlement is not complete yet. No respectable family would allow a dowry to remain unpaid—it would lead to suspicions and ill-feeling.

συναλλάττων, "arranging."

ὁστισοῦν, "anyone," "anyone at all." Cf. Smyth, 339e; GG. 410b.

μὴ διαλυσάμενος γάρ. Two sentences of explanation are given to show why it is not normal practice to "owe" the amount of the dowry. The participle has conditional force, "if he does not pay it" (cf. Latin solvere).

ἄδηλος. It is Greek idiom to say that a debtor is "uncertain whether he will pay"—meaning that others are uncertain about him.

οἰκεῖος. Cf. οἰκειοτέρους ποιεῖν in 27.5. Paying the dowry is thought to cement the bond between the families, and to make the marriage more secure for the wife.

13. δίκαια. Justice, as so often, means paying one's debts and fulfilling obligations.

ὧν εἶπον. Better in English to say "of the reasons that I mentioned."

οὐδὲ βουληθέντων ἄν. ἄν can be used with participles, giving an effect which can be achieved in English only with a finite verb—"nor would they want it."

οὐκ ἐπίστευσαν. Satisfied now that he has proved his point, the orator can speak of them as "not feeling confident" about letting the money out of their hands—it was not poverty or temporary shortage of cash or the need for haste, but "fear of losing it."

14. ὁμολογουμένως, usually "admittedly," but here the meaning is more like "beyond question."

ὡς οὐδ'. . . . This clause is the object of ἐπιδείξειν, and there is a pause after ἐξελέγχων.

κἂν εἰ, "even if," the ἄν anticipates the ἄν with ἀπέδοσαν and προεῖντο. Cf. Smyth, 1765; GG. 1312. Having proved, or claimed to prove, that Onetor and Timocrates never paid or intended to pay Aphobus the dowry, Demosthenes now argues that even if they had in fact intended to pay the full amount in time, events (i.e. the trial of Aphobus) would have prevented them from doing so.

ἐπὶ τούτοις, ἐπὶ τῷ ἀποδοῦναι. ἐπί denotes the intention, "with this intention," "with the intention of paying soon."

εἶχον, "retained."

ἀνάγκας, "pressure" or "emergency" (the plural is difficult in English).

15. τὰ μεταξύ κτλ. The accusatives and infinitives are best thought of as nouns: "the time between her marriage and their statement (φῆσαι τούτους) that she separated," i.e. "the so-called separation." This is the supposed separation from Aphobus, not Timocrates.

ἐπὶ Πολυζήλου. Polyzelus is archon 367–66, and Sciro-phorion the last month of the Attic year: June 366. Timocrates is archon 364–63, and Posideion would be about December 364.

ἐγράφη, "was recorded."

μετὰ τοὺς γάμους, though in all manuscripts, can hardly be right, and is generally rejected by editors as a mistaken addition, since Demosthenes did not come of age "immediately after the marriage"; without these words the meaning will be "as soon as I came of age." This would conform with what we know of the facts.

τὰς δίκας ἐλάγχανον, "filed suit," "was allotted a hearing."

16. ὁ δὴ χρόνος οὗτος. A difficult sentence: "This passage of time admits their being in debt, in accordance with the agreement, but makes it incredible that they paid." This must mean: "There is no reason why they should not have remained in debt, as the terms of the agreement per-mitted, but it is quite incredible that they paid within this period . . ." This argument depends on accepting the view that their reason for not paying the full amount was to keep the money out of Aphobus' hands, for fear it would be subject to a claim by Demosthenes; once suit was brought against Aphobus, it is not credible (οὐκ ἔχει πίστιν) that the money was paid over to him.

τότ', "in the past," back in 366; τηνικαῦτ', "now," after suit was brought against Aphobus.

17. ἐγήματο. The middle is regularly used of the woman, the active of the man who marries.

ἀντίδικοι . . . κατέστημεν, like καθίστασθαι εἰς ἀγῶνα, cf. 27.2 and note. "We" are Aphobus and I.

ἀπεγράψαντο, "registered," "recorded." Very little is known of the formalities required in this kind of divorce— was anything more required than a simple registration with the archon (see 26 below)? The witnesses called at this point are apparently intended to establish the chronological sequence of events. The divorce was evidently recorded *after* Demosthenes started proceedings against Aphobus, but presumably *before* the verdict. If the divorce was genuine and legal (which Demosthenes disputes), does this mean that the transfer of the land, as surety for the dowry, was also legal? If so, it is surprising that he should go to so much trouble to establish chronological details that are to his disadvantage. Our knowledge of the law is inadequate at this point, and we should have welcomed some more precise legal information from the orator.

ἐπὶ Τιμοκράτους. Thus we know that the suit against Aphobus did not come into court until 364-3. Cf. note on 15.

18. οὐ δόντες, ἀλλ᾽ ἐπὶ τῷ διασῴζειν. The emphasis in this sentence is on these phrases, not on τολμῶσι, i.e. "it is not as a consequence of paying the dowry, but with the intention of preserving . . . that they venture . . ." This is, of course, exactly what has to be proved; and only arguments from probability can be offered.

οἵ, relative with φασίν and the infinitives, "persons who say that . . ."

ἐν τοσούτῳ χρόνῳ, as the argument shows, means "in such a short (not long) space of time." The speed of such legal procedure excites suspicion; an interesting point! προῖκα is the object readily understood of the infinitives that need an object.

προστάντες, literally "standing in front of the business," cf. 5 above, προιστάμενον Ἀφόβου, where the meaning is "acting for Aphobus," and 30, προστασία, where the meaning is more like "collusion," "acting as a false front for someone." The word conveniently combines the notions of protection and concealment.

τὰ γνωσθέντα, cf. 27.1 where it means "verdict, decision," before the verdict was known; but here the verdict was for restoration of property, and it is the property itself which was "decided" to be Demosthenes'.

ἀποστερέω takes an accusative of the person deprived and the thing of which he is deprived.

19. ὡς δέ. This clause is the object of διδάσκειν ὑμᾶς.

ἐξ ὧν . . . ἀπεκρίναντο, "from what they replied" or "to judge from their replies."

ἐναντίον, "in the presence of," a proper legal word. Cf. 28.7.

ἀπελάμβανεν, imperfect, because Aphobus is supposed to have "been receiving" the money in instalments.

20. καθ' ὁποσονοῦν, "at whatever rate" (indefinite relative). κατά indicates the rate ("at how much a month") he wanted payment.

τῷ, interrogative, "to whom of you."

οὔσης. The genitive absolute comes first to establish the situation, "when a whole talent was involved."

ᾧ, "to whom," meaning Aphobus; after the verdict of the jury against him, is he the kind of person to whom one would give money without witnesses to the transaction? Not "lightly" or "rashly" (εἰκῇ) is the answer.

μὴ ὅτι. The phrase is elliptic (cf. Smyth, 2763; GG. 1519) like Latin ne dicam, "not to mention." The μή shows that some negative wish or command is implied, e.g.

"Do not imagine that anyone would treat him this way." English can equally well begin with "far from" or "not only" or "not to mention," but will not leave so much to the imagination as the Greek does.

ἀποδιδούς, a conditional participle, "if paying him" or "if one paid him." After the verdict of the previous trial it will not be easy to contradict this presumption that Aphobus is an unreliable character.

21. μὴ γὰρ ὅτι. See note in preceding section. "Not only not" may serve best as a translation here.

πρὸς τοῦτον, "in dealing with this man," cf. note on πρός in 27.2.

οὐδ᾿ ἂν εἷς οὐδένα, the negatives are piled up, as English might repeat "any" and "ever," to insist on the improbability, "no one ever dealing with anyone."

τῶν τοιούτων ἔνεκα, to be explained by the ὅτι clause which follows.

γάμους, "wedding feasts," which are solemn occasions.

ἀναγκαιοτάτους, persons with whom we have close bonds, as well as members of the family.

πάρεργον, "side-issue," i.e. unimportant.

τὰς ἀσφαλείας, "the safeguards, the safety." It is difficult to find a word in the plural which will tolerate the definite article, in contrast with "the risks." The article, equally in English as in Greek, emphasizes the general and normal regard for such things. This speech is particularly full of references to "the way things are done in proper families."

22. εἰκός, the argument is expressed with unusual completeness, the "unlikeliness" of his account insisted upon again.

καὶ τοῦτον, "this man too," i.e. like anyone else.

ὧνπερ ἐναντίον, the relative comes first, with τῶν αὐτῶν τούτων following in solemn legal style. An English translator may prefer to reverse the order of the three clauses in this sentence, beginning with the "if" clause.

πράξας, conditional participle, "if he acted" or "by acting."

ἀπηλλάττετο, "freed himself from," a common verb for escaping from trouble or hardship.

ὡς κατ' ὀφείλοντος ἂν αὐτοῦ may puzzle the reader, since a translation like "as against himself being in debt" does not help much. Demosthenes is describing the situation that Onetor created, assuming for the moment that he did in fact pay his debt without calling in the men who had been witnesses to his contract of loan. They could have testified against him "as against a man still in debt," i.e. thinking that he was still in debt. This is the situation in which he left them. The grammatical difficulty is to decide what verbal form ἄν qualifies. Not ὀφείλοντος, though it could be ὑπελείπετο ("if he did that, he would have left them"). It is possible that μάρτυρας implies a participle, μαρτυροῦντας ἄν, "persons who could testify," "potential witnesses."

23. νῦν τοίνυν. Now "as things are." This phrase brings us back into the realm of actuality, after the speculation about what might have happened—if Onetor had really acted as he said.

βελτίους αὐτῶν, "their betters," who would not have wanted to commit perjury.

ἀποδεδωκέναι σφᾶς, "that they had paid," because there would have to be evidence of two payments—Onetor's payment to Aphobus and Aphobus' repayment.

ἀθρόαν, "all at once, in a lump sum." Cf. 27.35.

φάσκοντες, conditional participle, "if they asserted."

τοὺς ἀπενεγκόντας, "who carried the cash;" it would be quite a heavy load.

ἐξαιτήσομεν, future indicative in the so-called "vivid" construction, since this is the tense Onetor and Aphobus would use in expressing their thoughts.

ἠλέγχοντ' ἄν, "they would be shown up, proved to be lying." If there was no payment and there were therefore no slaves who carried the cash, it may seem not entirely logical to say that they "refused to hand them over" (for questioning); though the meaning is clear enough. Refusal to hand over a slave for questioning under torture could always be claimed as proving the master's fear that an examination would reveal the truth. For praise of *basanos* as a useful procedure, see 37 below. There would be occasions when it was more convenient to complain that evidence given under such conditions was worthless. We have remarkably little information about the actual procedure of *basanos*—just how cruel it was or what efforts masters could or did make to protect their slaves. For an example of brutal application in a murder trial see Antiphon, *On the Murder of Herodes*.

ἐνόμιζον, a written version needs δήπου ("no doubt") to show the tone of voice in which the word was spoken.

24. διὰ τοῦτο τοῦτον. The conclusion is justified only by the assumption that Demosthenes' version of the facts is accurate.

ὡς ἁπλοῖ τινες εἶναι δόξοντες, the sarcastic tone continues, "as though they are likely to be thought simple people."

ἁπλοῦς (like εὐήθης) has the double meaning of "stupid" and "honest."

ἁπλῶς. The emphasis on this word is heavy—as soon as the orator has come out with it, he expects the jury to recognize what a totally unsuitable word it is to describe anything that these men would do. ἄν goes with πράξαντες, but there is no hurry to introduce a verb that can easily be supplied mentally.

τῶν διαφερόντων. "Their interests" is an exact translation.

ἀκριβέστατα, the opposite of "simply"—with great care and ingenuity. Though ἀκριβεία commonly denotes correctness or accuracy (cf. ἀκριβῶς in next section), it is the opposite of careless as well as of incorrect speech or behaviour.

25. τὴν γυναῖχ'. We never learn her name.

λόγῳ μέν . . . ἔργῳ δέ. This contrast is very common in Greek, and not as limited in meaning as the contrast between "word and deed"—theory and practice, fancy and fact, appearance and reality, what should be and what is—or, as here, "supposedly, reportedly," as opposed to "really."

τὰ δίκαια βοηθήσειν, cf. 27.3 and note.

τῶν μέν, neuter, "of some things."

μεγάλα τεκμήρια, "strong indications," which might be regarded as circumstantial evidence.

πίστεις, "arguments." As Aristotle points out (*Rhet.* 1.2) these can be ἔντεχνοι, thought out and cleverly presented by the τέχνη of the speaker, or ἄτεχνοι, observations, documents, or "exhibits" which are independent of any "art" of speech.

26. γεγράφθαι, cf. note on ἀπεγράψαντο in 17.

τῷ ἄρχοντι, cf. note on 6.

τὸ φάσκειν. Governed by μετά like the preceding infinitive, "after Onetor's statement that . . ."

ὁρῶν. The subject is "I," as the following verb shows.

ὁμοίως ἔχοντα, "behaving in the same way as before"— the καί that follows is explanatory, showing the respects in which his habits have not changed.

λόγος. This picks up the λόγῳ of 25: "lies."

παραγωγή. παράγω means "lead astray," so a "misleading account."

27. ἐξελέγχειν αὐτὸν ἠξίουν. Grammatically this could mean either "I decided to refute him" or "I invited him to refute me." If we try to reconstruct what Demosthenes actually said to Onetor, the second is the more attractive alternative. Cf. ἀξιώσαντος in the next sentence.

εἰ μὴ φάσκοι, optative because it is reported speech in secondary sequence; what Demosthenes said to Onetor was "if you deny."

οὕτως ἔχειν, "is as I say."

παρεδίδουν. The offer of a slave for interrogation is to be taken as a token of good faith, in contrast with Onetor's refusal.

κατὰ τὴν ὑπερημερίαν, i.e. because Aphobus was ὑπερήμερος, "beyond the day," "in arrears," had let the day pass when his payment was due and rendered his property liable to seizure.

ἔφυγε, "refused," more positive than "avoided."

ὡς δ' οὐκ ἐκεῖνος . . . οὐκ ἐδύνατο. The first negative here is redundant, contrary to modern usage, unless we use a neutral word like "maintain" instead of "deny." Cf. Smyth, 2743.

28. ἐκέκτητ' ἔτι, "was still in possession"; the pluperfect has imperfect force, cf. Smyth, 1952; GG. 1265.

πρὶν γενέσθαι τὴν δίκην, the expression is perhaps deliberately inexact—before I filed suit or before the case was heard? The difference might be important. It seems that Demosthenes did not know the exact date when Aphobus abandoned possession (note how the same expression is used in 30); he therefore quickly goes on to describe his behaviour after the verdict was given.

ὡς γὰρ οὐκ. ὡς introduces a comparison, and here it qualifies both participial phrases, οὐκ ἀποτετιμηκώς and ἐμῶν ἐσομένων, "not like a man who has pledged his property, but as if with his property likely to become mine by the lawsuit," i.e. like a man faced with the prospect described in the genitive absolute.

ᾤχετο λαβών, "he went off with" is the simplest rendering.

πιθακνῶν, wine casks, which were probably too large and too difficult to move. Aphobus, then, took many things that would normally have been considered part of the property, and left only what he could not help leaving (ἐξ ἀνάγκης)—not the kind of behaviour to be expected of a man who has given the property as surety for a debt.

αὐτῆς τῆς γῆς, "just the land and nothing else," a common use of αὐτός, cf. Smyth, 1209. ἀμφισβητεῖν with the genitive means "to dispute" or "lay claim to." Cf. 32.9.

29. τὸν μέν, Onetor. For the middle meaning of ἀποτιμᾶν see 8 above and note.

φαίνεσθαι, with participle, frequently used in legal speeches of someone who is discovered, proved, shown as

doing something. Cf. φανερὸς εἶναι. With φάσκειν
Onetor is the subject again. The changes of subject in
this sentence are not difficult to follow, now that the line
of argument is familiar. The μέν . . . δέ contrast is
important here to emphasize the contradictions in
Onetor's story—leading up to his apparent willingness to
let Aphobus take everything away from the farm.

ἡσυχίαν ἔχοντα, "keeping quiet," not raising any
objection.

30. πολλὴ περιφάνεια (cf. 27). It is the truth or the
conclusion that can be so described—"did you ever see
anything so obvious?"

προστασία, cf. προστάντες in 18 and note. Onetor's
strange behaviour is intelligible only if he is in collusion
with Aphobus.

ὑπὲρ τοῦ, "in defence of," i.e. "in defence of his
statement that . . ."

ἐξεσκευάσθη, "dismantled," when the σκεύη were
removed.

τῶν ἐγγείων, literally "the things in the ground," the
usual expression for objects that could not be removed,
like the four walls of the house and anything that was
"built in," as the wine casks perhaps were.

31. οὐκ ἀληθινὴν ἐποιήσατο τὴν ἀπόλειψιν. The sister,
not Onetor, is evidently the subject. "Not genuine did
she carry through the divorce" is the regular Greek form
of expression. The definite article is used, because "the
divorce" has already been mentioned and is a familiar
topic. More idiomatic English: "The form of divorce
that she went through was a pretence."

ᾧ γὰρ προσῆκεν. This is Onetor again: "The man for

whom it was fitting," or "whom we might have expected."

ἀμφισβητούμενον, "disputed," i.e. of disputed ownership, since Onetor would know that Demosthenes could claim it.

συνηγωνίζετο, συναποστερῆσαι. The συν- compounds underline the "friendly co-operation" of Onetor with Aphobus. Cf. 3 above and note.

ἦν πεπονθώς, third person singular. If Onetor has "no quarrel with me," his support of Aphobus can only be explained by his wish to help him—though if his story were true, he would have a serious grievance against him. All through this paragraph there is a strong contrast between what was "fitting" or "might have been expected" and what actually happened, so finally περιποιεῖν ἐζήτησεν is what Onetor actually did. περιποιεῖν, "acquire," not for himself (which would be middle) but "for Aphobus."

32. κατεγνωσμένης, "decided against him."

ἐδεῖτο . . . ταλάντου τιμῆσαι. Onetor, as a friend of Aphobus, asked the jury "to estimate the amount as of a talent" (for the genitive of price or value see Smyth, 1372–74; GG. 1133). The suit against the guardians was a δίκη τιμητή, involving an "estimate of the penalty," after the verdict of guilty was given, plaintiff and defendant proposing alternatives between which the jury had to choose (as in the trial of Socrates). In fact the jury awarded Demosthenes ten talents.

πολλαχόθεν, "from many quarters." Though it is more normal English idiom to say "on all sides," it is reasonable to think of the statements coming "from all directions."

τῶν ἔξωθεν παρόντων, "persons present from outside," a similar use of the -θεν adverb. People who have "come from outside" are "strangers."

παρέξομαι, middle, because it is "for my advantage."

33. τεκμηρίῳ. Not positive proof, but a strong indication that the divorce was a pretence. Later the evidence of witnesses will be offered, but it is first pointed out that the lady was not in the habit of doing without a husband, so that the defendant's story does not fit her character.

συνῴκει, "was living with her husband;" contrast the aorist συνῴκησεν, "married," in next sentence.

ἐχήρευσεν, aorist, "became a widow." Here again the contrast with the present χηρεύειν, "remain a widow," is worth notice.

παρὰ ζῶντος Τιμοκράτους, cf. 11 and note.

ὡς τότε μέν . . . νῦν δέ. It is the combination of events which is hard to believe.

ἠνείχετο, imperfect indicative middle of ἀνέχω, with the initial syllable carrying the augment, as well as -ειχετο. There are a few verbs in which this procedure is followed, although it is contrary to the regular rule. Cf. Smyth, 451; GG. 567.

ἐξόν, "it being possible," as it would be if she were in fact divorced from Aphobus.

κεκτημένου. Further reasons why she might easily have married again, if she were in fact divorced.

34. ταῦτ', "this story."

ἀλήθειαν . . . πιθανήν. An unexpected expression, until one remembers that a "true story" is sometimes not helpful to a defendant unless it can be made "convincing." Aristotle (Rhet. 1, 1) says it is the task of rhetoric ἰδεῖν τὰ ὑπάρχοντα πιθανά, "to discover the available ways of convincing people," and that since truth is "naturally stronger than falsehood," it is the fault of pleaders if a wrong verdict is given. The argument here, which Demosthenes does not develop or complete, seems to be that since Aphobus and Onetor are both capable speakers, if they cannot make their story convincing, it cannot be the truth; it cannot be through lack of skill, in their case, to make a true story convincing.

λόγοι, cf. 26.

οὐκ ἐπικρύπτεται. This is one more sign of Onetor's contempt for the courts and for justice; he does not even take the trouble to hide what damages his case.

μαρτυρίαν. The evidence has been postponed until arguments have been presented which will predispose the jury to believe the witness; this ought to be the truth, and now here is a witness to say that it is.

ἀρρωστοῦσαν, "when she was not well." νοσοῦσαν would suggest a more serious illness.

εἰληγμένης, perfect passive of λαγχάνω.

δίκην λαγχάνειν, conveniently translated "file suit," means "to be allotted a hearing, to have one's suit placed on the calendar."

τούτῳ, Onetor, as always in this speech.

35. καὶ . . . καὶ . . . καί, three very damaging items of knowledge.

μετὰ τὴν δίκην. A transfer of the property was of course no longer legal after the trial, when judgment had been given against Aphobus.

κύριον, "in possession of," but not necessarily with any legal right.

καὶ τῶν ἐμῶν ἁπάντων γεγενημένων. The property which has come into Onetor's hands is "property that has become mine, all of it." This is the meaning, not "and all my property."

καί is explanatory, not co-ordinate.

θεραπαίνας, "serving-women," i.e. slaves.

παρὰ τούτοις, Onetor and Timocrates, whose part in the business must not be forgotten.

μὴ λόγοι μόνον, "not just statements," made by me, but evidence given under torture by slaves.

36. προκαλεσαμένου, cf. 1 and note on 27.50. The meaning here is "demand," not "offer."

τῶν παρόντων, since the demand would be made before witnesses.

τοῦτο τἀκριβές, "this exactness," i.e. "anything as precise as this."

καταφυγεῖν. The verb commonly denotes refuge or resort; "come down to" would suit this context well.

ὥσπερ . . . μαρτυρίων. This is the reason Onetor is imagined as presenting for his refusal to let the slaves be interrogated; when it is convenient to maintain that statements of witnesses and slaves under torture are more convincing than logical argument, an orator will of course argue in this way; but there are occasions when he has to maintain that such evidence is misleading.

ὑβριστικῶς. The speech ends, as it began, with the display of *hybris* by Onetor—the refusal to speak with me is supposed to be as characteristic as his rough refusal to allow me on the land.

37. The praise of *basanos* as a useful and trustworthy procedure is a stock argument—a *topos* or commonplace— that speakers found useful on occasion; in a different situation it might be more convenient to argue that the evidence of slaves given under torture was of little value compared with voluntary statements of free men; it would

certainly be more in Onetor's interest to show distrust for
basanos. The present passage resembles very closely a
passage in Isaeus (8.12), and since Demosthenes is
supposed to have been his pupil, it is generally supposed
that Isaeus supplied him with this *topos*.

καὶ ἰδίᾳ καὶ δημοσίᾳ, a very common contrast—"in
private and public matters alike," or "in a private and
public capacity."

ὡς οὐκ ἀληθῆ τὰ ἐκ τῆς βασάνου εἶπον, "that not true the
statements after torture did they make," i.e. that the
statements they made after torture were false.

38. δίκαια, "right and proper procedures." The neuter
plural adjective is used like a noun, qualified by τηλικαῦτα.
Where two adjectives are used, they are normally joined
by καί (as in the phrase that follows immediately). The
procedures are called "so large" because they are so
important, just as by calling the proofs "large" Demosthenes means "strong and convincing." More commonly
the neuter plural δίκαια means "rights," and there is an
implication here that Onetor is denying me my rights by
refusing to let me question these servants. In fact he is
fully entitled to refuse, but his refusal may easily appear
prejudicial to him, like a defendant's decision not to give
evidence in our own courts; ancient orators are quick to
make this refusal look like a sign of guilt—though according to modern principles such argument would be
disallowed.

Ἄφοβον, a worthless witness, it is implied—and an
interested party, as also is Timocrates.

τὸν μέν, Timocrates, τὸν δέ, Aphobus—this chiastic arrangement, ABBA instead of ABAB, is not uncommon.

πιστεύεσθαι, passive, "to be believed."

193

τὴν πρὸς τούτους πρᾶξιν, i.e. all the supposed transactions involved in paying dowries and arranging for loans and securities.

κατέγνωκεν. Though commonly this verb means "condemn" and takes as its direct object the sentence passed (θάνατόν τινος καταγνῶναι), it can also, as here, have as its object the act or attitude of which a person is convicted, even when the conviction is tacit, "considered you guilty of folly."

39. οὔτ' ἀληθείᾳ ἐοικότα, nec veri similia, "nor likely." Attic orators like to supplement what they claim to be positive proof by arguments from likelihood (τὸ εἰκός). In this case Demosthenes lacks positive proof (particularly since the evidence, which he says would be decisive, has been withheld), and has to be content with showing that their story is "unlikely." It is curious that he does not actually claim to have proved the charge that was the proper subject of the trial—that he was illegally ejected from the property, because it did not belong to Onetor but was part of the property of Aphobus on which he had a legal claim. He appears content to have shown that their story will be "a pack of lies." The formal tone in which he finishes this speech is in contrast with the more emotional style in which he ended the earlier speech.

AGAINST ONETOR II (31)

A few new details, and some replies to arguments from the other side, as in the second speech *Against Aphobus*.

1. ὃ παρέλιπον . . . τεκμήριον, "an indication which I left out," literally: "which indication I omitted," but English idiom does not easily tolerate putting the noun into the relative clause. See note on περὶ ὧν διεφερόμεθα in 27.1. An infinitive phrase, in the genitive, follows, to show what the indication is "of."

τοῦτο, i.e. the *tekmerion*.

ἀμφισβητεῖν, with a genitive, cf. 30.28.

δεδωκέναι. The word may come as a surprise; one might have expected εἶναι or no infinitive at all.

ὅρους, "markers," "stones" to indicate that the property is mortgaged to Onetor, and cannot be sold or transferred until his claim is satisfied. The word commonly means "boundary-marker" or simply "boundary." The amount of money for which the property is pledged (2000 drachmas = 20 minas on the house, a talent on the land) is indicated on the marker. The property may be worth more than this, but perhaps not much more. Cf. 27.10 for a house in Athens worth 3000 drachmas.

2. ὡς διάκεισθε, "what attitude you take." As the

195

passive of διατιθέναι (cf. note at end of 27.3) the verb means "to be disposed."

ἔννους, "thoughtful," i.e. he comes to his senses. Note the shift from the historic present γίγνεται to the aorist ἡγήσατο.

μηδ' ὁτιοῦν, "not even anything," i.e. absolutely nothing.

ἔξοιμι, future optative; according to the rule of *oratio obliqua* in secondary sequence, this represents a future indicative used by the speaker, "if Demosthenes shall have," and in the next clause the "vivid" future indicative is used (γενήσομαι).

3. ἐν ᾧ, "at which figure."

δικαίως . . . ἀληθεῖς, "properly, legally, accurate, correct." There may be an innocent explanation for removal of the markers, but Demosthenes expects the jury to take for granted that Onetor's intention was dishonest from the start. The "if" clause, εἰ δ' εὐθύς, is almost the equivalent of a "since" clause. The emphasis is on the participle, ἀδικεῖν βουλόμενος, and a translator might say: "If his intentions were dishonest from the beginning when he set up these incorrect markers."

4. As though to distract attention from anything that Onetor may say in his defence, Demosthenes tells the jury to deduce his intentions from his actions—"not from anything that I have said."

οὐδ' . . . ἀναγκασθείς. The negative refers to the participle, not the finite verb; he *did* remove the markers.

ταῦθ' ὡς ἀληθῆ λέγω, "as for the truth of these statements, in proof that what I am saying is true." English can hardly be quite as simple as the Greek expression.

προσωρίσατο. Note the προς- compound: "put an additional *horos* on the house."

τοὺς εἰδότας ... μάρτυρας, not "the knowledgeable witnesses," but "knowledgeable persons as witnesses."

5. ἔμελλεν, "intended, expected." ὡς with the participle shows the line he was going to take in his argument.

τεκμήριον, followed by an infinitive phrase in the genitive, as in 1 above.

μὴ ταὐτὰ λέγων. The orators love to point out "inconsistency" in statements or action; it is easily represented as an indication of dishonest dealing.

ἂν δοκεῖ. In this type of phrase ἄν is commonly placed next to δοκεῖ and some distance from the infinitive which it qualifies: "seems that it would be found."

6. ὅς. Strict grammar requires "of the man who," but the antecedent of the relative is easily supplied mentally. "Onetor says he is not depriving me of any amount above a talent that the property is worth" (literally: "the amount by which it is worth more than a talent"). This evidently means that Onetor will be content if he can recover a talent, the amount of the dowry which he says is due to him; if the property is worth more than a talent, he will not grudge Demosthenes the surplus—in other words, he will let him have the property if he pays him a talent. If Demosthenes agreed to this, a new *horos* could have been set up recording the agreement, as on a stone found in Attica, on which it is noted that a property is pledged for a talent as security for a dowry to Hippocleia, and the surplus value is pledged as security to the members of a tribe and a genos (Cecropidae, Lycomidae) and the demesmen of Phlya (we can only guess at the details

behind this agreement):

> ὅρος χωρίο προικὸς
> Ἱπποκλείαι Δημοχά
> [ρ]ος Λευκονοιῶς Τ.
> [ὅσ]ωι πλείονος ἄξι
> [ον] Κεκροπίδαις
> [ὑπό]κειται καὶ Λυκ
> [ομί]δαις καὶ Φλυεῦ
> [σιν]

(SIG³ 1188, IG. II² 2670; M. I. Finley, *Studies in Land and Credit in Ancient Athens*, p. 160, no. 146, cf. no. 147 and pp. 99, 294, n. 7).

Demosthenes says that Onetor's offer is quite worthless, because the land is not worth more than a talent. It is useless for us to guess what it might in fact have been worth. We must go on to the next section, if we are to understand the argument.

7. At first, before the trial, Onetor argues that house and land are mortgaged for their full value—20 minas on the house, a talent on the land; he says this when he wants and expects to keep them entirely out of Demosthenes' hands. But after the trial, when the situation is different, "when your interests are no longer the same" (ὅταν δέ σοι μὴ συμφέρῃ), now that house or land or both may have to be surrendered to Demosthenes, in part payment of the ten talents due to him, Onetor and Aphobus want to have the property valued as high as possible. They will claim that neither house nor land was mortgaged up to its full value—that the house is worth a talent and the value of the land at least two talents more than it is mortgaged for (τὸ περιόν, "the balance over and above a talent").

Their present design, then, it seems, is to let Demosthenes have the property at this high valuation, but to refuse to let it go until Onetor is paid a talent; this he maintains is due to him from Aphobus as a prior debt, which was incurred before the trial; Demosthenes cannot deny that the divorce (if genuine) was registered before the trial (cf. 30.15–17 and notes). The object is to make Demosthenes appear in the wrong (ἵν᾽ ἐγὼ δοκῶ βλάπτειν τοῦτον) when he claims the land for himself; and offering to let him have it in return for a talent is made to appear like a concession—but is the land in fact worth even as much as that?

This passage has given rise to a discussion about the details of Athenian mortgage law (see Gernet's note in the Budé edition); but the design of Onetor seems clear enough.

8. ὑποκρίνει, "you pretend" (middle voice), like an actor (ὑποκρίτης).

μὴ κακουργούμενα . . . ἁπλῶς, "plain and unvarnished" might be a fair English equivalent.

τοὐναντίον, adverbial accusative, "contrariwise."

ἐξελέγχει, passive, "you are proved."

εἰς τὴν καθ᾽ ἡμῶν ὑπηρεσίαν, "for the purpose of serving Aphobus' interests against mine."

9. εἴ τις ἔδωκεν. The object is ὅρκον ὀμόσαι, the opportunity to swear an oath. Would he have been ready to swear that the dowry was 80 minas, as he said it was? Of course he would, if he didn't have to part with the cash! The only purpose of the paragraph is to insist that Onetor would not be particular about perjury. And in any case, since the dowry was never paid, it would be perjury

equally whether he swore that it was 80 minas or 60.

ὃς γὰρ ... ἔφη, "the man who said," i.e. Onetor, no change of subject.

ἔδωκεν ὁμόσαντι. This time the object of the verb is κομίσασθαι, "to take or keep for himself, if he swore" (the participle is conditional).

τί γὰρ καὶ λέγων οὐ φήσει, "what actually saying will he deny it," i.e. what in fact can he say if he tries to deny it?

τοῦτ' ἀξιῶν. He now "thinks fit" to swear that the dowry is only a talent.

ἐπιώρκησεν, from ἐπιορκέω, "commit perjury." Cf. ἐπίορκος, "perjurer," at the end of the section.

ἐκεῖνα, "the former figure" as opposed to τάδε. There is indeed no point in wondering whether "that" is more of a lie than "this." But if not both, one at least must be.

ῥᾳδίως οὕτως, "so readily," without any scruples.

10. Ἀλλὰ νὴ Δία, the usual way of introducing a supposed objection: "But, it will be argued ..."

πανταχόθεν, "from every direction, from every point of view."

τεχνάζων, "scheming, contriving, cheating."

τιμώμενος ... ταλάντου. Cf. note on τιμητόν in 27.67. When the verdict was given against Aphobus, Onetor proposed (τιμᾶσθαι) that the penalty against him should be one talent, in reply to Demosthenes' demand for ten talents; and he guaranteed this sum himself (ἐγγυᾶσθαι, "guarantee, pledge"). His willingness to pay this sum is taken as an indication that he owes a talent in any case— it is the sum that he claims to have paid (but never did) for his sister's dowry. And so this apparent generosity suggests not only that he never paid the dowry, but also that his sister never left Aphobus and is still living with him and that he is on good terms (οἰκείως) with Aphobus. The argument is ingenious, if not quite legally valid.

11. ἠλίθιος, "simple," like εὐήθης. The motives of Onetor in his apparent generosity towards Aphobus are further scrutinized. Can one really believe that he was prepared to part with another talent after already losing one to Aphobus? It would have been a direct loss, since the property which he claimed to receive as security was "disputed" (ἀμφισβητούμενον) in respect of ownership.

ἐζημίωτο, "lost," not necessarily "was penalized."

τὸν ἀδικήσαντα . . . προσεγγυήσασθαι, "act as guarantor for the guilty party" in respect of the ὄφλημα, the penalty he was ordered to pay. Could Onetor be willing to treat a dishonest man like Aphobus as a man likely to behave honourably (ὡς δίκαιόν τι ποιήσοντα)? It is simply not "within the bounds of reason" (λόγον ἔχον), says Demosthenes, that a man who cannot recover a talent that is owed him should be willing to pay the same amount to another person. He must be doing it "in exchange for" (ἀντί) something—the large sum which he expects his sister to get as "heiress (κληρονόμος) to my property in conjunction with Aphobus" (μετ᾽ ἐκείνου).

τῶν ἐμῶν (repeated) carries heavy emphasis.

12. παρακρούσασθαι, "cheat," literally: "strike aside for one's advantage." The original meaning is supposed to be "push the scale to one side," so as to give short weight.

πρότερον . . . ἢ κεῖνον . . . ὀφλεῖν. Onetor was speaking the truth here, but Demosthenes insists that it is a misleading statement all the same.

παρὰ σοί, i.e. τὴν δίκην ὀφλεῖν, as the next sentence shows.

καταγνοὺς ἀδικίαν. Hitherto it has been assumed that Onetor and Aphobus were working together; now it is suggested that Onetor was protecting himself against him —no honour among thieves!

σκοποῦσι, "consider carefully."

τότε γιγνώσκεται, "then he is revealed, as the kind of man he really is," i.e. then and only then.

13. πάσχειν. It is Onetor's feelings and his experience in dealing with Aphobus that are now reconstructed.

φέρε, "look here," "don't you see." The conventional "come now" hardly suits this mood.

πῶς ἐστι δίκαιον. Onetor will naturally argue that the *horoi* are valid evidence of his story, and so Demosthenes has to insist that they do not coincide with "the facts."

καταφεύγειν. If Onetor is content with the *horoi* as proof of his story, he will not feel obliged to "seek refuge" in any "fair test." For the expression cf. 30.36.

παρεσκεύασεν ἐξεπίτηδες, "specially contrived," cf. 27.2 and note.

14. τὸ δεινότατον. Cf. the similar expression in 27.53.

δεδωκότες ἦθ', plural, because it means Onetor and Timocrates.

ὡς μάλιστα. "As much as possible" is hardly the right expression here. "A hundred times over," perhaps.

ἐπεὶ ⟨ἐπὶ⟩ τἄμ' ἔδοτε. ἐπί, though not in the MSS, is accepted by most editors because Demosthenes cannot have said "you gave my property away," but, if their story was true, he could accuse Onetor and Timocrates of "granting a loan on the security of my property."

ἐπί with the accusative can be used in this meaning; cf. 27.27 and note. The presumption is that some scribe seeing *ΕΠΕΙΕΠΙ* thought it was a case of ἐπεί being written twice by mistake, and "corrected" the text without seeing that he had spoilt the meaning.

ὧν ὦφλεν τὴν δίκην, parenthetic, "this property in respect of which he lost his case," so that it is now forfeit to me.

καταδικασάμενον, middle, since it refers to Demosthenes, "who secured a conviction." But the perfect participles which follow are passive.

προικὸς ἀληθινῆς, the dowry that should have been paid to his sister, cf. 27.65, 28.21.

οὐδέ, with κινδυνεύειν: "should not even have had to risk *epobelia*." Cf. note on 27.67.

κεκομισμένον, middle voice, "having recovered." Cf. 30.8.

ποιεῖν ἐφ' ὑμῖν, "put it in your power, leave it up to you."

This unexpected, breathless outburst at the end, with its brief reminder of his misfortunes, is an effective conclusion; it puts his opponent at an immediate disadvantage, and may leave him facing a hostile jury.

FOR PHORMIO (36)

This speech can be dated about 350 B.C., by which time Demosthenes was an experienced and well-known speech writer and was starting on his political career.   He had written a number of speeches for political prosecutions in which prominent men were involved, starting with *Against Androtion* in 355, and made his first speech in the Assembly, *On the Symmories*, soon after.   His series of Philippic orations begins in 351, and since we are told that he gave up writing for individuals in civil cases once he entered public life (32.32), we must believe that this is the latest or at least one of the latest of the speeches that he wrote for clients to deliver.   It is not in fact delivered by his client Phormio, who is apparently incapable of making a speech, but by a nameless friend.   There is no positive reason for believing that Demosthenes delivered it himself.

It is a speech in support of a παραγραφή, a Counter-indictment or Special Plea entered by a defendant who can argue that the suit brought against him by the plaintiff either has no basis in law or is an illegitimate suit that should not be admitted, i.e. is not εἰσαγώγιμος.   There are a number of speeches of this type in the Demosthenic collection, not all of them genuine.   This form of legal procedure secured a tactical advantage; it gave the defendant the chance to present his case to the jury before the plaintiff, and he might hope to represent him as a dishonest *sycophantes* and raise a strong prejudice against him before he could speak for himself. In fact this particular speech made such an impression on the jury that they would not listen to the reply that Phormio's adversary Apollodorus wanted to make. He therefore attempted to renew the conflict by bringing suit against one of Phormio's witnesses, Stephanus, charging him with false testimony in a δίκη ψευδομαρτυρίων (just as Aphobus had sued Phanos, cf. Introduction to the speeches *Against Onetor*). The speeches that Apollodorus delivered in that case are included among the private orations attributed, rightly or wrongly, to Demosthenes (Orations 45 and 46). In 45.6 he describes how the jury would not listen to him after Phormio's case had been presented.

Phormio had been a slave and was presumably not of Greek origin, since Apollodorus accuses him of not speaking correct Greek (45.30). He had been employed by the Athenian banker Pasion, who gave him his freedom, promoted him to be his chief assistant, and helped him towards acquiring Athenian citizenship. We are told in this speech that Pasion had a high regard for him and in his will made him guardian for his younger son, entrusting him with the management of the bank until the boy should come of age; he also stipulated that he should marry his widow, which he did. The elder son, Apollodorus, an ambitious young man who had become quite prominent in politics by 350, objected very strongly to these arrangements, maintaining that Phormio had robbed him of a considerable sum of money and that the will and other documents which gave him authority to act as he did were forgeries.

Apollodorus' quarrel with Phormio goes back to the time of Pasion's death in 370. He objected strongly to his mother's marriage with Phormio and threatened legal procedure, but was dissuaded by family friends and mollified by financial concessions. The younger son Pasicles came of age in 362, no objections were raised about the administration of the property that had been held in trust for him, and Apollodorus signed a formal release, which should have made it impossible to press any further claims against Phormio. Such at least is what we are told in the speech. It appears that he decided on further action when his mother died in 360. On this occasion too a settlement was made out of court, and Phormio claims to have made generous concessions so as to pacify him. But now, twenty years after his father's death, Apollodorus makes yet another attempt. A statute of limitations debarred him from bringing action about matters so far in the past; this is one of the grounds for Phormio's *paragraphe*, and if it could be properly established should have been enough to block the action effectively. Equally good reasons were the releases which he had signed, which should have made it impossible to raise the issue again. But litigants in Athenian courts are very rarely content with technical argument. The object of this speech, therefore, is to show not only that there is no legal basis for Apollodorus' action, but that his behaviour and his character are totally deplorable and that Phormio is an honourable and careful man, with a good reputation in the world of business which he has earned by his skill and integrity. The result is an exceptionally interesting speech.

1. τὴν μὲν ἀπειρίαν. It is evident that Phormio has gone

through the form of attempting to speak and has stumbled through a sentence or two, so that the speaker can say to the jury: "You see for yourselves (αὐτοί) how helpless he is."

τοῖς ἐπιτηδείοις, "his close friends." Cf. 35.6 ἐπιτήδειοί μοί εἰσιν καὶ χρώμεθα ἀλλήλοις ὡς οἷόν τε μάλιστα ("we are on the closest terms"). Not quite the same as οἰκεῖοι (27.1), "members of the family."

ἃ σύνισμεν, "matters which we know about together," i.e. "the knowledge which we share."

διεξιόντος, genitive of the person heard, "from him describing," i.e. "from his description."

τὰ δίκαια. Not just "the facts" but "the rights of the case." Some editors would omit, because of δίκαια following; it is not necessary to repeat the word, but this is not a sufficient reason for altering the text.

ἂν ᾖ = ἃ ἂν ᾖ. The neuter plural calls for a noun in translation, "whatever verdict . . ."

εὔορκα, "in accordance with your oath," since the jury has sworn to give a *just* verdict.

2. παραγραφήν, "a counter-plea to his suit;" see pp. 205-6 above. Some editors omit τῆς δίκης as unnecessary.

ἐκκρούοντες, literally "knocking out," has acquired the obstructive sense of "postponing, gaining an adjournment." Cf. 19.144 ἐκκρούσας οὗτος εἰς τὴν ὑστεραίαν.

χρόνους ἐμποιῶμεν, "make" or "gain time."

τῶν πραγμάτων . . . ἀπαλλαγή. For πράγματα, "troubles," cf. 27.1, and ἀπαλλαγή, "release," cf. 18.145 οὐκ ἦν πολέμου πέρας οὐδ' ἀπαλλαγή.

ἐὰν ἐπιδείξῃ (from ἐπιδείκνυμι), "if he proves." The subject, οὑτοσί, is Phormio, "this gentleman," as a gesture would make clear. Gestures are needed especially in this paragraph, where οὗτος means sometimes Phormio, sometimes Apollodorus.

κυρία, "final" or "authoritative."

ὅσα γάρ. In this sentence, as so often in a speaker's opening remarks, it is insisted that Phormio has taken all the proper steps to satisfy Apollodorus and make litigation unnecessary; he has made generous concessions and fulfilled all his obligations, but even so Apollodorus has brought an action, which Phormio counters with a *paragraphe*. English idiom needs nouns instead of the Greek neuter plural adjectives. "All the things which in the eyes of other people (παρὰ τοῖς ἄλλοις) are solid and firm" means "the steps which other people (unlike Apollodorus) regard as proofs and assurances."

πάντα πεποιηκώς. The various steps which Phormio has taken are described in participles, "though he has done all these things."

3. εὖ πεποιηκώς, the normal expression for "doing kindnesses, conferring benefits," with a neuter plural adjective πολλά ("many kindnesses") and the beneficiary (Apollodorus) in the accusative also. See Smyth, 1591; GG. 1071–72.

πάντα ... διαλύσας καὶ παραδούς. The two verbs will call for different English nouns as their objects, though πάντα is all that is needed in Greek: "discharged all the obligations and handed over all the properties for which he was made responsible" (κύριος).

ἀφεθείς, aor. part. passive of ἀφίημι, "released from all claims." Thus his account of his trusteeship was accepted.

φέρειν τοῦτον. After the series of participles in the nominative, one expects Phormio to be the subject of the verb; but Apollodorus is clearly the subject of συκοφαντεῖ and τοῦτον is Phormio. Gestures would help, but this is a distinct grammatical irregularity (*anacolouthon*), deliberately introduced, perhaps, to indicate or suggest disturbance on the speaker's part. An abrupt change in the tone of voice might be suggested to the speaker. But φέρειν τοῦτον is a puzzling phrase, "cannot tolerate (accept?) Phormio," and some attempts at emendation have been made. If the change of subject could be postponed until the next clause, πείθειν might be possible, "since Phormio cannot satisfy Apollodorus."

δίκην . . . λαχών, the ordinary expression for "filing suit." Cf. 30.15 and 34, note on εἰληγμένης.

διὰ βραχυτάτων, cf. 27.3.

εἰσαγώγιμος, "admissible." The two objects of the speech, therefore, are (1) to show that Apollodorus is a *sycophantes*, (2) to show that his suit is not legally admissible.

4. Instead of a narrative, the speaker presents his documentary evidence first.

ἀναγνώσεται, "he (the clerk) will read."

συνθήκας, "terms of agreement, contract."

ἐμίσθωσε. Cf. the use of the word in 27.15. Pasion leased or "farmed out" the bank and the shield factory to Phormio in return for a fixed rent. There should, therefore, be no dispute about the sum due to the two sons, if they accept this contract as a genuine document; but Apollodorus will argue, in Oration 45, that it is a forgery. We have no details about these businesses comparable to what we learn of Demosthenes' properties.

πρόκλησιν, "challenge." Cf. 27.50 (προὐκαλεῖτο) and note. This would be a record that Apollodorus was invited to question the authenticity of these documents or demand further proof of it, if he chose (an invitation which he is said to have rejected). Subsequently, in Oration 45, he will deny that such a challenge was offered.

ἤδη καθ᾽ ἑαυτὸν ὄντι, "being by this time on his own," i.e. a free man and no longer a slave.

ἐκ τίνος τρόπου, "in what way." Various prepositions are used with τρόπος to express "how." The adverbial accusative is also used. Cf. 7 below.

τὰ ἔνδεκα, "the eleven talents," as mentioned in the documents.

προσώφειλεν. The προς- compound shows that the sum was "in addition to" the other assets of the bank.

5. ἀπορίαν, "lack of means" (πόροι), i.e. inability to pay.

ἔγγειος οὐσία, "landed property," as opposed to ἀργύριον. The sums of money involved here are much larger than in Demosthenes' suit against his guardians.

παρακαταθηκῶν, "deposits" in the bank.

ἐνεργά. Money invested is said to be "put to work." Cf. 27.10. The fifty talents thus included eleven talents from the bank-deposits, lent out at interest. It is therefore inaccurate to describe the fifty talents as Pasion's "private property," and ἴδιον in the previous sentence must be a foolish interpolation.

6. μισθούμενος τὴν ἐργασίαν, "when he took over the operation" in accordance with the μίσθωσις. The middle is used of the tenant, the active of the owner, just as δανείζειν means to lend, the middle to borrow.

λαμβάνων, "taking over," is omitted as unnecessary by some editors.

πολιτείας, "citizenship."

εἰσπράττειν, "recover," commonly used of collecting debts.

ἐπί with the dative shows the security on which the loans were made.

συνοικίαι are buildings in which more than one family lives, "tenement blocks" or "apartment houses."

χρήστης, "debtor." Cf. χρέα, "debts" in 27.49.

προειμένος ἦν, perfect middle of προίημι, which in the active means "abandon, give away;" but "to give away for one's advantage" is "to lend" (just as ἀποδίδοσθαι means "sell"). Cf. the cynic in 32.15 who says: τοῖς προϊεμένοις ἀπολεῖται τὰ χρήματα.

ἐγράφη, "was entered."

7. τοῦ ἐπικαθημένου, "the manager," who sat at the desk in charge. Cf. ἐπιστάτης, "the supervisor" who "stands over" the workmen.

ἀρρωστία is a gentler word than νόσος, though it means that his health has begun to fail.

ἀντίγραφον, "copy." The original text of the will is not produced, and there is therefore a "challenge" in case anyone doubts the authenticity of the copy.

παρ' οἷς, elliptical, "of persons in whose keeping," but the relative clause may be an interpolation.

8. ἐπετρόπευεν, "became guardian for the younger son, Pasicles," for whom property was to be held in trust until he came of age. There are other trustees, but we never learn their names.

ἁρπάζοντος τούτου, "when Apollodorus starts helping himself" to the funds which are being held for both of them in common.

οἰομένου δεῖν, "thinking it to be necessary," means no more than "seeing fit."

There was evidently no way of stopping Apollodorus from making inroads on the fund; we are not told any further details about the administration of this trust fund. Demosthenes is often careful not to overburden the jury with details which are not essential to his argument; perhaps he is afraid of confusing them, and thinks it will be sufficient to let it appear that the trustees were conscientious and careful in looking after the interests of their ward. The only way to protect Pasicles from the inroads of Apollodorus on the fund is "to remove from the fund portions equivalent to what Apollodorus spends" (ὅσ' ἂν αὐτὸς ... ἀναλώσῃ, τούτοις ἐξελόντας ἀντιμοιρεί), and "make the distribution of what is left" (τὰ λοιπὰ νέμειν) between the two, and when they consider that if they wait any longer, "there will not be anything left at all" (οὐδ' ὁτιοῦν ἔσται περιόν), they decide on immediate distribution of what is still in the fund in the interest of the boy (ὑπὲρ τοῦ παιδός).

ἀντιμοιρεί, an adverb which means literally "counterpartwise" or "correspondingly." The relative clause, as so often, is put first (ὅσα ἂν ... ἀναλώσῃ), "with respect to what sums Apollodorus spends, removing corresponding sums to them" (i.e. putting them aside for Pasicles). "Having done A to do B" would be better expressed in English: "To do A before doing B."

9. ὧν ἐμέμισθωθ' οὑτοσί, i.e. the bank and the shield factory, which Phormio had taken on a lease. Gestures are needed here, since οὗτος is Phormio and τούτῳ is Apollodorus.

ἀπεδίδοσαν, imperfect, "handed over regularly as it became due."

ἐγκαλεῖν ... μισθώσεως, "raise any complaint against

him in respect of the lease," the genitive particularizing the complaint.

οὐ γὰρ νῦν, with normal ellipsis, "because (if there had been any ground for complaint) they should not be complaining now, but then was the time."

χαλεπαίνοντα φαίνεσθαι, "show himself being angry," i.e. show his anger.

οὐδέ, "not even," qualifying the words that follow immediately, "not even with respect to the rents that came up can he say that he did not receive them."

10. οὐ γὰρ ἂν . . . ἀφήκατε. Ellipsis again, "for (if you had not received the money) you would not have released." ἀπηλλάττετο is third person singular (passive), but ἀφήκατε and ἀπητεῖτε are second person plural active; the speaker is addressing Apollodorus, "you and your brother." The genitive absolute, δοκιμασθέντος Πασικλέους, gives the date of the release: "When, as Pasicles came of age. . . ." For δοκιμάζειν see note on 27.5.

ἀπητεῖτ' ἄν, "you would have been making demands." The imperfect with ἄν, which usually refers to present time, "you would be demanding now," can also be used for repeated and continuous action (unfulfilled) in the past. Cf. Smyth, 2304; GG. 1407.

ἐνείματο. The speaker turns to the jury again, and οὗτος is Apollodorus.

παῖδ' ὄντα, i.e. before he came of age.

11. ἀφεῖσαν, 3rd. plural of 2nd. aor. indic. active of ἀφίημι. In the singular the 1st. aorist, ἀφῆκα, is used.

νέμονται, i.e. the two brothers "divide among themselves."

ἀφορμή can mean a "starting-place" or "something to start with," and hence, as a business term, it means "capital." The contention of Apollodorus is that Pasion, far from owing the bank eleven talents, had put eleven talents of his personal fortune into the bank and this is therefore "private capital" which his heirs can claim as their own property. The speaker's argument that Apollodorus would have recovered this "private capital" if he had chosen the bank as his share of the inheritance is a worthless argument, because it assumes that Phormio has not falsified the accounts. If Apollodorus can lead the jury to suspect that this documentary evidence is in part forged, his case will be dangerously strong. But his case, as presented here, appears to expect that the jury will be ignorant of simple bookkeeping. He apparently proposes to argue that the bank is being robbed by Phormio, because he has not produced money that is "owed" to it—as though they will not realize that this is a credit, not a debit.

σωφρονῶν, "showing good sense," because he is content with the safer business.

ἐργασία, "operation" or "business." By contrast the shield factory is a κτῆμα, in which the capital actually belongs to you instead of being "other people's money."

12. ἐγκαλοῦντ᾽ ἀφορμήν, "in claiming that there *is* an *aphorme*," that the eleven talents constituted a private investment of Pasion in the bank. σημεῖα are "signs," a more general and less precise term than τεκμήρια, "indications." The speaker does not produce any σημεῖα, contents himself with three strong indications that there was no such *aphorme*, that Phormio had never received it

(λαβεῖν). The first two are in accusative and infinitive form, the third in a ὅτι clause:

(1) τὸ ... γεγράφθαι προσοφείλοντα, as already explained in 4. Pasion was entered in the books as "owing" not as "having put capital in."

(2) τὸ ... μηδὲν ἐγκαλοῦντα φαίνεσθαι, the point already made in 10. Apollodorus does not "show up" (φαίνεσθαι) as complaining at the time of the division.

(3) A new point. Apollodorus is still the subject. He subsequently leased the bank to other tenants "for the same rent" (the genitive of price, τοῦ ἴσου ἀργυρίου) and "will not be found" (οὐ φανήσεται) including an *aphorme* in the contract of lease. If Phormio had more money at his disposal, when he managed the bank, than the later tenants, there should have been a difference in the rent; but there wasn't.

13. καίτοι, "and yet." This third point is insisted upon.

εἰ ... ἀπεστερεῖτο, "if he was being deprived by Phormio of the *aphorme* which his father had provided." As so often, the relative clause comes first—ἣν ... παρέσχεν, "the *aphorme* which ..." The verb ἀποστερεῖν, "to deprive," takes an accusative of both the thing and the person deprived, and in the passive the accusative of the thing is retained (cf. Smyth, 1632; GG. 1240). The argument is that, if Phormio had had a private *aphorme* at his disposal, Apollodorus, when he charged subsequent tenants the same rent, should have provided them with a similar sum of money "from some other source" (ἄλλοθεν). And the subsequent tenants know nothing of any such *aphorme*.

ἀπὸ τούτων, i.e. τῶν παρακαταθηκῶν.

αὐτήν, "itself," and nothing else, "by itself."

ὡς . . . εἵλετο, deleted by some editors, as a later addition. The evidence of the division of property has already been given.

14. ἐλευθέρους ἀφεῖσαν. This appears to mean that they were slaves, and Apollodorus and Pasicles gave them their freedom, when their terms as tenants came to an end, behaving therefore "like men who have been very well treated at their hands."

εὖ πεπονθότες is the passive of εὖ πεποιηκότες.

ὃν . . . χρόνον, accusative of duration of time, "as long as she was alive." Her name was Archippe, cf. *Argument*, I.

πρὸς αἷς . . . δισχιλίαις, "in addition to the 2000 which she had given to her children by Phormio." These were two boys (32, cf. 45.75). This account of Apollodorus' behaviour is difficult to reconcile with the account in 32 below, where he appears to recognize the rights of these children to their mother's estate as equal to those of himself and Pasicles, since he is content with a quarter share. Archippe did not inherit any of her first husband's estate; her property consists only of her dowry and some household possessions. If the dowry was 22,000 drachmas, as Apollodorus says (45.28), the 5000 which Apollodorus gets by this claim is nearly a quarter of it, but we cannot expect to discover the truth by combining the statements of the contending parties.

χιτωνίσκος, an article of dress, but the word appears to denote various different garments (see the passages cited in LSJ), and books on ancient costume are reluctant to reach definite conclusions about its precise meaning in any context. Here it is presumably a valuable possession, comparable perhaps to the χιτώνισκοι listed in the inscriptions recording articles dedicated by women to Artemis of Brauron (IG II² 1514–1516).

15. λέγων φανήσεται, "will be found saying." Cf. 12 above.

ἐπιτρέψας, "entrusting the matter for arbitration."

συγκηδεστῇ, "brother-in-law."

δωρεάν, "as a free gift."

τὸ προσόν, "the extra amount," i.e. the 2000 drachmas.

τὸ ἱερόν, the Parthenon. Hearings and private settlements of this kind were sometimes arranged in temples. Cf. 33.18 (the Hephaesteum, at the edge of the Agora).

16. συμπλάσας, "inventing, concocting," or "digging up out of the past." "The time before this" is only a way of saying "the past."

γνῶσιν, "judgment," i.e. of the arbitration committee.

ἀφίει, imperfect, "was ready to grant a release."

17. ὥσπερ, with participial phrases, "as though."

οὐ γενησομένης, "not going to be revealed."

τολμᾷ, "has the effrontery." Thus in Aristophanes, *Peace* 182, ὦ βδελυρὲ καὶ τόλμηρε κἀναίσχυντε σύ.

18. ἐξ ἀρχῆς ἅπαντα. This was what the speaker promised he would tell them (cf. 3 above), but in fact it has been a very scanty narrative, and it is the documents that have provided the details. He has tried to establish the following:

(1) During Pasion's lifetime the bank and shield factory were leased to Phormio, and Pasion withdrew 11 talents from the bank's deposits, wishing to handle the loans himself. This sum was never repaid to the bank,

and it is therefore the responsibility of Pasion's heirs to re-cover the money from the borrowers. Phormio probably believes (though he does not say so) that Apollodorus has already recovered the money, as he has recovered money from a number of his father's debtors.

(2) When Pasion died Phormio married his widow, Archippe, in accordance with the terms of the will, and became one of the guardians of young Pasicles. A formal division of Pasion's estate between the two sons was made, and the rent from the two businesses leased to Phormio was divided between them. There was no dispute over the accounting, and Phormio was given a full release from further claims.

(3) When the leases of the two businesses ran out, Apollodorus took over the shield factory and Pasicles the bank. The bank was subsequently leased to other tenants on the same terms as to Phormio.

(4) When Archippe died, Apollodorus made some new claims, which Phormio conceded, for the sake of keeping peace in the family. He was then granted a full release from all claims for the second time.

If this is a true and accurate narrative, Apollodorus has no case at all; but he will dispute many points in the story and his arguments will have to be met.

οἶμαι, "I imagine, I suppose," a special use of this verb, different from νομίζω.

ἅπερ παρὰ τῷ διαιτητῇ λέγειν ἐτόλμα. For the phrasing cf. 27.49. The relative clause precedes the demonstrative, as so often.

ἠφάνικε, a more literal use of the word than in 27.24, "has destroyed, made away with." Cf. διεφθαρκέναι in 20 below.

πεισθεῖσα, "influenced by," often with the meaning of undue influence, as in Isaeus (2.1) Menecles is said to have acted γυναικὶ πιθόμενος.

οὐκ ἔχει τίνα χρὴ τρόπον, "he has not what way he should" (τίνα is interrogative), i.e. "he has not any proper way to . . ."

19. ἡλίκα . . . τεκμήρια. It is impossible to prove by evidence that no documents have been lost, but there may be "strong indications" that Apollodorus is lying.

ἐνείματο, "divided for himself," used of one who receives a share, i.e. "accepted a division of the property."

μὴ λαβών, conditional participle, with negative μή, cf. 27.17. Question and answer, instead of a plain statement, is a common rhetorical device.

ἐξ ὅτου ἐνείμω. From this indication of the time-interval, and other remarks in this speech and those of Apollodorus (45 and 46), it becomes clear that Pasion must have died in 370–69, having arranged for the lease of the bank to Phormio a year or so before his death; and that the "division of property" took place probably in 367, after Apollodorus returned from serving as trierarch in Sicily. On this basis the date of the trial is 350.

20. τίς οὐκ ἄν . . . ἐδήλωσεν. There is a long interval between the negative and the verb. Cf. the first sentence of 10 above.

ἐκομίζετο, imperfect, "was receiving," because checking the account was a proceeding, not a momentary act.

εἰ δὲ αὐτοῦ τὰ γράμματα. The order of words is carefully chosen. Once he has said "if on his own account in respect of the documents he was hesitant," it is easy to anticipate what will follow. Apollodorus, as the elder son, might have been in a better position to complain than Pasicles.

ὅπως . . . ἠλέγχθη. The indicative is used to indicate the purpose of something that might have been done, but was not. Cf. Smyth, 2185c; GG. 1381.

τὰς δίκας, "those suits of yours." Oration 49 (not the work of Demosthenes) shows Apollodorus trying to recover a debt supposedly owed to his father by Timotheus.

ὁ δεῖνα, "so-and-so" or John Doe. Cf. Smyth, 336; GG. 398.

ὃ . . . ὀφείλοντα, "owing which." The relative is the object of the participle. The meaning can be seen clearly, if we start with a statement like: "My father, in his written record, left him owing this sum," and then try to say the same thing beginning with "which sum . . ."

21. ταῦτ' ἀληθῆ λέγω. He has not made "this statement" at all, but speaks as though he had answered his own question: "Of course he had the necessary documents."

λήξεων, corresponding to λαγχάνω as λῆψις to λαμβάνω, "legal suits," "pleas."

μοι, ethical dative, cf. Smyth, 1486; GG. 1171.

οὐ γὰρ δὴ συκοφαντεῖν γε. This infinitive, as well as δικάζεσθαι, is governed by φήσειεν ἄν. The separation of negative from verb can be reproduced in English by saying: "You would hardly expect him to say that he . . ." It would be *sycophantia* to sue for a debt if he had no documentation, a mischievous legal action with mere "nuisance value."

22. πολλῶν ὄντων. No noun is necessary in Greek, but

he means τεκμηρίων, "indications thanks to which we can see . . ."

ἐγκαλεῖ does double duty, as main verb and verb in the relative clause.

οὐ δήπου τὸν μὲν παῖδα . . . οὐκ ἂν ἠδίκει . . . σὲ δέ. As always, when a sentence takes this form, it is the μέν . . . δέ complex that is negatived: "It cannot be, surely, that he would refrain from cheating *him*, but would cheat *you*." Detail is added to emphasize the differences between Pasicles and Apollodorus.

τὸν μὲν παῖδα . . . καταλειφθέντα, "the one, left a boy," not "the boy, left . . ." The pause comes after τὸν μέν. The intention is to contrast the position in which each one was left when Pasion died, Pasicles a mere boy, Phormio as his guardian, Apollodorus a grown man of twenty-four, fully capable of looking after himself.

τὰ δίκαια, "your rights," as in 27.1.

τούτου, Pasicles, who is presumed to be in court, though not associated with his brother's plea.

23. ἃ . . . δεῖ σκοπεῖν ὑμᾶς. There is no place for the voice to pause in this long clause, and περί modifies the whole accusative and infinitive phrase "itself" (αὐτοῦ), "with respect to the actual admissibility of the case."

ἀναμνήσθητε, aorist imperative passive, "be reminded" or "remember."

γεγενημένου μὲν διαλογισμοῦ καὶ ἀφέσεως, "after a final accounting had taken place and a release" (it would have been clumsy to add γεγενημένης). The release is not "from the bank" but "from the contract of lease for the bank and shield factory," so that the Greek order of words may seem surprising. When there is no way of avoiding a series of words in the genitive, the orator will try to get the important words in first—"release in respect of the bank and the shield factory (from the contract of lease)." More genitive absolutes follow to show the circumstances which led Phormio and his supporters to enter the *paragraphe*.

δίαιτης, "a hearing before the διαιτητής."

δίκας ὧν ἂν ἀφῇ τις ἅπαξ, a magnificently simple expression of which the literal translation is very clumsy, "suits in respect of matters which one has once let go." It is easier in English to say "when one has once granted release." Cf. the opening words of Oration 37: δεδωκότων τῶν νόμων παραγράψασθαι περὶ ὧν ἄν τις ἀφεὶς καὶ ἀπαλλάξας δικάζηται, γεγενημένων ἀμφοτέρων μοι τούτων πρὸς Πανταίνετον τουτονί, παρεγραψάμην.

24. μὴ εἶναι. The negative μή is proper, since a *paragraphe* is a petition, not a statement.

25. ὧν μὴ εἶναι. The law gives its commands in the infinitive, with negative μή, so that this infinitive phrase is like a quotation from it, "of which 'there shall not be lawsuits permitted.'"

εἰκότως. In an Athenian court it is not always enough to say what the law is; in case the jury may think that "justice" or "equity" oblige them to ignore the law, it is useful if it can be shown that the law is "reasonable."

ὧν ἂν ἅπαξ γένηται δίκη. There is no appeal against an Athenian court decision, but an attempt to modify or nullify its effect can be made by bringing suit on other grounds.

τῶν ἀφεθέντων, i.e. ὧν ἂν ἀφῇ τις. The meaning might be more immediately clear if these words came before δικαιότερον instead of after it, but the present position gives greater emphasis to the idea of "release."

καταγνούς. By granting release and discharge a man can be said to "condemn himself," admitting that he has no case.

τίν' ἂν ἑαυτὸν αἰτίαν, "accusing himself what accusation." The double accusative is normal with αἰτιᾶσθαι.

τῶν αὐτῶν, genitive of the matter at issue.

ὁ τὸν νόμον θείς. Modern idiom prefers a noun to the participial phrase, "the legislator."

ἃ τῷδε γέγονε, cf. the passage quoted in notes on 23.

προθεσμίας νόμον, "statute of limitations" (cf. the verb ὥρισεν used in the next sentence).

26. περὶ πλείονος. A modern reader might prefer to have this phrase after ὑμᾶς, but the present position gives it greater emphasis. Cf. note on τῶν ἀφεθέντων in 25. It also avoids the hiatus of ἀξιοῖ ὑμᾶς.

περὶ πλείονος . . . τὸν νόμον. Cf. the final appeal to the jury in 27.68.

27. ὁ Σόλων. Like the other law this one also is explained and justified. By convention most of the established rules of legal procedure are attributed to Solon, as the "father of the constitution." An appeal to Solon is like an American orator's appeal to the ideals of Washington, Jefferson, and Lincoln.

τά πέντ' ἔτη. The article shows that "five years" was mentioned in the text of the law.

ἱκανόν, singular, "a sufficient space of time to . . ."

τὸν χρόνον. The logic of the remark may not be obvious at once. Time makes it possible for people to tell lies, since they are more readily believed when told about events of long ago; but if the law makes it useless to tell such lies after five years have passed, the liars will have been found out by time, since they will fall silent when their lies can no longer help them.

τοὺς συμβάλλοντας, "signers of contracts and witnesses to them." It is suggested that the statute of limitations provides a man with a substitute for witnesses, so that he will not be entirely alone and defenceless. This is a happy thought, but we cannot know whether it is original to Demosthenes or part of the conventional praise of the law.

28. τί ποτ' ἐστὶν ἅ. This type of expression is very common in modern English, but Greek is more often content with a simple τί.

οὐ γὰρ ἐκεῖνό γε. A very good illustration of the force of γε. Whatever notions Apollodorus may have, here is something which he certainly cannot have imagined.

μηδὲν ὁρῶντες, "if (or while) you saw," hence μή not οὐ.

τοῦτον, Apollodorus, not Phormio.

It is interesting to see the language Demosthenes uses in a protest against social and racial prejudice, a weapon which in Athens might often seem to have the support of the law, since the distinction between citizen and non-citizen, and between Athenian and non-Athenian descent was so important legally. Instead of deploring such prejudice, Demosthenes shows, by choosing suitable examples, that foreign-born former slaves have often deserved and won the confidence of their former masters; and that ex-slaves have often followed the examples of their former masters in promoting their own slaves—like Pasion, who is a former slave and not a native Athenian (despite the pretentious efforts of his son to be so *very* Athenian).

ἐκεῖνος, like *Alexander ille magnus*, "the well-known banker."

τῶν κυρίων, his employers, who had complete control, since he was their slave. Like Pasion's employers these men will have been active in the closing years of the fifth century. These are the earliest Athenian bankers known to us.

29. τῷ ἑαυτοῦ οἰκέτῃ. It appears that, when Strymodorus made his will, Hermaeus was still his slave; presumably he manumitted him in his will.

τελευτησάσης ἐκείνης. It is not clear whether Strymodorus' wife pre-deceased him and he accordingly made a new will giving Hermaeus his daughter as wife, or if the original will contained the proviso "and if my wife shall die."

τοιούτους, "such persons," i.e. persons behaving in such a way.

30. ὑμῖν μέν. Demosthenes wants to protect Phormio from possible prejudice on the part of the jury. A native-born Athenian (he admits) might shudder at the thought of marrying a foreigner; but men who have been granted Athenian citizenship because they have proved themselves worthy of it by their successful careers in business, must ensure the continued success of their business if their children are to enjoy the benefits of citizenship. The legal objection to an Athenian woman marrying a non-citizen is that their children will not be citizens. But that objection does not apply here, since Phormio is now a citizen. The only objection to him would be that he is unacceptable because of foreign birth or unsound character; and it is the task of the speaker to show that neither of these complaints is valid.

οὐδὲ ἕν, stronger than οὐδέν, "not *any* amount."

καλόν. To marry a wealthy foreigner and deprive unborn children of Athenian γένος would be αἰσχρόν.

τοῦτο μὲν δωρεάν. Grammatically τοῦτο might mean γένος, but it evidently means "the gift of citizenship." So also αὐτῶν τούτων ἀξιωθεῖσιν must mean "thought worthy of these same privileges." The plural is appropriate, since the argument has been extended to cities outside Athens.

παρ' ὑμῶν, i.e. from the Athenian people, whom the jury represent. It might be thought that the speaker is not a native Athenian, because he says "you" instead of "us," but this is not a proper inference.

τῇ τύχῃ. We might have expected more emphasis on qualities of character or services rendered to Athens as earning a man the gift of citizenship. But τύχη means success, not just good luck, and success has to be earned by talent. The way in which Pindar speaks of τύχη in describing the victories of athletic contenders shows that it has to be earned and the gods do not grant it lightly.

ἐξ ἀρχῆς. One would expect "initial success" to be balanced by something like "established prosperity" or "public recognition." The words that follow in the text, καὶ ἑτέρων πλείω κτήσασθαι, "and acquiring more wealth than others," seem hardly suitable and are rejected by many editors (they are omitted in one of the manuscripts); but something more than "success in business from the beginning" seems to be needed as a reason for the gift of citizenship, and it is possible that something has been lost in the text.

αὐτῶν τούτων appears to mean "the privileges of citizenship" (see previous note on τοῦτο), but ταῦτ' ἐστὶν φυλακτέα can hardly refer to anything but the money (χρήματα) which the business has accumulated. The next sentence points out that the purpose of bringing Phormio into the family was to preserve the business; such treatment of a valued ex-slave had good precedent, and a man who owed his Athenian citizenship to the wealth he had acquired would naturally have a special kind of regard for it.

ὑβρίζων. Apollodorus had chosen to regard the marriage as an "outrage," and had tried to frighten Phormio by a charge of ὕβρις (45.4), which never came to court and could hardly have been sustained, as these words are intended to remind him.

οἰκεῖον, "a member of the family" (cf. 27.1). The tie (ἀνάγκη) of marriage would mean that he could not escape his obligations.

31. πρὸς ... τὰ συμφέροντα, "if you look to the advantage (of the family)." Whether an act is καλόν or not has to be considered "relatively to something" (πρός τι). τὸ συμφέρον is often contrasted with τὸ δίκαιον, but there is said to be no conflict here between justice and expediency. Another point of view is "pride of race," but Apollodorus is advised not to make himself ridiculous about that.

κηδεστήν, "as a relative."

χρηστόν. We could put the word in quotation marks.

τὸν τρόπον, accusative of respect. It is assumed that the jury will know something about Apollodorus and his extravagant way of life, of which we shall hear more later.

σοῦ, genitive of comparison.

32. ἀλλὰ μήν, "but of course," shows that the speaker is anticipating another objection—that Phormio married Archippe without Pasion's approval.

ὅτι γε δόντος . . . ἐπράχθη. There is greater emphasis on the genitive absolute than on the finite verb, "this was done with your father's approval." For the verb ἐπισκήπτω cf. note on 28.15.

τὰ μητρῷα, "your mother's property," i.e. her estate after her death.

ἠξίους, "thought fit" rather than "asked." The division that he accepted was πρὸς μέρος, "relative to his share," so that he got no more than his share, τὸ τέταρτον μέρος.

κυρίως, "with proper legal force and authority," i.e. in a will.

οὐκ ἦσαν. There is no need for ἄν. This is a type of conditional sentence like "if he said that, he told a lie"— "if they were not legitimate children, they were not legitimate heirs." The legal validity of the argument is doubtful; only legitimate children had a claim to a father's estate, but the law may not have been so definite about a mother's estate.

⟨τῷ⟩ before τὸ τέταρτον, added by Reiske, makes the grammar easier.

33. Since Apollodorus has no real case, he has fallen back on "barefaced lies."

κατ᾽ οὐδέν. κατά denotes the level, as of a line in a page, "along no line of argument."

μὴ γενέσθαι. Apollodorus will continue to maintain this in Oration 45.

ἔνεκα τούτου, refers forward, "for the following reason."

συγχωρεῖν. It is the imagined words of Apollodorus that are being quoted; it is he, not the speaker, who talks of "concessions."

τηνικαῦτα. Here we have the actual words of Apollodorus, "now, finally . . ."

34. ταῦτ' ἀμφότερα . . . ψεύσεται. The order of words is important, "these statements will both be lies."

πρεσβεῖα λαβών. These two words are best taken as a quotation from Apollodorus' statement, "getting his rights, as he says."

πρεσβεῖα must mean "rights of the eldest son," but there is no sign that any legal right of primogeniture existed in Athens, and this passage should not be taken as evidence of it. Cf. Lipsius, *Att. Recht*, p. 542, n. 12. On the contrary, the speaker insists that he could not have obtained what he calls "his rights" without the will; and he is acting oddly in saying the will is a forgery, when it gives him what he wants.

συνοικίαν, cf. 6 above, a rental property or apartment house. Another συνοικία was part of Archippe's property, worth 100 minas according to 45.28, whereas the family house of the elder Demosthenes is valued at only 30 minas (27.10).

οὐ γὰρ ἐκεῖνό γε. It is of course exactly what he is saying, though it would be awkward for him to admit it.

τόνδε means "him" (Apollodorus) and ἔγραψεν is treated as a verb of command, "what advantages his father said he was to have." In the next sentence τοῦδε is Phormio, so that gestures will be necessary.

35. ὅταν δέ. Now we have the reply to Apollodorus' second "shameless statement," balancing ὅταν μέν above. To accuse Phormio of not paying the rent is absurd, since he was released (ἀπηλλαγμένος) from all claims before other tenants took over the bank and shield factory, and

230

"we have produced these tenants as witnesses." The genitive absolute χρόνον πολὺν τοῦδ' ἀπηλλαγμένου gives the circumstances in which these tenants entered upon their lease, with the accusative of time showing that Phormio had been released "a long time" at this stage.

μισθωταὶ τούτοις ἐγένοντο, i.e. ἐμισθώσαντο ἀπὸ τούτων.

καίτοι τότε, "and yet then was the time that . . ." In similar fashion in *On the Crown*, Demosthenes says that Aeschines or "any good citizen" should have voiced his complaints many years ago: ἦν μὲν τοίνυν τοῦ δικαίου πολίτου τότε δεῖξαι πᾶσιν εἴ τι τούτων εἶχεν ἄμεινον, μὴ νῦν ἐπιτιμᾶν (18.188).

τότ' ἀφείς. The speaker must pause before and after these two words.

τούτῳ balances ἐκείνοις (the tenants), but it may be a late addition and is omitted by some editors, since Phormio appears as τῷδε in the next sentence.

36. If Apollodorus' charges are absurd, his attempt to present himself as a poor man is even more ridiculous.

ἐκ τῶν χρεῶν, the debts due to Pasion that he has collected.

πολλῶν τὰ μέρη, "his share in many (of these sums)." The Greek has "shares" because the instances are many. The charge that he cheated his younger brother is not substantiated; but if the jury have been convinced by the portrait of Apollodorus presented so far, they will readily believe this extra suggestion of dishonesty.

37. ὀκτὼ μὲν ἐτῶν, i.e. eight years' rent.

τὸ ἥμισυ, half of the combined rent of bank and factory, 100 minas for the bank, 60 for the factory, see 11 above. The contracts with Euphraeus and the others are said to have been at the same rate as with Phormio (13). The subsequent reduction in Apollodorus' income must be because he now owns the shield factory (Pasicles owns the bank) and receives only the income that it produces. No proof is presented that it actually produced a talent per annum. Cf. the assumption of a "normal" income in 27.18.

38. ἐτῶν ἴσως εἴκοσι . . . τὰς προσόδους, "the income for about twenty years from the property . . ." How much income he got from it will depend, of course, on how well he managed it. It included a συνοικία (34), and if, as is likely, Demosthenes is reckoning at the conventional rate of 12% per annum (cf. 27.9), an annual income of 30 minas means that he is valuing this property at about four talents.

τετταράκοντα τάλαντα. Apart from any capital sums, the three items of income already mentioned, when added up, come to over 30 talents (1800 minas):

8 years at 80 minas	640
10 years at 60 minas	600
20 years at 30 minas	600
	1840

εὖ πεποίηκεν. Cf. 15 above.

ὧν . . . ἔχων οὐκ ἀποδίδωσιν, i.e. τούτων ἃ ἔχει καὶ οὐκ ἀποδίδωσιν.

πένθ' ἡμιτάλαντα, "five half-talents," though πέμπτον ἡμιτάλαντον would mean 4½ (four talents and half the fifth one). We cannot interpret these figures without the documentary evidence.

39. Ἀλλὰ νὴ Δία, "but, it will be objected . . ." This is

the regular formula for introducing an anticipated reply or objection. Cf. Smyth, 2785. It would be normal practice to tell the court how generously he had spent money in the service of the state, and the speech of Apollodorus, *Against Polycles* (Oration 50), shows that he did in fact spend considerable sums on his trierarchy of 362–1; and he had also been trierarch in 369 or 368, and therefore had been absent from Athens at the time when his mother married Phormio (45.3). The statement that his trierarchies were financed by the "joint fund" which he shared with his brother (cf. 8 above), though not supported by any evidence presented here, may be quite true.

μὴ ὅτι, "not to mention," "let alone," as when we deny that someone has done a fraction of what he is supposed to have done: "He is not guilty even of an indiscretion, let alone a crime," "He has not spent five dollars, not to mention five thousand." The analogy with Latin *ne dicam* shows that the meaning must be "I need not say that . . ." Cf. Smyth, 2763; GG. 1519 and note on 30.20.

μηδέ, with λέγε. For this separation of the negative from the verb cf. 10 and 20 above.

αἰσχρῶς. The "shameful extravagance" of Apollodorus has not yet been described or documented; this will come later.

40. καθ' ἕν ἕκαστον, more precise than καθ' ἕκαστα, "according to each individual detail."

41. χρέα . . . ἔχων, "recovering debts," not "having debts." Cf. 36 above.

παρ' ἑκόντων, "from willing payers," a common type of expression. The Athenians claimed to have taken over the hegemony of Greece παρ' ἑκόντων τῶν Ἑλλήνων (Aesch. 3.58).

ἐκείνῳ, Pasion.

παρειλήφασιν. These are credits that they have inherited, money owed to them by others.

τοσαῦτα, "only so much," as the context shows.

μὴ ὅτι, cf. note on 39.

ἀλαζονεύσεται. The "boastful braggart" is such a familiar figure of comedy that this means something like "put on an act."

χορηγίας, the other expensive liturgy, cf. 28.3.

42. ἐπέδειξα. Did the documentary evidence prove anything of the kind? Probably not, but it may have convinced the jury that Apollodorus was quite a rich man, and that was the purpose of presenting it.

κάλλιον. In this instance justice will not be in conflict with τὸ συμφέρον (advantage) or τὸ καλόν (what is worthy and satisfying).

τόνδε must be Phormio, and τούτῳ Apollodorus, and the subject of δόντας and μετασχόντας is "you" (the people of Athens); there is no need to include the word ὑμᾶς, since ὑμῖν has already shown that "you" are the third party in the sentence: "Better that Phormio should serve you, than that you should give Apollodorus Phormio's wealth, getting very little of it yourselves."

ὑβρίζοντα. The speech is reaching its climax, in which it will be argued that Apollodorus is hybristic in character, and *hybris* is a very serious criminal charge, which he foolishly tried to bring against Phormio (cf. note on 30). A year or two later Demosthenes himself will discover the difficulties and dangers of this kind of accusation in his action against Meidias, whom he will charge with violent assault in a public place. The implication here is that Apollodorus might be prosecuted for *hybris* himself. No

234

actual evidence of any violent conduct is presented, but the jury might suspect that it could have been, if Phormio had wanted to be vindictive.

ἅπερ εἴωθε. We shall hear what they are in 45 below.

43. ἀλλὰ μήν should indicate a change of subject, but the objectionable character of Apollodorus is still being pursued; he is now represented as an absurd snob, affecting to despise people who have earned their wealth.

ὧν ἐρωτήσειν, i.e. περὶ ὧν.

εὑρών, the exact opposite of "by hard work."

ἀλλά. The old MS A reads ἄλλη, and Reiske's suggestion ἀλλ' ἤ is adopted in some editions. While ἀλλά offers an alternative, ἀλλ' ἤ offers an exception to the preceding negative statement—"unless it was a lucky chance to win the confidence of his employers." Cf. Denniston, *Greek Particles*, pp. 24–26 for this kind of apparent modification of a negative (especially his examples in (iii)). He does not discuss this passage. Pasion acquired the bank of Archestratus and Antisthenes (presumably by purchase) before 395, as we learn from Isocrates, *Trapeziticus*. Cf. T. R. Glover, *From Pericles to Philip*, chap. X.

44. The characters of Apollodorus and Phormio are about to be compared, and some gnomic remarks about the value of honesty in business form a suitable introduction. The first sentence must be phrased rightly if it is to be understood, with pauses only after ἔστι δέ, ἀνθρώποις, and τὸν αὐτόν. First we have the people in the dative, "for people working in commerce and dealing with money," then the accusative and infinitive with "the same man" as subject, and finally "it is amazing how big

(important) it is." Cf. 19.24 ταῦτα δὲ θαυμάσια ἡλίκα καὶ συμφέροντ᾽ ἐδόκει πεπρᾶχθαι τῇ πόλει.

τοῦτο, i.e. the all-important accusative and infinitive. This is not a quality of character that can be acquired from others, and it is not necessarily inherited (though Apollodorus would like the jury to think so).

ἐπ᾽ ἐκείνῳ, "in his power," see Smyth, 1689, 2c; GG. 1217b.

πίστις, an extraordinarily important word in Greek ethical language, which lays so much emphasis on "keeping faith" and "mutual trust." Here it combines the ordinary meaning of "trustworthiness" with the business meaning of "credit."

ἀφορμή, cf. the discussion in note on 11 above. Certainly credit is "as good as money in the bank." It is also an essential "starting point" for any business operation and a "capital asset."

ἂν ἀγνοήσειας. A little less rude than the blunt indicative.

πολλά, adverbial, "in many ways," with γέγονε χρήσιμος.

οἶμαι, parenthetic, "I imagine." The interrogative τίς comes as a surprise instead of "nobody." The genitive is used with ἐφικνέομαι as with ἐφίεμαι and τυγχάνω.

45. The moralistic tone continues. A rich man's son may lose his money, and has no special right to live a life of luxury and self-indulgence. The misfortune of Pasion's former master's son should be a warning to Apollodorus. It is taken for granted that the members of the jury are good family men of strict morals. As Gernet points out, "bourgeois respectability" is part of the *ethos* of the speech.

δεινά, "shocking" or "undeserved" treatment.

χλανίδα, a cloak or cape of fine quality wool, such as poorer men could not afford. Demosthenes (21.133) says that Meidias wore one when on active cavalry service and it was most irregular and unsuitable. Examples in vase-painting are difficult to identify (cf. M. Bieber, *Die Entwicklung der griechischen Tracht*, p. 32).

λέλυσαι. The middle is regularly used of freeing slaves or ransoming prisoners of war, who would otherwise become slaves.

ἐκδέδωκας. Giving in marriage would mean providing with a dowry. At least Apollodorus is not accused of treating his former mistresses shabbily.

παῖδας, slaves, who are called "boy."

ἀσελγῶς, the word implies *hybris*, as in the opening words of the *Meidias*, τὴν μὲν ἀσέλγειαν καὶ τὴν ὕβριν. Apollodorus replies briefly to these charges in 45.76–77; he also complains that it is unfair to blame him because he walks fast and speaks in a loud voice.

46. προσήκειν. In the meaning "to belong" this verb can have the property as subject; but here, as often, the property appears in the partitive genitive (τῶν τούτου). Does Apollodorus think "any of the property belongs" or that he has any claim to it? Cf. Smyth, 1342; GG. 1097b.

τοῦ πατρός, "your father's," i.e. his slave, his property.

ἐκείνῳ, Antimachus. Legally it is unlikely that one has any more claim than the other, that either of them would have any title to the property of his father's former slave. The property of a freedman who dies without issue can, it seems, be claimed by his former master (Isaeus 4.9), but this is not a relevant consideration here. The speaker in fact is not appealing to law but to equity; if you claim rights over Phormio, you should allow Antimachus a similar claim against you; his case, at least, is more deserving; and Pasion was Archestratus' slave before Phormio was Pasion's.

ἅ is the object of τοὺς λέγοντας, and the idiom here is puzzling because untranslateable. The easiest way to understand it is first to see how it will be expressed with a demonstrative (cf. note on 20 above): τοὺς λέγοντας ταῦτα προσήκει σοι ἐχθροὺς νομίζειν, "it is fitting to regard persons who say these things as hostile." But the sentence cannot be finished (in English) if we put it in the form: "You force us to say the things, persons saying which . . ." The Greek order can be kept if the sentence is given the following form: "The kind of statement which, when it is made, entitles you to regard the speakers as your enemies, this very statement you are yourself forcing us to make." Thus Apollodorus is inviting insults.

47. Certainly Apollodorus, as the son of a former slave, may find his weapon turning against himself if he disparages the non-Athenian origin of Phormio; and as one who has enjoyed the gift of Athenian citizenship, he is in no position to complain of its being granted to others, who may have earned it by their own merits (which he has not). None the less it was permissible in Athenian courts to question the legitimacy of an opponent's citizenship; Demosthenes himself maintains that Aeschines was of servile origin with a very questionable right to citizenship (*On the Crown*, 129, 261).

ἀπολαύσας, "enjoying," "having the benefit of," with a genitive. Cf. Smyth, 1355.

τουτωνί, the Athenians, whom "these jurymen" represent.

ἃ ... ηὕρετο, "the privileges which he won." "Finding" often suggests a lucky chance (cf. note on εὑρών in 43), but these men earned their good fortune.

κοσμεῖν καὶ περιστέλλειν. "Cherish" and "prize" are the words that seem appropriate, though less exact translations than "adorning" and "embellishing;" we think of a man "being an ornament" to his city or his profession, not to his honours.

ἵνα, with indicative, cf. note on 20 above.

ἄγεις εἰς μέσον, δεικνύεις, "drag through the mud, point a finger at," is what he means.

ἐποιήσαντο, the regular word (in middle voice) for adoption, equally appropriate of a city "adopting" a new citizen.

48. The speaker has to prove his statement that Pasion is a former slave, but he tries to give the impression that he would have said nothing about it, unless Apollodorus had forced him to do so by claiming to be a superior person to Phormio; thus he makes it appear that Apollodorus is not only an undesirable character but lacks simple intelligence.

εἰς τοῦθ' ἥκεις μανίας. For this idiom cf. Smyth, 1325; GG. 1088.

ἀξιοῦντες, "thinking fit" in the sense of "asking;" later in the sentence the verb has the sense of "allowing."

ἀπηλλάγη, "released" from slavery is clearly the meaning here.

μηδὲν ὑπόλογον. The adjective can be applied to persons ("subject to account") or things ("taken into account"). The MSS read μηδέν, adverbial, "not at all," but many editors prefer to read μηδέν', following Dobree.

δίκαια, "rights." These must be allowed to work both ways, against you as well as for you. The verb ἥξει suggests movement, a tide which "will move against you from Pasion's masters," just as surely as it works in your favour.

49. The evidence must have covered the better part of Pasion's life and the story of his success in business, and his employment of Phormio, who "saved the day" for him. By presenting evidence of this extensive nature time has been saved for argument and comment which would otherwise have been spent in narrative.

ἑλὼν τηλικαύτην δίκην, "winning a case of such proportions," i.e. getting Phormio condemned to pay such a large sum. αἱρεῖν δίκην, like λαμβάνειν δίκην, means "exact a penalty, obtain judgment." The malicious intentions of Apollodorus are now made clear, when it is seen what the consequences will be for Phormio if the verdict goes against him (ὃ μὴ γένοιτο, cf. 27.67 and note). The speech has told us nothing definite about Phormio's present life, but what follows indicates that he now owns a banking business and, if suddenly called upon for a large sum of money and faced with a run on the bank when the news spreads that he has lost his case, will be utterly ruined.

ἐκβαλεῖν, because he will have to leave the country, as Aeschines did, when he lost the case against Ctesiphon.

ἔχοις, preferable to ἔχοι, the reading of one MS. It is better to avoid the hiatus, and Apollodorus is certainly the subject, not Phormio: "This is the result you would achieve," thus showing what a savage revenge is intended.

εὑρήσεις ὧν ἔστιν, "you will discover to whom they belong." These "things" must be the money that he is seeking, and this is what τὰ ὄντα means (not "the facts"). The "vast wealth" which Phormio is supposed to "own" is really nothing but the deposits in the bank, which do not "belong" to him; he is a banker and his wealth depends not on capital but on credit. Examples are therefore given, to show what happens to bankers if depositors suddenly start reclaiming their money.

50. The banker Aristolochus and his misfortune are mentioned by Apollodorus in 45.63–64. It does not follow that his father Charidemus is the well-known mercenary commander of that name, who was active in the service of Cotys in Thrace.

πολλοῖς ... ὀφείλων αὐτὸν ἐκτήσατο, an accurate description of a banker's operation, when he uses the deposits to buy land. The persons "to whom he owes money" are the depositors.

ἐξέστησαν ... τῶν ὄντων, "withdrew from their property," i.e. were dispossessed of it or abandoned it, if they went into exile without attempting to convert it into cash. The expression is semi-technical and occurs in several other passages in Demosthenes, e.g. 45.64 (of Aristolochus) and 37.49 (of borrowers who cannot repay their loans).

οὐδέν ... οὐδ' ὧν ὁ πατὴρ ... ἐβουλεύσατο, "nothing, not even of the plans that he made." This is the object of σκοπεῖν, and pauses must be made in the right places, so that it will be clear how the sentence is constructed when it is spoken.

51. In a further attempt to humiliate Apollodorus it is now suggested that his father did not really trust him, since he preferred to leave Phormio in charge of his affairs.

ὦ Ζεῦ καὶ θεοί. The effect is something like "just imagine," "strange to say," "believe it or not."

τῶν ἡμίσεων, the half-share of his estate which was to be held in trust for Pasicles until he came of age.

δικαίως, "and rightly too." For this kind of comment, at the end of a sentence, cf. 18.208, where Demosthenes reminds Aeschines that Athens has always shown equal honour to all who give their lives in battle, not only the successful and the victorious—δικαίως.

πάντες ἀπώλοντο. The words suggest a financial panic in Athens. It is not recorded in the historians, but can be dated with reasonable certainty in 371–70. Cf. R. Bogaert, *Banques et Banquiers dans les cités grecques*, Leyden, 1968, 72–73. Pasion was still actively managing the bank in 372 (cf.49.29), but died in 370. Two talents and 40 minas is the combined rent that Phormio paid for the bank and the shield factory.

52. ἀραῖς, curses presumably against anyone who failed to carry out the terms of the will. The practice of inserting such curses in a will is not known from other sources, but a dead man's curse (especially a father's) might be felt as a restraining influence even by people who had little respect for the law.

ὦ βέλτιστε, an expression of protest, like "please" or "look here," but the speaker pretends for the moment that the words mean what they say.

τὸ χρηστὸν εἶναι, more idiomatic than χρηστότης, though modern English may prefer "honesty." Cf. 44 above.

ἐπιεικής, "a decent sort of man," "un homme comme il faut" (Gernet). If Apollodorus has lost his money, it is of course because of his deplorable extravagance.

53. One aspect of Apollodorus' character remains to be pointed out; he is constantly in the courts, and the jury

may decide that, in his refusal to let Phormio alone, he is simply "acting in character."

ἀλλ' ἔγωγε. The tone of personal protest continues, each excuse indignantly rejected with an ἀλλά.

πανταχῇ σκοπῶν, "looking at it every way" or "whatever way you look at it."

χρόνοις, "ages."

ἀπράγμων, often used of quiet people who mind their own business, in contrast to those who seek πράγματα.

ἰδίας, see Introduction, p. 5.

τίνας οὐ, object of κρίνων coming abruptly at the end, "whom didn't he prosecute?" All these men are known. In Apollodorus' speech *Against Polycles* (Oration 50) we learn of his activities as trierarch in 362–1 and he is highly critical of his commanders: "After I had received no pay for my men from the admiral for eight months, I sailed home with the official delegation on board . . . and then quickly put to sea again under orders from the people to take Menon to the Hellespont to replace Autocles, who had been removed from his command . . . And after we reached the Hellespont and the term of my trierarchy had run out and there was still no pay for my men, except for two months, a new commander came out, Timomachus, still bringing no replacement to take over our ships" (50.12–14). He speaks of the "lack of faith" in these officers, and we can assume from the present passage that he subsequently took part in their prosecution for incompetence or corruption. In another passage Demosthenes notes that Autocles was prosecuted for his failure to support the Thracian prince Miltocythes (23.104). Callippus is mentioned in 50.47–52 as guilty of cooperating with the admiral Timomachus in an effort to fetch the exiled Callistratus from Macedonia, using

243

Apollodorus' ship for the purpose. Apollodorus describes how he discovered in time that his ship was to be used for this illegal purpose; and it is likely that this story is the ground for his prosecution of Callippus and Timomachus, who is brother-in-law to Callistratus. Callippus is said to be "still in Sicily;" and he is commonly identified with the former student of Plato's Academy, who became tyrant of Syracuse after murdering Dion, but was expelled from Sicily and killed in Rhegium, about 350 or 349. Cf. Plutarch, *Dion* 54–58, Plato, *Ep.* 7. 333e, Diodorus 16.31, with Sherman's note in the Loeb ed. If the identification is correct, we have one more reason for dating this speech no later than 350.

Apollodorus' speech *Against Timotheus* is concerned with a private matter, and we have no way of knowing what part he may have played in the political attacks on Timotheus in the 350's, which led to his downfall.

It is not unlikely that Demosthenes had read Apollodorus' speeches and had copies of them in his possession, and that they were included in his collected speeches because they were found among his possessions after his death. Cf. L. Pearson, "Apollodorus, the eleventh Attic orator," in *The Classical Tradition, Studies in honor of Harry Caplan* (Cornell, 1966), p. 350.

54. Now that the character and reputation of Apollodorus have been shown, the jury may draw their conclusions. Is it credible that a man like this, if he had any real grievance, would have postponed legal action that was likely to bring him money in favour of political prosecutions, which would bring him no monetary reward? No, it is clear that he knew he had no case against Phormio. Apollodorus of course might choose

to argue differently, pointing to his public spirit and un-
selfish concern for public affairs, when he could have
spent his time collecting his personal debts.

Ἀπολλόδωρον ὄντα, "being what you are" is the meaning,
as though the name Apollodorus were a byword.

τῶν κοινῶν, neuter, "public misdeeds," "offences
against the state." The genitive goes with δίκην
λαμβάνειν, "obtain justice for" ("exact the penalty for").

ὧν μέρος ἠδίκου. The relative is attracted to the
preceding genitive; the accusative ἅ could have been
written, since the meaning is "in respect of which."
μέρος is adverbial, "in part," meaning "only in part,"
since Apollodorus suffered only part of the injustice
committed by public offenders; the city was the principal
sufferer.

οὐκ ἠδίκου. This is the final answer and explanation; if
Apollodorus had really suffered injustice from Phormio,
it would not have been in character to leave him in peace
for so long.

εἰς τὸ πρᾶγμα, "very much to the point."

ἀεί. The pause comes after this word.

55. It is also appropriate to offer evidence of Phormio's
character, and the speaker explains exactly what he means
by the argument from character. It is clearly expected
that this contrast of the two men's characters will have a
telling effect. The speech thus ends with a personal
appeal—Phormio deserves a favourable verdict because
he is a good man.

τάχ' ἄν. The argument from probability is set forth
quite fairly; an action that is in keeping with a man's
character is easily credible, an isolated act totally out of
character much harder to believe.

ἂν . . . ἠδίκει. The imperfect refers to present time, "could be guilty of an offence now."

ὁ δὲ μηδένα. The μή negatives show that the argument is about a man in general; in section 57 when Phormio is meant, οὐ is used with the participles.

56. κατ᾽ Ἀπολλοδώρου, with τῆς πονηρίας added as further specification, "showing his bad character," to distinguish the evidence that shows the worthy character of Phormio, οὑτοσί, his benefactions to individuals and to the city.

57. In case the evidence of Phormio's benefactions should be disbelieved or even ridiculed, like the statements of Apollodorus about his public services, it has to be explained that his wealth does not consist in cash, but is measured by the extent of the credit that he commands. It is likely that many members of the jury thought of wealth only in terms of cash or marketable possessions, and the speaker wants to show (as Sandys and Paley point out in their note) that Phormio "was enabled, as a capitalist in the enjoyment of extensive credit in the commercial world, to advance sums of money larger than the private resources of any single individual." Cf. note on 11 above and the remarks about credit in 44.

προσηυπορηκώς. The simple verb εὐπορέω can mean either "provide" or "be well provided," but here the meaning must be "provide generously for you." It is his credit, not his actual possessions that make these contributions possible. παρά with the dative indicates where the credit is recognized, and the genitive (πλειόνων χρημάτων) shows its value in terms of money.

58. ἅ, referring to χρήματα, but the verb ἀνατρέψαι shows that Phormio's wealth and position are thought of as a

fabric or structure which can be overturned. Elsewhere
Demosthenes uses ἀνατρέπειν of upsetting the ship of state
(9.69) or the peace of the Greek world (18.143). Cf. the
note in Sandys and Paley.

μιαρῷ, a more abusive word than any so far used of him,
"filthy, disgusting." There is no longer any doubt about
his character!

παράδειγμα, an example which will discourage possible
benefactors in the future and set a dangerous precedent
in the courts; and it is the city which will suffer. Thus
the jury are reminded that a just verdict will be in their
own interest as Athenians.

τοῖς δεηθεῖσιν, "to people who asked (or needed) his
help." The aorist participle seems to particularize better
than the present. The aorist middle of this verb is not
used.

59. Phormio helped people not with any idea of ultimate
profit εἰς χρήματα, but out of pure charity. The em-
peror Julian, who disapproved of the Christians, admired
their φιλανθρωπία.

πλέον. Greek prefers this comparative, while English
is content with "good" or "help." Cf. 32.17.

κύριοι, with infinitive, like other adjectives that denote
ability. Cf. Smyth, 2001; GG. 1530.

καιρόν. The "opportunity," the right timing and
placing of any action, is an important element in all
Greek thought; and it is a compliment to the jury to tell
them that they have a special opportunity, as well as the
power to do something worthwhile.

ἐν τίνι, an unexpected interrogative instead of a relative
pronoun.

60. The parting shot at Apollodorus is to set him the
tasks he should attempt in his defence. In contrast with

this kind of challenge we find Demosthenes in *On the Crown*, 2, insisting on the right of the defendant to conduct his defence "as he wishes."

λόγον, in a bad sense, "verbiage," "hot air."

συκοφαντίας, the plural has a concrete sense, "examples of *sycophantia*."

ὡς οὐ διέθετο. This is exactly what Apollodorus will argue in Oration 45.

διαλογισάμενος, cf. διαλογισμός in 23 above.

διδόασιν οἱ νόμοι. If he cannot prove that the facts are different, can he prove that the law is different? The jury are expected to recognize the difference between matters of fact and matters of law, though they may not always preserve the distinction.

61. αἰτίας, "accusations, complaints." The word is used in this sense by Thucydides in speaking of the recriminations and disputes that led up to the Peloponnesian War (1.23). It was naturally common for speakers to complain that their adversaries were using abusive language as a substitute for argument. Cf. e.g. *On the Crown*, 10–15, 123–24.

ἐξαπατήσῃ. The verb is singular, because, though there are formally two subjects, they express a single idea, "his loud-mouthed brazen manner." Gernet points out that Demosthenes does not demand any shouting of his speaker: "Ce qui est la marque du discours, c'est cette modération souveraine qui interdit les éclats de voix et qui donne toute leur force de conviction aux arguments et aux sentiments" (Budé ed., Notice, p. 204).

ἐξέρα, "pour out," to show that there is still water in the clepsydra and that he has not used all the time allowed him.

AGAINST ZENOTHEMIS (32)

This speech is only a fragment and may not be the authentic work of Demosthenes, but it is of such exceptional interest and offers such a good example of a complex narrative skilfully handled, that it seemed worth while to include it in the collection. It is delivered by Demon, a relative of Demosthenes, who tells us in the last surviving paragraph of the speech that he asked Demosthenes to help him in the case and was told: "Of course I will help you, but you must understand that since I started my political career I have ceased handling private cases." This ambiguous remark leaves us free to decide as we please whether he wrote this speech or not; but at least it indicates that the trial took place several years after the trial of Phormio and Apollodorus, perhaps as late as 340. Since the speech shows us that trade is going on with Syracuse, it is commonly supposed to be later than 344, when Timoleon restored order there.

Like the speech *For Phormio* it is in support of a *paragraphe*, but it concerns commercial dishonesty, not a family quarrel. The story is sufficiently complicated that an attempt to summarize it "from the beginning" would probably only confuse the student, and it will be better to let the speaker tell his story in his own way (since we cannot hope to know what really happened without

249

hearing the other side, and without even the whole of this speech available to us). But a few remarks of explanation about commercial enterprises, particularly the import-export business, and the laws which regulated them in Athens may be helpful.

An individual or partnership in Athens, preparing to export a cargo of Athenian products overseas, perhaps to Sicily or the Crimea or one of the other Black Sea colonies, could borrow money on the security of this cargo and the profit it was expected to make in the foreign port. Re-payment of the loan would not be due until the return cargo arrived back in Athens and was sold in its turn. On these loans on bottomry (to use the traditional legal term) a fairly high rate of interest was charged, over 20% and sometimes as high as 30% (cf. Lipsius, *Att. Recht*, 721–24), since the risks were considerable; but if the ship sank and the cargo was lost, and the borrower could prove this and also prove that it was an accident which he could not prevent, his debt was cancelled. This special clause in the loan contract was the equivalent of a modern insurance policy, and was of course subject to the same abuses. There might be occasions when the creditors suspected barratry—a contrived shipwreck to avoid repayment of the loan, if the trading enterprise had not been profitable.

There was a special court in Athens concerned with the hearing of cases that arose out of disputes with regard to such loan contracts. The lawsuits were called δίκαι ἐμπορικαί, and they belonged to the class of δίκαι ἔμμηνοι, suits which would be heard within one month of the time after they had been filed. The reason for this guarantee of a quick hearing was of course that the parties might not be residents of Athens, and if the hearing was delayed the chance of obtaining satisfaction might be very slim. Very often persons other than Athenian citizens would be involved, and this was one branch of the Athenian judicial system in which Athenians and non-Athenians faced one another on an equal basis. Zenothemis is not an Athenian but a citizen of Massalia.

Among the speeches attributed to Demosthenes there are several concerned with lawsuits of this sort, most of them almost certainly not the work of Demosthenes himself. Those delivered in support of or in answer to a *paragraphe* are collected together, beginning with the speech *Against Zenothemis*, and a good introduction is offered by the opening paragraph of Oration 33, *Against Apaturius*:

Τοῖς μὲν ἐμπόροις, ὦ ἄνδρες δικασταί, καὶ τοῖς ναυκλήροις κελεύει ὁ νόμος εἶναι τὰς δίκας πρὸς τοὺς θεσμοθέτας, ἐάν τι ἀδικῶνται ἐν τῷ ἐμπορίῳ ἢ ἐνθένδε ποι πλέοντες ἢ ἑτέρωθεν δεῦρο, καὶ τοῖς ἀδικοῦσιν δεσμὸν ἔταξεν τοὐπιτίμιον, ἕως ἂν ἐκτείσωσιν ὅ τι ἂν αὐτῶν καταγνωσθῇ, ἵνα μηδεὶς ἀδικῇ μηδένα τῶν ἐμπόρων εἰκῇ. τοῖς δὲ περὶ τῶν μὴ γενομένων συμβολαίων εἰς κρίσιν καθισταμένοις ἐπὶ τὴν παραγραφὴν καταφεύγειν ἔδωκεν ὁ νόμος, ἵνα μηδεὶς συκοφαντῆται, ἀλλ' αὐτοῖς τοῖς τῇ ἀληθείᾳ ἀδικουμένοις τῶν ἐμπόρων καὶ τῶν ναυκλήρων αἱ δίκαι ὦσιν. καὶ πολλοὶ ἤδη τῶν φευγόντων ἐν ταῖς ἐμπορικαῖς παραγραψάμενοι κατὰ τὸν νόμον τουτονὶ καὶ εἰσελθόντες εἰς ὑμᾶς ἐξήλεγξαν τοὺς δικαζομένους ἀδίκως ἐγκαλοῦντας καὶ ἐπὶ τῇ προφάσει τοῦ ἐμπορεύεσθαι συκοφαντοῦντας.

"In disputes which involve traders and ship-owners the law lays it down that their cases shall be presented to the *thesmothetai* (the six archons in addition to the *archon eponymos*, *basileus*, and *polemarch*, all nine of them being responsible for preliminary hearings on different subjects), when any injustice has been suffered by them in the trading-market here or on voyages to or from Athens; and the law says that the party at fault shall be punished with imprisonment until the sum which the court orders to be paid shall be paid in full. This is to prevent people from cheating traders with impunity. But when people are sued on the ground of non-existent agreements, the law grants them the *paragraphe* as a refuge to which they may have recourse, so that no one shall be the victim of *sycophantia* and hearings shall be restricted to traders and ship-owners who have suffered some genuine mistreatment. There have in fact been numerous instances of men sued in trading cases who have entered *paragraphai* in accordance with this law, and have come before you, gentlemen of the jury, and shown that the persons suing them were making complaints without any justification, were in fact using the excuse of a business complaint to indulge in *sycophantia*" (33.1–2).

The reason for entering a *paragraphe* given here is simple—the speaker says he never had any written agreement (συγγραφή) with Apaturius, who therefore had no right to sue him in a δίκη ἐμπορική. Demon's reason for his *paragraphe* against Zenothemis is formally the same, except that, like Phormio, he hopes not only to extricate himself from a vexatious prosecution, but to reveal a remarkable story—a story, in fact, of criminal conspiracy and fraud.

As an example of the kind of situation that might arise in this "traders' court," a brief account of Oration 34 (*Against Phormio*) may serve as a useful introduction to the speech *Against Zenothemis*. This is a different Phormio, not Demosthenes' client, and this speech can hardly be the work of Demosthenes himself, since the date of the trial is later than 330.

The speaker, Chrysippus, says he made a loan of twenty minas to Phormio, in Athens, to finance his voyage to the Crimea and back. The terms were that a cargo worth twice this sum was to be put on board; but Chrysippus had information that Phormio borrowed additional money in the Piraeus without increasing the amount of his cargo in proportion. Then when the ship reached the Crimea (the Cimmerian Bosphorus), Phormio found himself in trouble, because there was no market for his goods and he had creditors there waiting for him. Consequently he could not buy a return cargo and the ship's captain took on other freight instead, but overloaded his ship so badly (putting among other things a thousand hides on the deck) that it sank a short distance out of harbour, and thirty slaves who were on board were drowned. The captain, however, got away safely, and people congratulated Phormio on his good fortune that he had not been on board himself or lost any cargo on the ship. The captain, Lampis, reached Athens before Phormio and told this story, but when Phormio arrived he produced the story that he had given the captain a sum of money, in gold, to take with him to Athens and hand over to Chrysippus in payment of his debt. But since the captain gave no indication, until prompted by Phormio, that he had received this money and lost it (or saved it) when the ship went down, we are left wondering who is the greater liar.

Our chances of discovering the true facts in the case *Against Zenothemis* are not much better. The speaker represents himself as the victim of four dishonest men, but it does not follow that he is always speaking the precise truth himself, and he certainly does not tell us the whole truth. There is nothing to be gained by attempting to master the details of the story before reading the speech. The speaker tells his tale with considerable skill, revealing each piece of information at the time and in the manner that he thinks will suit his case best. If he tried to tell the whole story, accurately and completely, from the beginning, it is unlikely that he would have served his purpose better. We should not find fault with him if, for reasons of his own, he makes it difficult for us to understand everything that has happened and to grasp all the legal implications.

1. τῶν ... συμβολαίων. The genitive gives the proper subject matter of the lawsuits. They should be "concerned with συμβόλαια to and from Athens," i.e. with contracts or obligations or transactions relating to the import and export trade.

περὶ ὧν ἂν ὦσι συγγραφαί, "with matters about which there are written agreements." This statement of the law is fuller and probably more exact than the statement at the beginning of *Against Apaturius* (quoted in Introduction, above). The precise relation or difference between these two pre-requisites for a suit in the "traders' court" has been disputed by legal scholars (see Gernet in ed. Budé, p. 112). It is simplest to suppose that there is first a limitation to a particular type of claim (it must be related to the import or export trade), and secondly a written agreement, relevant to the claim, must be produced. This is the solution proposed by H. J. Wolff, *Die attische Paragraphe* (Weimar, 1966).

2. ὁμολογεῖ. If the legal basis for the *paragraphe* is as sound as it appears to be, one might think that the matter ended there and that Zenothemis could have no hope of

success with his action. But a mere legal technicality will not prevent Zenothemis from maintaining that he has been defrauded, and so the speaker takes the opportunity of getting in first with his version of the tale. As he says in the next sentence, his speech will serve two purposes, to prove his legal point and to tell an astonishing story.

At this stage of the speech he gives no indication what kind of complaint Zenothemis has made against him or what positive gain he hopes to obtain by frustrating it. We shall learn in due course that they both claim legal title to a ship-load of grain, that has been brought to Athens from Syracuse in a ship in which Zenothemis was a passenger. But it never becomes clear which of them at the moment is in possession of the grain, whether it is still on board the ship or has been sold or where it is. Instead of describing in full the legal moves that have preceded the action, the speaker prefers to tell the story in his own way, so that we are left to reconstruct many of the details as best we can. We cannot of course know how much better informed we would be if we had the whole text of the speech.

δανεῖσαι, "he *did* make a loan," but to Hegestratus, a ship-owner and captain.

τῷ πελάγει, "the open sea."

τὸ ναῦλον, "cargo." The word is also used for a passenger's "fare."

3. καὶ τούτῳ προσέχειν, "listen as you never listened before."

οὐ τὴν τυχοῦσαν, "no ordinary, everyday criminal enterprise."

πολλάκις when used in an "if" clause means "by any chance," "by good luck"—"if I am lucky enough to succeed." The speaker, as usual, is modest about his rhetorical ability and gives warning that his tale may be hard to swallow.

The introduction (1–3) has been brief and to the point; the speaker gives the legal reason for his *paragraphe* and warns the jury that he will have to tell the full story in order to make his position clear.

4. ὑπηρέτης, "employee," though it might be taken to mean something like "first mate."

ὃν . . . ἔγραψεν. One expects an infinitive to follow, but we have the ὡς clause instead. A purist might consider this "bad grammar," but it is well established in Greek usage.

πῶς δέ. There is no need to repeat the verb ἀπώλετο, just as in the next sentence δανείζοντας is not repeated with τοὺς ἐκείνῳ.

ἐδανείζετο. There is some manuscript authority for ἐδανείζοντο, but the singular verb is perfectly correct if the speaker pauses before κἀκεῖνος, so that it comes as an apparent afterthought: "and so did the other man," Hegestratus, who, being dead, can hardly be οὗτος.

πολύν, in emphatic position at end of the clause, "plenty of it."

γόμον, another word for "cargo."

οἰκεῖον, in predicative position, "he himself had the cargo of the ship belonging to him." It would be normal, but not inevitable, for the ναύκληρος to be owner of the cargo; in which case he would also be an ἔμπορος. ἐπιβάτης is "passenger."

ἃ . . . ἔλεγον, "they were believed what they said," a good example of a retained object with a passive verb.

5. ἀπέστελλον. The use of imperfects is significant, "as they got the money they went on to send it" or "set about sending it."

οὐσῶν δὲ τῶν συγγραφῶν, "the agreement being that . . ."

σωθείσης, conditional participle, "if the ship gets safely home," a regular use of the passive of σῴζω. The infinitive that follows is a command. But the purpose clause is not part of the agreement; it gives the purpose of their plan.

καταδῦσαι. The first aorist is transitive, while the second aorist (ὁ ἥλιος κατέδυ) is intransitive.

ἀπῆραν, aorist of ἀπαίρω, which means "depart, set sail," and it is surprising to find it with an expression of distance. One might have expected ἀπῆσαν.

εἰς κοιλὴν ναῦν, "into the hollow (belly) of the ship," a regular expression for "below." Cf. e.g. Herodotus, 8.119.

διέτριβε, a neutral word, "spending time," under the circumstances probably "lying down." The passenger's quarters would be on deck, perhaps under cover. In Antiphon, *On the Murder of Herodes*, 22, the passengers transfer to a vessel with a covered deck, when it is raining in port.

κακόν τι, something "wrong" or "queer."

6. ἡλίσκετο, a good example of imperfect in narrative, "his secret was being discovered." His conclusion, ὑπέλαβεν, is in the aorist; historic presents describe the chase, with aorists for the abrupt conclusion, "he missed the boat and was drowned." Greek uses the same word for suffocating and drowning.

κακὸς κακῶς ἀπώλετο, a tragic phrase in tragic metre; the orator is careful to avoid a second metrical phrase (he might have written ταῦτ' αὐτὸς παθών) and his word order avoids an appearance of tragic style that would have been in bad taste.

7. τὸ μὲν πρῶτον. The phrases that follow reiterate the idea of his "immediate" reaction. παρά is used of nearness of time as well as place (though here it might mean either or both).

ἐκπεπληγμένος, grammatically qualified by ὡς, but his shock cannot be entirely feigned.

ἔπειθεν, imperfect, "tried to persuade."

τὸν πρωρέα. With the captain dead, the officer in charge of navigation is in command.

σωτηρίας, i.e. saving the ship, getting it to port, cf. σωθείσης in 5.

τὰ συμβόλαι' ἀποστερήσαιεν. A personal object of the verb meaning "to rob" (ἀποστερεῖν) might be expected, but the verb acquires a meaning of "steal" as well as "rob." τὰ συμβόλαια is equally "the contract" or "the money in the contract."

8. τούτου, the purpose as described. Cf. the beginning of 9.

τοῦ παρ' ἡμῶν ἐμπλέοντος, "the person from us on board," i.e. "our man," of whom we have heard nothing so far. We shall be told in due course that his name was Protus (15), and that he had purchased the cargo of grain in Syracuse (12), with money borrowed from us (14). He is mentioned here partly to remind the jury that there are witnesses to this story, but he will not be formally introduced until it is time for him to play a more important part. Like the dramatists, Demosthenes is generally careful not to have more than three characters on the stage at the same time.

σωθείσης εἰς Κεφαλληνίαν, "when the ship got safe to Cephallenia" (cf. note on 5), "more by the gods' grace than anything else."

ἀρετήν, "good work," they showed themselves ἄνδρες ἀγαθοί.

πολιτῶν, "fellow-citizens, countrymen," a regular use of the word. These Massaliots are evidently passengers or members of the crew.

ἔπραττε has the preceding accusative and infinitive as its object, "he intrigued, negotiated to insure that . . ." The verb is used with ὅπως, with similar meaning, in 11.

οἱ δεδανεικότες, the captain's creditors, who had lent him money on the security of the ship (cf. 14).

9. γνόντων, "deciding, ruling."

ὅθενπερ ἀνήχθη, "whence it had set out." ἀνάγω means to take a ship "up on to the high seas," and so καταπλεῖν (11) means come "down" to port. No doubt "our man" was largely responsible for this ruling, when he explained that the cargo was bought with Athenian money. But Zenothemis turns up in Athens, and claims the cargo as his!

ἀμφισβητήσας, with genitive, "laying claim to." After the story of the voyage, we now learn how Demon's troubles start.

10. τῷ ποτ' ἐπηρμένος (from ἐπαίρω), "lifted up by what," i.e. with what kind of support or expectations?

ἀχθόμενος ("though I am distressed by it"), the tale is painful to recall.

ἐργαστήριον, "gang," cf. 27.9 and note.

συνεστηκότων, "got together, organized." In *Against Meidias* 139 there is said to be μαρτύρων συνεστῶσ' ἑταιρεία, "an organized association of witnesses," that will tell any lie if they are paid for it.

οὐδ' ὑμεῖς ἀγνοήσετε. As usual, the speaker recognizes that the jurors are respectable men (cf. note on 36.45), not familiar with characters of the underworld. But "even you will recognize" these notorious men.

11. ἔπραττεν ὅπως, see note on 8.

πρεσβευτήν, like Latin *legatus*, can mean "ambassador," but here merely "delegate" or "representative."

ἐκ βουλῆς, "as result of a discussion." Demon tells us nothing about his partners.

γνώριμον οὑτωσί, "perfectly well known," cf. σαφῶς οὑτωσί in 36.26.

ὅ τι, "what," i.e. what kind of man.

συμμεῖξαι, "getting mixed up with."

Μικκαλίωνος. This was presumably some notorious scandal; we know nothing of it.

νῦν, "only now." If we had known at the time, of course we would not have picked him to work for us.

ἠργολάβηκεν αὐτός, not just "has taken on the job," but "made the job his own," with the idea of handling it to his own best advantage; he resolves to see which side will pay him best, and Zenothemis (ὁδί) accepts his offer of help.

κατεπήγγελται. Cf. ἐπαγγειλαμένου in 8 above.

12. διήμαρτεν with genitive, like ἀποτυχών in 8 and 9. The object desired is expressed in a passive infinitive phrase, "the ship's destruction," which he failed to achieve. English idiom, in this situation, needs some kind of active verb like "achieve." Cf. the first sentence of Oration 30 and note.

ἃ . . . μὴ ἐνέθετο, "money which he had not put into the ship," as he would have done if the cargo was his investment. The middle voice is appropriate for an anticipated advantage. The negative μή makes the relative clause generic; the speaker is thinking of a general truth; no one can get money out of an enterprise, if he has not put money into it.

ἀντιποιεῖται, like ἀμφισβητήσας in 9 above.

'Ηγεστράτῳ, with δεδανεικέναι, not with φησί. Cf. 2 above.

ἐπί, "on the security of the cargo," which he did not own.

δανεισταί. Are these his Massaliot creditors (cf. 8 above) or Athenians who had lent him money on the outward voyage? and are they also the victims of a fraudulent transaction? had the ship been pledged to more than one set of creditors, for a sum far beyond its value? The jury are left to decide these questions for themselves; they do not really affect the argument, and the speaker usually avoids detail that does not bear directly on his own case.

ἄνθρωπον πονηρὸν χρήστην, "a dishonest man for a debtor."

ἐλπίδ' ἔχοντες. The rest of the sentence must be taken carefully, phrase by phrase. Their hope is expressed by a genitive absolute (the participial phrase is conditional) and a future infinitive.

παρακρούω, "to cheat." This is passive here, but middle is used in 31 below. Cf. note on 31.12.

ὃν ἴσασι ψευδόμενον. Clearly this is Zenothemis. We do not see how he fits into the sentence until τούτῳ συνδικεῖν ἀναγκάζονται picks up the relative: "They find themselves compelled to join him in his lawsuit, concerned as they are with their own profit."

13. ἐν κεφαλαίῳ. "To put it in a nutshell" would be the English idiom. κεφάλαιον means "main part" or "total" or "sum" (cf. its use in 27.7), and the phrase should help us to understand what "in summary fashion" really means.

μετὰ ταῦτ᾽ ἤδη. Witnesses will come first, and "only after that" (cf. the use of νῦν in 11) will I tell the rest of the story. The word διδάσκω is often used of "explaining" things to a jury, and has no "didactic" tone.

14. We are given no indication how much time has passed before the ship reaches Athens, how long it was in Cephallenia when all the intrigue and bargaining went on. Cephallenia was a busy place, and there was presumably plenty of traffic to carry the news back and forth.

γνόντων, cf. 9 above. The formal language of their judgment follows.

οἱ ἐπὶ τῇ νηὶ δεδανεικότες, Hegestratus' creditors. Since there is no cash forthcoming, they seize the ship.

τὸν δὲ σῖτον. Now we finally learn why Demon refers to the cargo as "ours." It was bought, we are told, by "our man" (we learn his name Protus in the next section), who borrowed money from us in order to buy it, and cannot repay us until he sells it, so that it represents "our" money. By introducing these details now (and not earlier) the speaker hopes to allay any doubts about the legal owner of the cargo, which may have risen in the minds of the jury. Modern critics have not all been so easily satisfied. It has been suspected that Protus did not in fact purchase the grain at all, and that perhaps Demon was aware of this (cf. Gernet, ed. Budé, p. 115).

οὗτος. Now Zenothemis comes along with his story.

ἠμφεσβήτει. But who actually remained in possession?

262

And where was the grain? still in the hold or on the quay? The conversation that follows, in which passengers on the ship take part, must be supposed to take place soon after arrival, presumably on the quayside.

15. ἄνθρωπε. An offensive and rather provocative form of address. Not "Man" but something more like "Buster."

σὺ χρήματα δέδωκας Ἡγεστράτῳ. Each of the four words carries full weight. Protus is represented as knowing the story of the fraud in Syracuse. Demon never tells us how he found this out.

λέγοντος. Hegestratus is subject of the participle.

τοῖς προϊεμένοις, middle participle, "people who let go their money for their own advantage," i.e. lenders. It looks as though the captain Hegestratus had been airing his opinions of business men.

προήκω, 1st aorist middle of προίημι, 2nd person singular.

ἔφη, "Yes, he said," as often in Plato's dialogues.

ἀναίδης ἦν, "he was shameless," he could not be shamed into taking back what seemed an obvious lie.

τὰ μάλιστ' ἀληθῆ, "truth in the highest degree," "the gospel truth."

αὐτὸς αὑτῷ θανάτου τιμήσας, "himself for himself estimating the penalty (τιμή) of death," i.e. passing his own death sentence. Now we know that the speakers were passengers on board the ship.

16. καὶ ὅτι γ', "and one thing that . . ." This is a strict use of γε. Whatever the whole story may be, there is evidence at least that the two were accomplices.

τίθενται . . . συγγραφήν, "deposit a copy of an agreement." There will be evidence to support this statement

(19). But we can only wonder what was in the text of the agreement, which, if plans had gone off smoothly, was expected to be lost with the ship.

τὰ βέβαια, cf. 36.2. The meaning is "steps to ensure safety," to solidify the agreement and ensure πίστις. This bystander is clearly an amateur detective, convinced that the "legal precaution" was a piece of play-acting, to allay any suspicion that the two were planning a crime; and it was a crime, if they expected everyone to go down with the ship, while they got away on the boat. The accusation of attempted murder, however, is never made.

τὰ δίκαια, the proper legal precautions.

17. τὰ πολλά, "the long argument" that followed.

οὐδ' ὁτιοῦν πλέον, "not the slightest progress." We were getting nowhere.

εἴχετο, "held on to," with genitive as usual. Cf. 34.8 οἱ δανεισταὶ εἴχοντο αὐτοῦ, "the creditors held on to him." The genitive is partitive, since they did not hold all of him (only his coat-tails). Cf. Smyth, 1345; GG. 1099.

ἐξῆγεν, imperfect, "tried to dispossess," the proper legal term. Cf. 30.4, where the aorist is used of successful dispossession or eviction, of Demosthenes by Onetor, after which Demosthenes brings a δίκη ἐξούλης against him. Protus' object is to make Zenothemis bring a suit of this kind against him, since, if the suit fails, Protus will be established as in lawful possession.

Does the "refusal to be removed" mean that Zenothemis is in possession and refused to budge unless removed by a greater show of force than the law would permit, or does it mean that he is not in possession and refuses to "trespass" in such a way as to invite eviction? It is not altogether clear whether the technical term ἐξάγειν is regularly used of a man in possession as well as of a "trespasser;" but in the present instance it is easier to believe that the grain is in Zenothemis' possession, perhaps still on board the ship, which would make it easier for him to defend it. In any case, Zenothemis wants to bring his case against Demon, not Protus. It is generally supposed, therefore, that Demon took possession by removing Zenothemis, who in his turn brought a δίκη ἐξούλης, and that Demon countered with a *paragraphe*. But Demon does not actually tell us that things happened like that.

18. προὐκαλεῖτο. A *proklesis* is the next step, an offer to put the case before the ἀρχή (the legal authorities) in Syracuse. This will mean looking up the records, to find proof of the purchase of the grain.

φαίνηται, with participle, "is revealed, is shown." Cf. 27.16 and note.

τὰ τέλη κείμεν' ἐκείνῳ, "the taxes put down as paid by him," i.e. export taxes or port taxes which were the rule in most cities.

τὰς τιμάς, "the payment" or "payments," if there was more than one lot of grain.

τοῦτον, Zenothemis. Protus is always ἐκεῖνος, since not in court.

τὰ διάφορ' ἀπολαβεῖν, "receive the difference," i.e. the expenses. Zenothemis is still subject of the infinitive; we might expect "us" to be the subject and a verb like ἀποδοῦναι, "we offer to repay."

τάλαντον, a generous offer of damages.

ἀφιστάμεθα, "we relinquish (stand aside from) the grain" on these conditions.

ἐκείνου προκαλουμένου . . . καὶ ἡμῶν, "and with us doing the same."

οὐδὲν ἦν πλέον, cf. 17.

ἦν αἵρεσις. "The choice" was either an active infinitive, ἐξάγειν, or a situation described with a perfect infinitive, ἀπολωλεκέναι . . . τὰ ἡμέτερα, "the loss of our property."

σωθέντα, "after it had come to port safely." Cf. 5.

19. διεμαρτύρετ' ἐξάγειν. διαμαρτυρία is a solemn declaration before witnesses, sometimes a protest against the action or the legal procedure of an adversary, warning him to desist; sometimes, as here, a man's formal announcement of what he proposes to do and why he is entitled to do it. Thus Protus states his intention to dispossess Zenothemis and his legal right to do so. Normally such a statement, if the response is not satisfactory, leads to litigation, but Protus is apparently not disposed to take the initiative in the courts.

βεβαιῶν, "confirming" or "assuring him." Evidently the offer to go to Sicily is represented as a sign of his *bona fides*.

εἰ δὲ . . . προησόμεθα, "but if we surrender the property (i.e. if we take no positive steps against Zenothemis) he does not care." This presumably means that he will refuse to repay his loan, regarding it as our loss if Zenothemis retains the cargo.

20. ἐπὶ τὰ δίκαια, "to face the legal procedure."

ἐνθένδε μὲν πεποιημένοις, "who had made the contract of loan from this end." It appears, therefore, that Demon and his partner decide to accept the cargo in lieu of cash from Protus, though it will take legal action to recover it. Thus Protus considers he has fulfilled his obligations; and he "does not care" whether we recover the grain or not, because, as we shall learn in 25 below, he did not expect any profit if he sold the grain himself.

21. τοῦτό γε, "this at least" was a possibility that we had not yet considered—a decision in Zenothemis' favour in the Athenian courts. This reference to a court decision in Zenothemis' favour is puzzling, because we have not yet been told of any actual litigation. The reference seems to be to a suit which Zenothemis brought against Protus, which Protus lost by default, having agreed not to contest the case (see 26 below and note). But what actually happened? We have been told of Protus' threats to dispossess Zenothemis, but nothing of any legal proceedings or of any act of violence which might give rise to legal action. If there had been a court decision which recognized Zenothemis as legal owner of the grain, it must have been, one would think, in a δίκη βλάβης, the proper action if Protus gained possession and Zenothemis tried to reclaim it, declaring that he had been "wronged."

This may be the correct reconstruction of events, if Demon is telling the truth (though we cannot be sure when he is telling the exact truth). If it is, Demon's case is much weaker than it has so far appeared to be.

καταδύντος. Cf. note on καταδῦσαι in 5 above.

σημεῖον, "an indication," not a proof. Protus is not available as a witness, and Demon has no documentary evidence that Protus actually bought the grain. Some modern scholars (cf. Gernet in Budé edition, 114–15) suspect that he did not, and that he had no intention of keeping his contract with Demon. Thus unless Demon can produce witnesses to the attempt at wrecking the ship, he is in grave difficulty.

μηδέν, adverbial accusative, "not at all." The subject of the infinitive is "the grain."

εἰς τὴν Σικελίαν. Refusal of a challenge like this is no real proof of anything. The offer to go to Sicily may have sounded well, but it is perhaps unlikely that either party was really willing to make the trip. Hence the generous offer described in 18.

22. οὐδὲ τοῦτ' ἐμέλλομεν ὑμῶν καταγνώσεσθαι. In addressing the jury "you" may mean the actual jury or the Athenian courts in general. Here Demon must mean the jury before him: "Even this verdict we were not likely to pass against you," i.e. we were not likely to consider you guilty of this error. The error has not yet been made, and the prospect of their making it is considered unlikely, so that οὐκ ἐμέλλομεν has the force of: "You could hardly expect us, knowing your intelligence, to think you so foolish . . ." The error which is so unlikely is that of rejecting the *paragraphe*, so that Demon claims to have entered his plea in perfect confidence. If we have reconstructed the facts correctly, it is unlikely that he felt so sure of himself.

τούτων τῶν χρημάτων can mean equally well "the cargo" or "the money at stake in this trial," and the ambiguity may be intentional. The word-play on εἰσαγώγιμον adds to the rhetorical artifice of this sentence; while I insist that his suit is not admissible, he seemed to think that this valuable cargo (and my legally earned money) was not "admissible" as import in Athens.

ἔπραττε, with the infinitive as in 8 above. His efforts to obtain a ruling that the ship should go to Massalia were perfectly reasonable and proper if the grain really belonged to him and not to Protus. He will of course maintain that the Cephallenian authorities ruled incorrectly. We can begin to see the lines the reply to Demon may take, but the truth remains very uncertain.

23. Here we have an appeal to the vanity of the Athenian jury not to fall short of the standard set by Cephallenians. The sentence is carefully designed to emphasize every possible contrast and incongruity. Foreigners gave a ruling that safeguarded the property of Athenian citizens; is an Athenian court to give a judgment that permits anyone to sink Athenian property? They ruled that the ship was to come to Athens and turned down the request of Zenothemis to take it to Massalia; he did not even ask to have his so-called property "admitted" or recognized in Athens; is an Athenian court, by declaring his suit "admissible," to grant him even more than he asked? The word-play on "admissible" has become more complicated, and it is hoped that the jurors will be properly impressed and confused.

τὰ τῶν πολιτῶν can be taken as object of both καταποντίσαι and δοῦναι. Cf. note on ἔδωκεν . . . καρπώσασθαι in 27.5.

ταῦτ' εἰσαγώγιμα. Grammatically "these things" are "the cargo." By voting his case "admissible" the jury will be declaring his "ill-gotten goods" admissible in Athens, and failing in their duty to protect Athenians against crime. The insistence on "admissibility" prepares the way effectively for reading the text of the *paragraphe* and the relevant statute.

24. ἐκ τῶν νόμων, "in accordance with the law."

τέχνην—σοφοῦ—συντεθηκότος. There is a sneer in each of these three words which punctuate the sentence. Not "skill" but "low trick," not "wise man" but "crafty

scoundrel" who has "devised" it. The narrative shifts
from Zenothemis and Hegestratus to Aristophon and
Protus; the object now is to show the jury how Protus'
mind worked.

οὐδέν . . . δίκαιον, "no justifiable claim open to them,"
i.e. no real case according to law. δίκαιος has not always
the moral tone of English "just," since δίκη often has a
purely legal meaning. These men find that the method
of δίκη will not help them, so they find another way.

ἐπικηρυκεύονται, the proper diplomatic word for a
"peace offer," made through a herald in war time.

ἐκδοῦναι τὰ πράγματα, in a dishonest sense like "sell the
game."

πράττοντες. Cf. the use of this verb in 8 and 10,
meaning "scheme" or "work for" an object, here with
τοῦτο as direct object.

καί, "actually," i.e. right from the start.

25. γάρ, explains why they could not persuade him.

τὸν σῖτον, subject of the infinitive with ἐλθόντα in
agreement. He expected the grain to "make a profit
when it arrived."

ἀντείχετο, cf. εἴχετο in 17.

αὐτός, not just "himself" but "all by himself," without
sharing the profit—which he will have to do, if he decides
to be dishonest.

ὠφελίας, genitive with μερίτας.

ἀδικῆσαι, as opposed to giving us τὰ δίκαια, "what he
owed."

πραγματευομένου. Since πράγματα often means "trouble," this verb probably has the sense here of "running
into this trouble," not just "being occupied with this
business."

ἐπανῆκεν, "relaxed," i.e. went down in price. High price is thought of as tension, and ἀνίημι regularly means to release the pressure, "let up."

In this and the preceding section the speaker is using a more colloquial style of language, with simple but highly idiomatic expressions that might enable the jury to see how Protus argued and justified his dishonest course, motivated by pragmatic "common sense."

26. The speaker now has to describe how he and his partner reacted to Protus' change of γνώμη, and he puts on a show of candour—he will not conceal from the jury how very angry they were.

προσεκρούομεν, literally "clashed with him." Latin *offendere* means "hit against," but in modern English "be offended" is used with little regard for the original imagery of the expression.

πικρῶς εἴχομεν describes our strong feelings, as revealed in our actions.

ζημίας. Not punishment, but the "loss" as result of the fall in price.

συκοφάντην ἀντὶ χρημάτων. Cf. 12 ὁρῶντες ἑαυτοῖς ἀντὶ τῶν χρημάτων ἄνθρωπον πονηρὸν χρήστην. αἰτιώμενοι is used instead of a verb of observation, like ὁρῶντες, because the speaker is describing his quarrel with Protus. τοῦτον is object of κεκομικέναι, a verb which reminds us that Protus had been expected to "bring money home."

οὐδὲ φύσει χρηστός, "not even naturally honest." The characterization of Protus continues. Normal people, it is presumed, incline to honesty rather than dishonesty, but not Protus, who readily "inclines" (ἀποκλίνει) to the suggestion made to him by Zenothemis and Aristophon.

τὴν δίκην ἔρημον ὀφλεῖν, "to lose the case by default"

271

(the adjective ἔρημος usually has the same terminations for masculine and feminine—this is the feminine accusative form, in agreement with δίκην). δίκην ὀφλεῖν (aorist infinitive) is the regular expression for "losing a case," i.e. "owing" it or, if one does not dispute it, "recognizing the debt." A suit is ἔρημος and lost by default if one does not appear to answer it. After συγχωρεῖ, "agrees," one might have expected a future infinitive, but there is no future of ὀφλισκάνω in use.

On this lawsuit, in which Zenothemis takes the initiative (ἣν οὗτος αὐτῷ λαγχάνει), see note on 21 above. When the course of events is not made clear, we are inclined to suppose that the speakers had some good reason for not making them clear.

ταὐτὰ ἐφρόνουν, "thought the same thing," i.e. were in agreement, in alliance.

27. εἰ μὲν γὰρ ἀφῆκε. As so often in γάρ clauses we must stop and ask what is being explained. The speaker imagines the jury asking why Zenothemis did not drop his suit against Protus, when they decided to work together; and he gives the answer: "Because if he had dropped it . . ." ἐξελήλεγκτ' ἄν, pluperfect passive; aorist passive might have been expected, except that ἐξηλέγχθη ἄν, with unavoidable hiatus no matter how the words are arranged, would have been less euphonious. The argument is not given in full—if Zenothemis had dropped his suit against Protus and sued me instead, it would have suggested very strongly that he and Protus were in league against me; but by being less explicit Demon is able to overstate his case—"he would have been proved."

ὀφλεῖν δὲ παρών, "to lose the case being present in court," i.e. by pleading his case very feebly. Why did

272

not Protus go through this form? Because he did not trust Zenothemis completely, and wanted to leave himself a loophole and a means of counterattack; so he let the case go by default. It would be easier for us if all this were stated clearly in so many words: "He lets the case go by default, so that if Zenothemis and his party carry out their agreement, all will be well, but if not . . ." The ellipse, after an "if" clause, of a phrase like "well and good" or "he will be content," is very common, and the speaker will make his meaning clear if he makes a pause before εἰ δὲ μή. Cf. Smyth, 2346d, n. 3 and 2352; GG. 1426.

τὴν ἔρημον ἀντιλάχῃ, subjunctive after ἵνα, "file a counter suit protesting the judgment by default." A protest of this kind was permissible if made within two months, as stated clearly by Pollux VIII.61: ἀντιλαχεῖν δὲ δίκην ἐξῆν ὁπότε τις μὴ παρὼν ἐν δικαστηρίῳ κατακηρυχθεὶς καὶ μὴ ὑπακούων ὄφλοι. ἀντιλαχεῖν δὲ ἐντὸς δυὸ μηνῶν ὑπῆρχεν. Cf. Lipsius, Att. Recht, 960–61.

ἀλλὰ τί ταῦτα; This time the speaker asks the question, and then gives the answer in a γάρ clause: "But what was the point of this? There was a good reason, because Protus had to be very careful about appearing guilty of the charges made against him by Zenothemis."

εἰ . . . ἐποίει, "if he had been doing." The imperfect shows that Protus was accused of a course of action, not a single act. But what were the accusations? We have to be content with the vague remarks that follow about excessive drinking, in stormy weather at sea, and theft and unauthorized opening of sealed papers.

οὐκ ὀφλεῖν, "not merely lose his case, but . . ."

ἐν κακοῖς, "in time of danger," when faced by κακά.

ἔπινεν. The imperfect has the force of "went on

drinking." And the imperfect that follows shows the succession, "and proceeded to steal."

ὑπανέῳγεν, the compound shows that surreptitious opening is meant. The papers were presumably sealed.

28. ταῦτα μέν. The hint of deplorable behaviour is one more useful indication of Protus' character; but the speaker hastens to warn the jury that it is not part of their responsibility to decide whether these accusations are true.

διακρινεῖσθε, future indicative, "you will decide," that is, "I cannot stop you from forming your own opinion, though the matter is not really relevant."

πρόσαγε. The switch to singular imperative shows that the speaker turns from the jury to Zenothemis.

τί σ'. It is interesting to see how the elided σέ can bear so much emphasis.

ὡς ἔοικε δίκην. The implication is that Protus never paid any damages for "losing" his case, but Zenothemis can hardly deny having "obtained justice."

παραιτεῖται, "plead for him," especially used of an attempt to mitigate guilt.

περιεργαζόμεθα. The περι- compound suggests excessive or meddlesome concern, since it is supposed to be not relevant to our case whether you cheated Protus or Protus cheated you.

29. νὴ Δί' ἀλλ', the imagined reply of Zenothemis: "Yes, but damn it the fellow's got away!" The tone is colloquial, in contrast to the speaker's more formal style.

διά γ' ὑμᾶς, "yes, thanks to you." For this use of γε see Denniston, Greek Particles, pp. 130–138.

λίπῃ, "miss," in the sense of missing an appointment; he failed us, instead of appearing to give evidence for us. It

274

has been apparent all through the narrative how important the evidence of Protus would have been, if he had been faithful to Demon.

λέγητε. Since Protus has apparently left Athens, nothing that Zenothemis says now can do him any harm.

δι' ὑμῶν, "through your agency," not quite the same as δι' ὑμᾶς. The plan to let the case go by default gave Protus the chance to disappear. It appears that things had not gone so far as issuing a personal summons for him to appear in court.

προσεκαλοῦ (middle), "summon," in the presence of witnesses called κλητῆρες.

κατηγγύας πρὸς τὸν πολέμαρχον, "demanded bail (ἐγγύη) before the polemarch." Protus, like Zenothemis, was not an Athenian citizen, and would have had to put up bail or provide sureties (ἐγγυηταί) to guarantee his appearance in court. Legal matters affecting noncitizens were the concern of the polemarch (see General Introduction, pp. 8–9).

ἤ, "or else" (if he did not remain in Athens).

παρ' ὧν λήψει δίκην, "persons from whom you could get satisfaction," i.e. the sureties. The future indicative λήψει is used as preserving the tense of the verb that Zenothemis might have used himself: "I have people from whom I *shall* obtain satisfaction." This kind of relative clause in future indicative, in secondary as well as primary sequence, is often called a relative clause of purpose (cf. Smyth, 2554; GG. 1454). Thus in Thuc. 3. 16, ναυτικὸν παρεσκεύαζον ὅτι πέμψουσιν εἰς τὴν Λέσβον, the meaning is "they prepared a fleet to send to Lesbos," but the Athenians are represented as saying to themselves "a fleet which we shall send to Lesbos."

ἑτοίμους εἶχες, "you had them ready to hand." There

is no need for ἄν, because the guarantors were there, whether the defendant skipped bail or not.

τὸ οἴκημα, "the jail."

30. ἔκδειαν. This means "shortage" or "arrears of payment" (cf. Thuc. 1. 99), and in Dem. 33. 10 the speaker says he took possession of some slaves to cover the price due to him, "in case there was any shortage." Protus' debt will have increased, with interest mounting up.

σὺ δ'. The verb of thinking is not repeated, but the infinitive shows that something like οἴει is taken for granted.

κλητεύσω, "summon" to appear as a witness, formally, through a herald, after a witness has not responded to an ordinary private request. In 59.28 the speaker says he will compel a witness to appear or κλητεύσω αὐτόν. There was a fine of 1000 drachmas for ignoring this official summons; but if Protus had left Athens, he was beyond reach.

31. παρακρούσεσθαι. Cf. 31.12 and note.

αἰτιάσονται, not "accuse" of anything illegal, but simply "blame" him for what I am doing, so that τὴν αἰτίαν (at end of sentence) is simply "this allegation." It was of course easy to say that Demon relied on the political influence of Demosthenes.

ἐξάγειν, the first definite indication that Demon had made a formal move to dispossess Zenothemis (cf. 17–19).

ἦ μήν, the usual formula for introducing a statement under oath. The formality of the statement may seem exaggerated; perhaps it is felt that an elaborate show of candour will convince the jury that no "pressure" was being exercised by Demosthenes.

32. εἴ τι ἔχοι, "if he could help at all," as supporting speaker or in any other way.

276

ὡς ἂν σὺ κελεύῃς, indefinite, "whatever you ask," not ὡς σὺ κελεύεις.

δεινόν, "shocking (if I did not)."

τὸ σαυτοῦ, "your situation."

We have no reason to doubt that what Demosthenes says is true, that he had not made any appearances in court in private cases; but there was no reason why he should not give Demon some legal advice and help him with the composition of his speech. The last phrase, before the text breaks off, is not intelligible as it stands.

INDEX TO THE INTRODUCTION
AND COMMENTARY

(For an *Index Verborum* to the Greek text see Preuss, *Index Demosthenicus*)

279